American Visions ✳ Readings in American Culture

Series Editors

Michael Barton
Associate Professor of American Studies and History
Pennsylvania State University at Harrisburg, Capital College

Nancy A. Walker
Professor of English
Vanderbilt University

This unique series consists of carefully assembled volumes of seminal writings on topics central to the study of American culture. Each anthology begins with a comprehensive overview of the subject at hand, written by a noted scholar in the field, followed by a combination of selected articles, original essays, and case studies.

By bringing together in each collection many important commentaries on such themes as humor, material culture, architecture, the environment, literature, politics, theater, film, and spirituality, American Visions provides a varied and rich library of resources for the scholar, student, and general reader. Annotated bibliographies facilitate further study and research.

D1373876

WHAT'S SO FUNNY?

WHAT'S SO
FUNNY?

HUMOR IN AMERICAN CULTURE

Edited by
NANCY A. WALKER

American Visions ※ Readings in American Culture
※
Number 1
※
A Scholarly Resources Inc. Imprint ※ Wilmington, Delaware

Scholarly Resources Inc.
104 Greenhill Avenue
Wilmington, DE 19805-1897

Library of Congress Cataloging-in-Publication Data

What's so funny? : humor in American culture / edited by Nancy A.
  Walker.
       p.   cm. — (American visions)
    Includes bibliographical references.
    ISBN 0-8420-2687-8 (cloth : alk. paper). —ISBN 0-8420-2688-6
(pbk. : alk. paper)
    1. American wit and humor—History and criticism.   2. United
States—Civilization.   I. Walker, Nancy A., 1942–   . II. Series:
American visions (Wilmington, Del.).
PS430.W49   1998
817.009—dc21   98-13440
                                                              CIP

∞ The paper used in this publication meets the minimum requirements of
the American National Standard for permanence of paper for printed library
materials, Z39.48, 1984.

ABOUT THE EDITOR

NANCY A. WALKER, professor of English at Vanderbilt University, has written about American humor since the 1970s. One of the first scholars to focus attention on the humor of American women, she is the author of *"A Very Serious Thing": Women's Humor and American Culture* and the coeditor of *Redressing the Balance: American Women's Literary Humor from Colonial Times to the 1980s*, both published in 1988, as well as numerous articles and book chapters on the humor of such authors as Dorothy Parker, Margaret Halsey, Emily Dickinson, and Phyllis McGinley. Professor Walker is also the author of *Feminist Alternatives: Irony and Fantasy in the Contemporary Novel by Women* (1990), *Fanny Fern* (1992), and *The Disobedient Writer: Women and Narrative Tradition* (1995), and is at work on a study of American women's magazines of the 1940s and 1950s. She is co-editor, with Michael Barton, of the Scholarly Resources book series "American Visions: Readings in American Culture."

CONTENTS

I

NANCY A. WALKER

Introduction
What Is Humor?
Why American Humor?

We begin with a paradox: humor—that is, the ability to smile and laugh, and to make others do so—is a nearly universal human trait, and yet most people who attempt to write about humor acknowledge that it is difficult to define, grasp, and pin down. Why should this be the case? Why should something so common be at the same time so elusive? Most of us claim to have a sense of humor, yet we would be hard-pressed to say just what that sense is. Because this volume is a collection of essays about the humorous expressions of America as a nation, essays which in some way do attempt to define that humor, we should first consider why the study of humor presents such challenges.

Humor takes many forms, ranging from the casual level of the joke told to friends to the sophistication of a Shakespearean comedy. Some humor, such as a slapstick routine or a pun, is intended primarily for amusement, while such forms as political satire have quite serious purposes; for well over a hundred years, political cartoons in daily newspapers have attempted to influence public opinion on important issues. Humor may take the form of what is called "light" verse, such as the writings by Ogden Nash and Phyllis McGinley, or it may be an element in what we consider "serious" literature, such as the novels of Mark Twain and William Faulkner. In fact, many writers use humor to call the reader's attention to a serious message. Dorothy Parker, for example, although known as a humorist associated with *The New Yorker* magazine and the Algonquin Round Table in the early decades of the twentieth century, used the medium of light verse to convey biting commentary on relationships between men and women, as in her "Unfortunate Coincidence":

> By the time you swear you're his,
> Shivering and sighing,
> And he vows his passion is
> Infinite, undying—
> Lady, make a note of this:
> One of you is lying.

Humor may, then, be written or spoken; it may take the form of song lyrics, physical clowning, or the comic strip.

This diversity, in turn, suggests that in addition to its many forms, humor appears in numerous media—especially in the late twentieth century. Whereas in colonial New England most people experienced humor in the form of spoken and written jokes, political satire, and comic songs, today there are television situation comedies and stand-up comics, comedic films, and humorous pieces circulating on the Internet. The comic strip, an American invention that observed its hundredth anniversary in 1995, is a feature of virtually every newspaper, and comedy clubs bring comedians and audiences face-to-face in cities throughout America. And just as developments in technology have changed the ways in which we experience humor (the seventeenth-century colonists had the printing press; we have electronic media), so American humor has changed over time. Humor, like all forms of communication, requires *context*: to find it amusing, the audience must have certain knowledge, understanding, and values, which are subject to evolution from one century or even one decade to the next. For example, readers today probably would not find much humor in a political satire related to obscure events of two hundred years ago, nor would most of us be much amused by a pun in the Elizabethan English of the seventeenth century. While racist humor has certainly not disappeared, the minstrel show, featuring white actors in blackface and turning upon the stereotype of the African American as childlike and gullible, is a thing of the past. Since humor often depends upon the context of a particular time, topical humor seldom lasts past its own day. In his introduction to *A Subtreasury of American Humor,* published in 1941, E. B. White notes that he and his coeditor, Katharine White, had originally intended to include newspaper humor, but found that it became stale with age: "Even the perfect newspaper story, by the most expert and gifted reporter, dies like a snake with the setting of the sun."[1]

Another dimension of the challenges involved in defining and analyzing humor is that there are many purposes for and methods of doing so. Those who study humor are usually not interested in explaining why something is funny, for reasons that E. B. White also expressed in the *Subtreasury*: "Humor can be dissected, as a frog can, but the thing dies in the process and the innards are discouraging to any but the pure scientific mind" (xvii). Sociologists commonly study how humor works in social settings—the relationship between humor and such matters as social class, power relationships, and gender differences. Psychologists, on the other hand, have been inclined to look at humor as a manifestation of human mental and emotional development. How, they ask, do people use and respond to humor at different stages of the life cycle and in different psychological states? What is the usefulness of humor to the human psyche? Sigmund Freud, who is often credited with helping the field of psychology achieve mature status, was extremely interested in humor, especially in joking behavior. For Freud, humor functioned as a sort of release from the rule-bound superego that he believed regulated human social behavior. In his 1927 essay, "Humor," Freud termed humor "liberating," a release from "reality."[2] More recently, a number of medical professionals have investigated the function of humor in the processes of healing and recovery; they are interested in the *function* of humor, but in a physical rather than a psychological sense.

Students of American culture are likely to ask an entirely different set of questions about humor than do those who are concerned with what effects it has on either groups or individuals. Reduced to its simplest level, the difference might be stated as follows: rather than asking "what does humor *do*?" they ask "what kinds of humor have Americans created?" "Why?" "What can humor tell us about American values, experience, and aspirations?" Put a different way, the study of humor becomes yet another way of understanding social history, cultural institutions, and the development of both a sense of national identity and threats to that identity. To use again the minstrel show as an example: students of American culture are interested in what this form of humorous expression can tell us about race relations in the nineteenth century and how elements of such performances were later carried over into the vaudeville theater and into popular radio programs such as *Amos 'n' Andy* in the 1930s. Similarly, a study of the witty but world-weary verse of a writer such as Dorothy Parker can provide insight into changes in literary taste as America became a more urban than rural country by the 1920s, when magazines such as *The New Yorker* (founded in 1925) helped to define a kind of city sophistication that was in sharp contrast to the boisterous frontier humor that had flourished in the nineteenth century.

Another consideration in the study of humor is the extent to which we should take it seriously. In the field of literature in particular, scholars have tended to value tragedy over comedy, viewing the comic as a form that has less to tell us about the important moments of human experience. E. B. White also addresses this point in introducing the *Subtreasury*: "The world likes humor, but treats it patronizingly. It decorates its serious artists with laurel, and its wags with Brussels sprouts. It feels that if a thing is funny it can be presumed to be something less than great, because if it were truly great it would be wholly serious" (xviii). White goes on to point out that because writers themselves are well aware of this distinction, a number of them have signed their real names to their serious work and used pseudonyms when they wrote humor. And yet when we consider some of the classic works in the American literary tradition, we cannot say that they are wholly serious. Mark Twain's novel *The Adventures of Huckleberry Finn*, for example, achieves much of its effect through Twain's use of many of the major techniques of humor, including slapstick, satire, mistaken identity, wordplay, and exaggeration. While it can certainly be argued that identifying comic elements in a novel about slavery is a different matter than assessing the value of a comic strip or a television situation comedy, it is nonetheless true that many of America's prominent writers have found the various techniques of humor quite congenial to their purposes, including authors as otherwise different as Herman Melville, Henry James, Gertrude Stein, and Eudora Welty.

Before considering the ways in which scholars have, for more than a hundred years, attempted to characterize American humor, we should address one more question: why should a nation have a particular kind of humor? In other words, why should American humor be significantly different from the humor of England or Japan or Peru? If, indeed, the creation of humor is an impulse shared by all human beings, what would make the humor produced by one culture different from that produced by another? One reason could be that cultures differ in their histories, values, and geography. For example, the fact that the United States originated as a group of colonies in rebellion against domination by Great Britain, with its monarchy and various levels of aristocracy, led to the creation of the American comic figure frequently known as Jonathan, a country bumpkin who was treated humorously for his ignorance of city ways but simultaneously admired for his innocence and lack of pretentiousness. The title of Royall Tyler's 1787 comic play *The Contrast,* which includes a Jonathan character, points to the significant distinctions that the earliest Americans believed existed between their rural, democratic values and the highly stratified cultures of Europe. Also America, from its earliest years, has been largely a nation of immigrants, which brings former residents of many countries together. This circumstance gave rise to humor dealing with ethnic groups, highlighting customs, accents, and other characteristics which served to distinguish one group of settlers from another. Of course, ethnic humor can be quite negative when it is used to disparage people perceived as "different"; those who feel themselves to be superior to blacks, Jews, the Irish, or any other group have used humor as part of the process of stereotyping them. On the other hand, members of racial and ethnic groups have also developed their own forms of humor as a way of coping with such discrimination, and these traditions have contributed to the complexity and distinctiveness of American humor.

One of the most important features of America, especially for the three centuries following initial European settlement, has been the country's physical size. Until the end of the nineteenth century much of its territory was not marked by what Europeans regarded as "civilization." For many years there was always a "frontier" of some sort, which had an influence on America's humor as well as other aspects of American life and thought. The earliest settlers sent back descriptions to Europe of a vast wilderness, new and strange plants and animals, and encounters with what they largely regarded as uncivilized people. Such accounts, because of ignorance and from a desire to impress those on the other side of the Atlantic, often exaggerated the physical features of the new land. This habit of exaggeration led to the creation, in the nineteenth century, of one of the distinctive forms of American humor—the tall tale, which is "tall" because of the larger-than-life depiction of man's encounter with the natural world. In one of the best-known tall tales, Mark Twain's "The Celebrated Jumping Frog of Calaveras County," a man trains a frog to win jumping contests—thus exerting his human will over one of nature's creatures—until a competitor fills the frog with buckshot so that it is too heavy to move (another of the tale's exaggerations is that the frog survives this experience).

Also contributing to America's uniqueness as a nation is its institution of a democratic form of government at a time when most other nations were still ruled by hereditary aristocracies. The fact that democracy encourages the participation of its citizens in the development of its institutions allows those same citizens freedom to criticize both the nation's leaders and its laws, and such openness has no doubt contributed to the long American tradition of political humor. From the colonial period onward, in songs, poems, cartoons, newspaper columns, plays—and, later, on radio and television—Americans have devoted a large share of their humor to the expression of political beliefs. And, because the ideals embodied in the promises of democracy are just that—ideals and not necessarily realities—a great deal of American humor, whether overtly political or not, has pointed to the discrepancies between the grand promises of equality, prosperity, and fulfillment and the actualities of socioeconomic class differences, discrimination, and corruption. One of the most common purposes of humor is to point out such distinctions, and American culture has provided a particularly fertile setting for this development. According to Thomas L. Masson, who assessed American humor in his 1931 book *Our American Humorists,* humor is important because it deals with the problems of a culture. Masson declares that his purpose in writing his book is "to show . . . that there is no other class of writers in America that is actually doing more for the country than the humorists," and it is precisely because of the ills of the nation that this is the case. According to Masson, "God knows that when we consider the hopeless welter of slums and bad finance, and utterly banal patter wasted upon our outstanding problems, such as education, one could cry aloud for some new satirist to arise who, with a truly illuminated pen, would show us the utter folly of so much that we accede to—for example, the frightful stupidities of prohibition . . . . And the humorists are working like nailors, constantly trying to correct the things that they see are wrong."[3]

To speak of "American" humor, then, is to assume that these factors and more have produced both themes and forms which address a particular cultural experience that is widely shared. But it is important also to acknowledge significant differences within this experience, for the diversity that is one of America's distinctive qualities has in turn produced much humor expressive of these differences. For example, scholars have known for some time that different regions of the country have given rise to humorous writing that reflects regional dialects, customs, and values. The Jonathan figure, who in the earliest years of the nation's existence represented honest agrarian values in contrast to the superficiality of aristocratic pretensions, is very much a product of New England. Although untutored and naive, he is morally upright and law-abiding (if sometimes a bit crafty). In contrast, the corresponding rural figure that emerged in the humor of the South and the West in the early nineteenth century was apt to be a lawless renegade who was contemptuous of both secular and religious authority. An example is George Washington Harris's character Sut Lovingood, who inhabited the hills of Tennessee in the decades before the Civil War. The product of the frontier rather than the more settled Northeast, Sut is a practical joker who likes nothing better than to disrupt a church service with one of his pranks, and who declares his atheism in heavily dialectical speech: "I haint got nara a soul, nothin' but a whiskey proof gizzard."

Those who study American humor were much slower to understand that American women had produced a body of humorous work that is in many respects quite different from that created by men. Indeed, despite the publication of two early anthologies of women's humor— Kate Sanborn's *The Wit of Women* in 1885 and Martha Bruère and Mary Ritter Beard's *Laughing Their Way* in 1937—until the 1980s most analyses of American humor were predicated upon a largely male canon, and therefore emphasized the centrality of the frontier, politics, violence, and individualism to the humorous tradition. With the recovery and study of a great deal of humor by women during the past two decades, we now have a more complete picture that includes gender as well as regional and ethnic differences among the varieties of American humor. We can see, for example, that while male authors were writing about jumping frogs and practical jokes, women were concerned with the gossip of sewing circles and the mishaps of homemaking. While women did not generally write tall tales, they did sometimes write humorously about the frontier experience, which they perceived somewhat differently than did their male counterparts. The women emphasized, as did Caroline Kirkland in her 1839 *A New Home—Who'll Follow?,* the interdependence of people in isolated areas rather than individualism and competition. When women created political satire in the nineteenth and early twentieth centuries, they often focused on the battle for female suffrage; and, as Dorothy Parker's verse attests, women's humor frequently has been concerned with the battle between the sexes. Thus, while humor in general may deal with discrepancies, women have been interested in those discrepancies that have most directly affected their own lives.

Theories of American Humor

Two of the earliest scholarly studies that attempted to come to terms with the essence of American humor rest on a belief in an American "national character." The notion that there is or could be a unitary character that represents everyone in this diverse culture has largely been discredited in favor of a perception that people from vastly different backgrounds retain vital differences from one another that are to be celebrated rather than erased. But beginning in the years following the American Revolution—and intensifying in periods of such crises as wars—public rhetoric has, understandably, sought out ways to create unity in a spirit of nationalism. While all citizens of the United States do share certain things, such as federal laws, some holidays, and the system of public education, the concept of a national character goes beyond these experiences to suggest fundamental similarities in values, beliefs, and behavior that make Americans essentially different from people in other cultures.

Part of the impetus for a belief in an identifiable national character came from the desire for a body of literature that could be regarded as distinctively American, rather than borrowing its themes and forms from European models. This movement gained momentum in the nineteenth century with a series of writers, including Ralph Waldo Emerson, Walt Whitman, and William Dean Howells, who encouraged Americans to find subjects and modes of expression that could represent what was indeed unique about the American experience, from its geographic features to its possibilities for social mobility. Since humorous writing tends to focus on the concrete, immediate aspects of a culture, it is not surprising that it was America's humorous literature that seemed to some observers to first represent a unique American culture.

Thus, for example, H. R. Haweis delivered a series of lectures on "American Humorists" at the Royal Institution in London in 1881, and collected the lectures in book form the following year (excerpted in Chapter 1). Of the six authors about whom Haweis chose to speak, three represented the Northeastern region (Washington Irving, Oliver Wendell Holmes, and James Russell Lowell) and three were identified with the frontier (Artemus Ward, Mark Twain, and Bret Harte). However, considering the work of all six, Haweis found sufficient commonality to declare that American wit had three main sources. The first of these he described as "the shock between Business and Piety," by which he meant the paradox that although the earliest New England settlers were motivated by a search for religious freedom, they were also shrewdly aware of the commercial possibilities of the New World, and hastened to take advantage of them. The second contrast that Haweis found at the heart of American humor was the clash between the European settlers and the native inhabitants of the continent—a clash that certainly led to a great deal of tragedy, but that also had the potential for comic misunderstandings. The third element that Haweis identified was geographical—"the contrast between the vastness of American nature and the smallness of man." Haweis believed this third feature of the American experience caused the tendency toward exaggeration in American humor, as well as a certain boastfulness about the ability to cope with the "immensities" of the American scene. For Haweis, then, commenting as a British observer, these three "shocks" lay at the heart of the American national character and hence of American humor.

For American anthropologist Constance Rourke, writing four decades later, the link between a national character and a national humor was at least as close as it had been for Haweis; her 1931 book is titled *American Humor: A Study of the National Character* (excerpted in Chapter 2). In the foreword to the book, Rourke declares that "there is scarcely an aspect of the American character to which humor is not related, few which in some sense it has not governed." Rourke is in agreement with Haweis that one of the major contrasts apparent in the young American nation was that between the piety of the Puritan settlers and the practical business of earthly survival. But she differs from Haweis in maintaining that the New England atmosphere of religious strictness had to dissipate before an American comic spirit could emerge. Rourke's stance is informed by the theories of French philosopher Henri Bergson (1859–1941), who posited that the creation of humor had to wait until people were no longer concerned with sheer survival: "The comic comes into being just when society and the individual, freed from the worry of self-preservation, begin to regard themselves as works of art." Rourke locates the moment at which Americans were able to regard themselves and their culture as "works of art" in 1815, when the Jonathan figure had matured into the figure of the "Yankee." This Yankee, who was in turn the basis of the popular icon

"Uncle Sam," most often took the form of a shrewd New England peddler, who sold his various wares from town to town and was "rural, sharp, uncouth, witty." This Yankee was a clever man and storyteller who was given to mild practical jokes and the wearing of disguises. According to Rourke, it is not a contradiction that Americans could admire this sometimes unscrupulous, often tricky fellow, but instead evidence that one trait of the national character was "the habit of self-scrutiny." In other words, if what H. R. Haweis called "Business" involved an element of dishonesty, Americans were content to celebrate this as a form of practical shrewdness. Typical of the stories of the clever Yankee peddler is one from 1852 that Cameron Nickels cites in his book *New England Humor*: a peddler who cannot find anyone to pay cash for the brooms he has to sell finally locates a shopkeeper who offers to give the peddler half cash and half merchandise in exchange for the brooms; having pocketed the cash, the peddler then takes the brooms to settle the rest of the deal.

Rourke believes the essence of American humor is its irreverence, a kind of native exuberance that refuses to take life too seriously—even the foibles and failures of its own citizens. Walter Blair, who from the 1930s through the 1980s was the most dedicated and prolific of scholars of American humor, agrees with Rourke. In his 1937 book *Native American Humor* (excerpted in Chapter 3) (by which phrase he does not refer to the humor of those people we now call Native Americans), Blair lists "detachment" as the first of several requisites for American humor. This quality may be similar to Bergson's requirement that people be able to view themselves as "works of art." For Blair, the necessary detachment did not come about until around 1830; before that, he believed, Americans, who described their experiences in ways that we might find comic, did not themselves see the humor in what they conveyed. Blair cites, for example, parts of William Byrd's *History of the Dividing Line* (1728), in which Byrd describes the lazy men he encounters in the South, who, "when the Weather is mild, . . . gravely consider whether they had best go and take a small Heat at the Hough [hoe]: but generally find reasons to put it off till another time." Byrd's humor is unintentional; his intention is to criticize unproductive farmers. For a true American humor to flourish, according to Blair, one must not merely report such scenes, but "consciously exploit" them. Blair's second major requisite for American humor was that it be expressed in forms not borrowed from English and European models; agreeing with his nineteenth-century predecessors, such as Emerson and Whitman, he insisted that "native" literature must be couched in new forms and he found the tall tale and the habit of oral storytelling especially central to the American humorous tradition.

This second requisite explains why Blair dates American humor as beginning around 1830. For while he does sometimes speak of a "national character," Blair views the salient factor in the development of American humor as geography—specifically, the frontier—and the great westward expansion of the country was under way by the 1830s, assisted by such events as the opening of Texas for settlement by American citizens in 1825 and the incorporation of the first passenger railroad line in 1827. In his 1972 essay "'A Man's Voice, Speaking'", Blair identifies "the comic narrative modeled upon the oral tale" as the most enduring form of American humor.[4] Examples of this "comic narrative" reach beyond the tall tale itself; Blair includes Twain's *Huckleberry Finn* (narrated by Huck in the first person), J. D. Salinger's *The Catcher in the Rye,* and William Faulkner's *The Sound and the Fury,* among many others. But these works have in common an adventurous travel into the unknown (more psychological than physical in Faulkner's novel) that has its prototype in the story of frontier exploration. Implicit in Blair's selection of the frontier experience as central to true American humor—and somewhat more explicit in the title "A Man's Voice"—is a definition of that humor as male. With few exceptions, such as Caroline Kirkland's *A New Home,* women wrote neither published accounts of frontier exploration nor tall tales pitting "man" against nature. It should be noted that Blair was not alone among early commentators in defining American humor in almost exclusively male terms: H. R. Haweis's six examples of nineteenth-century humorists are all men, and Constance Rourke admits to an otherwise all-male pantheon only Emily Dickinson. Rourke, in fact, was one of the first to recognize the comic dimensions of Dickinson's poetry.

If for Walter Blair geography has been of central significance to American humor, Louis D. Rubin, Jr., has more recently located that centrality in politics, broadly defined. What Rubin identifies as "The Great American Joke" in the introduction to his 1973 book *The Comic Imagination in American Literature* (Chapter 4) is the gap between the ideal promise of American democracy—"freedom, equality, self-government"—and the ordinary quality of everyday life. For Rubin, this gap between the lofty and the mundane has two dimensions. One, the political, is that the perfection promised by the ideals of a democratic society is not—and cannot be—the reality of our daily lives. The second dimension, which has more direct implications for humorous expression, is what we might call the semantic: the difference between the formal language in which abstract ideas are articulated, and the concreteness of ordinary speech. What Rubin calls a "verbal incongruity" that "lies at the heart of American experience" provides a form for what he defines as American humor: the down-to-earth, "homely metaphor," which at once expresses and deflates the abstract ideal. Of the examples of this use of language that Rubin cites, perhaps the most engaging and instructive is Mark Twain's description of "the calm confidence of a Christian holding four aces." Not only does Twain point to the discrepancy between abstract faith and practical action but he also provides the concrete picture of the Christian sitting at a poker table—a specific visual incongruity that can make us laugh. Twain's comment also reminds us of the "shock between Business and Piety" to which Haweis points: the Christian's "confidence" comes from both his faith and from a winning poker hand. Thus, the religious and the secular, supposed opposites, are conjoined. Rubin's definition of the American "comic imagination" resides in such clashes of opposites. In his words, "the interplay of the ornamental and the elemental, the language of culture and the language of sweat, the democratic ideal and the mulishness of fallen human nature."

Finally, William Keough, in his 1990 book *Punchlines* (excerpted in Chapter 6), takes Blair's concept of the frontier and Rubin's notion of the clash between the lofty ideal and mundane reality a step further by declaring that the hallmark of American humor is its violence. If indeed, Keough argues, a nation's humor mirrors its dominant characteristics, then both the linguistic and the thematic violence of American humor simply reflects the fact—which many a foreign visitor has noted—that Americans have an unusually high tolerance, and even an enthusiasm, for lawlessness and brutality. The lines between Keough's characterization and those of Blair and Rubin are not difficult to trace. There is no doubt that life on the American frontier allowed a freedom from civilized restraint that has appealed to the American sensibility in both the tall tale and the film Western; the outlaw, from the actual Jesse James to the fictional Thelma and Louise, is an American hero. And the conflict between the ideal and the real to which Rubin points can be far from genteel or gentle. In Nathaniel West's grimly comic 1934 parody of the American Dream, *A Cool Million*, the central character lives according to all the Boy Scout virtues, but instead of succeeding, as the ideal of the Dream promises, he is physically mutilated during the course of the novel. The backdrop for such humor is a nation that systematically eradicated Native Americans, and in which persistent racism led to nearly five thousand recorded lynchings of African Americans between 1882 and 1927, and a culture in which many civilian adults routinely carry guns, and televised cartoons for children are noted for scenes of physical brutality. As a result, Keough maintains, our "native humor reflects the more menacing aspects of American society, and lampoons certain of our most cherished assumptions, such as the natural goodness of man and the inevitability of progress." In emphasizing the violence of American humor, Keough, like most commentators before him, envisions humor to be almost entirely produced by men. In the few pages of *Punchlines* devoted to women's humor, he acknowledges that although this humor may sometimes be verbally caustic, it seldom approaches the violence he associates with the rest of the humorous tradition.

Because these attempts to get at the essence of American humor have tended, for more than a hundred years, to assume that humor is the province of white men, the resulting definitions proposed are necessarily partial. By focusing on such areas of American life as religion, business, politics, frontier life, and the heroes of popular culture, these theories must omit segments of the population who have traditionally not played major roles in these areas and thus have seldom used them as material for humorous expression. Nonetheless, as we begin to look at the history of American humor, such theories are useful as ways to think about that humor.

Bearing in mind their limitations, the analyses offered by Haweis, Rourke, Blair, Rubin, and Keough point to some essential truths about the American experience, which in turn has given rise to our humor. All of the definitions point to some sort of contrast or even paradox. For Haweis, this is embodied in the "shocks" experienced by the colonists—the contrast between a European sensibility and the features of a new (to them) continent, including the necessity that one's piety be tempered by shrewd practicality. For Rourke and Blair, who by the 1930s could reflect upon the nineteenth century in ways that Haweis could not, American humor seemed to originate in that century's story of the individual at odds with the rules of "official" society—whether the Yankee peddler making his way by his wits (Rourke), or the frontiersman spinning tales of his encounters with the wilderness (Blair). Rubin and Keough, conscious of a twentieth-century history that included severe economic depression, continued racism, and corruption in business and politics, see the central paradox giving rise to humor given the fact that Americans could believe in and espouse certain national ideals and yet behave in a manner diametrically opposed to them, and, further, that many could find this situation more comic than tragic. What should be clear is that one's attempt to provide a definition of American humor is contingent upon one's tastes, values, and historical moment.

American Humor: History and Forms

When we speak of the history of "American" humor, it is important to understand that we do not mean the humor of "the Americas," which would include not only countries other than the United States, but also the humor of people who had inhabited the land that became the United States for hundreds of years before the European explorers and settlers arrived. It is the humor of those explorers and settlers and their descendants that scholars have in mind when they study American humor, and perhaps the term "United States humor" would be more descriptive, but that would leave out the humor of the 150 or so years before the United States became a nation. "Euro-American humor" would be more accurate, if a bit clumsy; however, "American humor" has become the standard designation. Unfortunately, little is known about the humor of the native inhabitants of this continent, the people for centuries called Indians (itself a sort of joke in that Christopher Columbus and his peers hoped they had found India but were lost). Language barriers, mutual distrust, and intermittent hostilities between natives and colonists made most encounters serious at best, and it was not until the late nineteenth century that native cultures began to be taken seriously on their own terms—including the values and beliefs that produce humorous expression.

Commentators who date the beginning of American humor from the early nineteenth century do so either because they wish to focus on humor that did not borrow heavily from English and European themes and forms, or because the kind of humor they find most characteristically American—for example, frontier humor—began to flourish in that period. But the seeds of many forms of American humorous expression were sown well before the Revolutionary War. One of these seeds was the habit of exaggerating the experience of the New World in reports to those back home—an exaggeration that is common to many forms of humor, but which shows up especially in the tall tale, in American political humor, and even in the films of Woody Allen. The explorers and settlers of the colonial period did not always set out to lie deliberately—often they were understandably overwhelmed by circumstances for which they had no frame of reference—but their accounts of the landscape and the native inhabitants frequently featured hyperbole that painted the New World as much better or much worse than it proved to be in reality. At one end of the spectrum, America was filled with gold (which no one ever managed to find), abundant food, and natives who would surely make fine slaves. At the other end were ferocious beasts, extreme cold or heat, and hostile "savages." Evidence that a colonial writer might even embellish his own story is offered by two different accounts by Captain John Smith of a trip up a Virginia river. In 1608, Smith reported that his party was met by "3 or 400 Salvages"; in 1624, writing of the same experience, he recorded being threatened by "three or four thousand Salvages." Rather than a failure of memory, the numerical discrepancy points instead to Smith's desire to blame the various failures of the Virginia Company on forces beyond its control.[5]

In the absence of any means of either substantiating or debunking such accounts, writers such as Smith were free to tell whatever stories they chose, and readers were equally free to believe or mistrust them. In any event, America in its early years was not so much *described* as it was *invented*. The habit of invention, closely tied to the habit of exaggeration, laid the groundwork for American humor. Long before the nineteenth century, Americans were known for their boastfulness and for their fondness for disguises. Aware of their own process of transformation from citizens of other countries to residents of a new land, settlers engaged in self-invention, and often tested out versions of a new reality on those new to the continent. As Walter Blair and Hamlin Hill put it in *America's Humor* (excerpted in Chapter 5): "Since peculiar things were always happening in America and uninformed newcomers always lusted for strange news, over the years merry fellows could unwind incredible yarns about flora, fauna, natives, and geography and then give true or untrue but more or less plausible explanations." Such lies—which we might give the term that Twain's Huck Finn uses, "stretchers"—could be put to more sobering purposes when the intent was to defraud rather than to amaze or amuse. It was this aspect of the American habit that Herman Melville captured in his 1857 novel *The Confidence-Man: His Masquerade,* in which man's desire to trust in others is thwarted time after time (hence our term "con man" for one who fools another for profit).

All of this fooling might seem at odds with our concept of the New England colonists as grim Puritans with their minds on heavenly rather than earthly matters, but, in fact, not all colonists of the area came for reasons of religious freedom, which created conflicts that gave rise to one of America's first satiric writers. In 1627, Thomas Morton angered his Puritan neighbors in Plymouth Colony by erecting a Maypole and conducting what the Puritans regarded as pagan rituals around it. The clash between them was not solely over religious observance; Morton, as a fur trader with the Indians, was also in commercial competition with the residents of Plymouth, who three times arrested him and shipped him back to England, only to have him return to Massachusetts. Morton's response to the Puritans was his 1637 *The New England Canaan,* in which he satirized Puritan society. Morton characterized them as anti-intellectuals who did not know that "learning does enable men's minds to converse with elements of a higher nature than is to be found within the habitation of the mole." He refers to Captain Miles Standish, a man of small physical stature, as "Captain Shrimp," and accuses Standish and his colleagues of making "a great show of religion but no humanity."

About a hundred years later, a different satirist expressed his displeasure (or at least mock-displeasure) with what he experienced in colonial America—this time in Maryland. Ebenezer Cooke, known in the 1720s as the poet laureate of Maryland, published several versions of his long poem *The Sot-Weed Factor* between 1708 and 1731. The title translates as "tobacco agent," and the poem tells the story of a young man bringing goods from England to trade for Maryland-grown tobacco and encountering a culture noted for its uncivilized inhabitants, lawlessness, and crude lifestyle. At the end of the poem, the beleaguered trader prepares to return to England to leave this "dreadful curse behind," and bestows upon Maryland his own curse: "May wrath divine then lay these regions waste/Where no man's faithful, nor a woman chaste." Cooke's subtitle leaves no doubt as to his intentions: "A satire in which is described the laws, government, courts, and constitutions of the country, and also the buildings, feasts, frolics, entertainments, and drunken humors of the inhabitants in that part of America."

Much of the humor of the colonial period dealt with such dissention between groups of people—religious factions, nationalities, men and women—and thus turned upon stereotypes that we may find disquieting today. Nathaniel Ward's *The Simple Cobbler of Aggawan* (1647), for example, targeted women's fashions in clothing, complaining that "it is no marvel they wear drailes [trailing headdresses] on the hinder part of their heads, having nothing as it seems in the fore part but a few squirrels' brains to help them frisk from one ill-favored fashion to another." The Native Americans and the Irish were similarly objects of such satire, and, as the eighteenth century progressed and the colonists increasingly felt united against a common enemy, the British were common subjects of American humor. But even as tensions began to build toward the inevitable revolution, residents of one colony could find those of another sufficiently different in beliefs and habits to provoke humorous derision. One of the best examples is the pronouncements of the aristocratic Virginian William Byrd on his Carolina neighbors in such works as the *History of the Dividing Line* (which, perhaps fortunately, was not published until 1841). Byrd, a hardworking Anglican, was particularly struck by the backwoods Carolinians' laziness and lack of religious observance. Remarking on the "Carolina felicity of having nothing to do," Byrd describes the indolence of one inhabitant: "Like the ravens, he neither ploughed nor sowed, but subsisted chiefly upon oysters which his handmaid made a shift to gather from the adjacent rocks." Byrd's ironic use of biblical phrasing marks him in contrast to the unpious Carolinians, who "seem very easy without a minister, as long as they are exempted from paying him."

Because it remained a private document until many years after his death, Byrd's *History* was not a source of amusement to his contemporaries. What published humor would the eighteenth-century American colonist have found available? One popular kind of publication was the almanac, which frequently combined such practical information as observations on the weather with wise and witty sayings known as aphorisms. The best-known of these sayings were created by the man who in his multiple roles as printer, inventor, and statesman has come to embody the American eighteenth century—Benjamin Franklin. *Poor Richard's Almanac* began in 1732, and was published for twenty-five years, reaching many New England families annually. Franklin's assumption of the persona of "Poor Richard"—one of the many masks and disguises of American humor—is yet another version of the Jonathan figure: a simple, unassuming country lad blessed with a fund of common sense that emerges in such aphorisms as "Three may keep a secret if two of them are dead," "Fish and visitors smell after three days," and "Creditors have better memories than debtors." To describe a figure such as Jonathan or Poor Richard, whose pose of humility is at odds with his wit and wisdom, Blair and Hill reach back to the Greeks for the term *eiron,* which Aristotle defined as the "mock-modest man" (and which gave rise to the term "irony"). Such a figure became a staple of American humor, combining homespun simplicity with penetrating insight into human nature and culture.

Periodicals other than almanacs also brought humor to colonial readers. The first known American magazine devoted expressly to humor was the Philadelphia *Bee,* which produced three issues in 1765. A decade before the American Revolution, the *Bee* was editorially loyal to the British monarchy rather than to the discontents of the colonists, and much of its satire was aimed at the governors of what the magazine called "Quillsylvania." Despite its allegiance to the crown, the *Bee* took the part of the common worker against their colonial rulers, who were described as "great Folks who stick themselves up for Quality, and turn up their Noses at honest Mechanics."

The heyday of the American comic magazine did not begin for another century, with the advent of such periodicals as *Life, Puck,* and *Judge;* in the meantime, most Americans would have turned to the daily or weekly newspaper for amusement. We now think of newspaper humor as limited to the comic strip pages and the occasional satirical editorial column, such as those by Molly Ivins and Art Buchwald, but from the colonial period through much of the nineteenth century, newspapers printed many kinds of humor, including light verse, humorous columns, and political satire. Whereas in the twentieth century we expect journalistic objectivity except on the editorial pages, earlier newspapers were not bound by such constraints, and many were fiercely partisan to specific political parties and factions, often using humor to espouse or attack political positions.

In the years before and during the Revolutionary War, newspapers and pamphlets were fully engaged in the conflict between the colonies and Great Britain. As Carl Holliday puts it in *The Wit and Humor of Colonial Days* (1912), "as we approach the prolonged struggle of the American Revolution, we find the American sense of the ludicrous becoming more and more alert. The colonist becomes eager to discern the weakness of his enemy, to discover all of that enemy's predicaments, and to set them with taunting laughter before the world."[6] Of course, many in the colonies remained loyal to the British crown, so the taunts came from both sides in the controversy. However, given the outcome of the war, most commentators on American humor have chosen to focus on that which viewed the British as the enemy. For example, of the many humorous sketches that dealt with the subject of tea after the famous Boston Tea Party, Holliday singles out as "perhaps the best" a series of pamphlets titled *The First Book of the American Chronicles of the Times* (1774–75), which parodies biblical language as a way of maintaining the righteousness of the American cause. After the colonists refused to "bow down to the Tea Chest, the God of the Heathen," they "assembled themselves together, in a Congress in the great city of Philadelphia, in the house of the Carpenters, the builders' house, in the land of Pennsylvania, on the seventh day of the ninth month, with their coaches, their chariots, their camels, their horsemen, and their servants, a great multitude and they communed together."

One of the sins of the British, according to the *First Book,* was soldiers who "abused . . . the young children of Boston by . . . calling them Yankees." The term "Yankee," like the figure of the New England Jonathan, is complex, and that complexity is tied up in the development of American humor and in how Americans regarded themselves. While the British used the term during the period of the Revolution as an insult (and used it to refer to all colonists, not just those in the North), for Americans developing a sense of national pride it came to stand for qualities on which they put high value. As Cameron Nickels notes in *New England Humor,* the figure of the Yankee represented those qualities that most differentiated the American from his European background. "As a rustic, he stood emphatically free of influences derived from the city, where, it was believed, foreign values and practices tended to prevail and inhibit, even corrupt, native growth. From those rural origins come the other indigenous, distinguishing features of the Yankee—his homespun dress, manners, and speech. . . . [T]he rustic Yankee embodied the American common man who had become the principal element in the experiment in democracy and thus who, more significantly, seemed to give substance to the hope of achieving an indigenous national identity."[7]

Yet at the same time that this hearty agrarian figure represented the simple virtues that embodied American democracy, his very lack of sophistication could make him a figure of fun, a target of ridicule. As America showed signs, shortly after becoming a nation, of developing more and more into an urban, industrial culture, the rustic Yankee could be seen, as Nickels puts it, as "a comic anachronism"—"Machinery overwhelms him, often injures him, and in the city he is awed by the diversity of people and activities, confused by modern conveniences, and duped by more knowledgeable city types" (9). Both of these views of the Yankee type can be seen in the character of Jonathan in Royall Tyler's late eighteenth-century play *The Contrast,* especially in the scene in which he attends a play in the city, but, knowing nothing about the theater, assumes that he and the rest of the audience are peeking into an actual house when the curtain rises. While both we and *The Contrast's* original audience may laugh at Jonathan's ignorance, it is also true that the simple values he embodies are clearly preferred by the playwright over the European pretensions of the urban dwellers.

For a long time, Americans remained ambivalent about being identified with the rustic Jonathan and Yankee figures, and especially resented English and European visitors who characterized American culture as crude and backward. At the same time, however, humor that featured the wisdom of a homespun figure flourished throughout the nineteenth century, and endured well into the twentieth. Perhaps the best-known such character is Twain's Huck Finn, an unsophisticated adolescent boy who provides an excellent example of the *eiron* as he unmasks various forms of hypocrisy—especially that surrounding the institution of slavery. A century after Tyler's *The Contrast,* Twain's novel has many of the same targets, including social climbing, pretentiousness, and affectation. In fact, Huck's greatest fear is being "sivilized," which he understands as involving Sunday School, table manners, uncomfortable clothing—and, implicitly, the inhumanity of slavery. The fact that Huck never explicitly condemns slavery testifies to his position as the apolitical innocent, and also allows for a moment of supreme irony in the book, when, having decided not to turn in the runaway slave, Jim, Huck reckons he will go to hell for this "sin" against the values his culture has taught him.

Before *The Adventures of Huckleberry Finn* was published in 1885, a number of other humorous writers had used the mask of the untutored rustic to comment pithily on the American scene. All of these figures used vernacular speech, which means literally that they speak "the language of the people." The term signals the use of dialects, which often contributes to the humor of their observations. The earliest of these vernacular figures were New England Yankees such as Jack Downing, whom Seba Smith began creating in 1830 as a way of remarking upon politics in Maine. Jack's letters from the state capitol to his relatives in Downingville reveal both Jack's ignorance of the political process and Smith's understanding of political pettiness and corruption. Jack's enthusiasm for politics eventually takes him to Washington, where he becomes an adviser to President Andrew Jackson. When Jackson is awarded an honorary doctorate of laws degree by Harvard University, Smith has the president remark to Jack that this seems appropriate because "I have had to doctor the Laws considerable ever since I been to Washington." While we might easily see the humor in Smith's play on words, the incident gains comic force when we understand that, as president, Jackson represented frontier culture rather than well-educated Easterners, and there was considerable resistance to him from the latter group. The vernacular figure did not remain a white male New Englander such as Jack Downing, but moved West with the development of the nation; as Nickels notes, the "various vernacular characterizations . . . reflect the nation's persistent faith in a dynamic, democratic pluralism."

By the end of the nineteenth century, two popular vernacular characters illustrated just how diverse the original Yankee figure had become. Finley Peter Dunne's "Mr. Dooley" was an Irish bartender in Chicago who brought his own common sense to matters of politics and culture in conversation with his patrons. When Mr. Hennessey voices support for President William McKinley taking over the Philippines, Mr. Dooley cautions that American imperialism may have gone too far: " 'Tis not more than two months since ye larned whether they were islands or canned goods. . . . If yer son, Packy, was to ask ye where th' Ph'lippeens is, cud ye give him anny good idea whuther they was in Rooshia or jus' wast ov th' thracks?" Mr. Dooley is also skeptical about the get-rich-quick promise of the American Dream, as he opines, "Me experyence with goold minin' is it's always in th' nex county."

A very different kind of sage was created by Marietta Holley, whose "Samantha Allen" spoke in favor of women's rights from her position as a hardworking homemaker in rural New York State from the 1870s into the twentieth century. Samantha's observations, like those of Mr. Dooley, emerge in conversations with those who do not share her common-sense views, including her husband, Josiah, and her neighbor Betsey Bobbet, both of whom hold traditional opinions of woman's proper role in society. Holley uses dialect in a more complex way than do many creators of such rustic observers; when Samantha speaks of women as a "sect" and of the "spear" in which she wishes to see them occupied, she is not merely mispronouncing "sex" and "sphere," but announcing a group's engagement in battle for the right to vote, receive equal pay, and hold positions of authority. Samantha repeatedly counters the standard nineteenth-century arguments against women's rights by showing them to be illogical; one of her signature lines is, "I love to see folks use reason if they have got any."

One of the earliest full-length studies of American humor focuses precisely on this American tradition of the rural philosopher. Jennette Tandy's 1925 book *Crackerbox Philosophers in American Humor and Satire* takes the first word of its title from a common feature of the country general store: a box (or barrel) of crackers from which those who gathered for conversation might help themselves while they discoursed upon weather, crops, and politics. These "philosophers" are, for Tandy, a type of "folk-hero, the homely American" who "represents the man of the people," and whose continuity in American writing "suggests a national ideal."[8] (Tandy's term "man" is descriptive of the fact that all of her examples are male; the work of Marietta Holley, although in its own day as popular as that of Mark Twain, was not rediscovered until the 1970s.) Tandy, like other observers, points out that crackerbox philosophers were historical figures as well as fictional creations, including such people as Benjamin Franklin, Abraham Lincoln, and Davy Crockett, all "living examples of the sages whom Democracy delights to honor" (x). During the decade in which Tandy's book was published, Will Rogers emerged as one of the most popular real-life rustic philosophers. The fictional tradition continued as well, with Langston Hughes's character "Simple" introducing the black vernacular figure in the 1940s, and is alive today in Garrison Keillor's folksy stories of Lake Wobegon.

It is interesting and somewhat ironic that Tandy's celebration of the crackerbox philosopher was published in 1925, for the same year saw the debut of the magazine *The New Yorker*—a periodical consciously designed to appeal to the urban sophisticate and featuring a humor that relied for its effect upon linguistic play, in-group allusions, and the creation of a somewhat world-weary, well-educated persona. One signature of *The New Yorker* was—and continues to be each February—the cover drawing of the top-hatted and monocled Eustace Tilley, a figure far removed from Downingville, Maine, and Samantha Allen's kitchen. *The New Yorker* humor favored irony over common sense, and dealt far more commonly with the arts and the social scene than with politics. The success of *The New Yorker* was due in part to demographic fact: the 1920 census revealed that for the first time in America's history, more people lived in towns and cities than in rural areas, and the urbanization that had begun with the development of industry in the nineteenth century would continue throughout the twentieth. Many of those who wrote for *The New Yorker* in its early years—including Dorothy Parker, S. J. Perelman, Robert Benchley, E. B. White, and James Thurber—were among the most popular humorous writers of the first half of the twentieth century. By the time Jennette Tandy published *Crackerbox Philosophers,* then, the tradition that she traced was in the process of being superceded by one that sprang from city pavements rather than from native soil.

Tension between urbane sophistication and what Tandy calls the "homely American" was, however, not a new phenomenon in the 1920s. In the popular tall tale of the nineteenth century, for example, the actual tale, narrated in the dialectical speech of the frontier, was frequently distanced from the reader by what has come to be called a "frame narrative." That is, the tale and its teller are introduced by a visitor to the frontier setting, often a well-educated Easterner to whom the untutored storyteller is an amusing curiosity. In Thomas Bangs Thorpe's "The Big Bear of Arkansas" (1841), for example, the "frame" narrator is traveling on a steamboat on the Mississippi River; describing himself as "a man of observation," he finds the mix of people on a steamboat an opportunity for "amusement or instruction." Such an opportunity takes the form of a fellow traveler from Arkansas, who boasts of killing forty-pound wild turkeys and of his hunting of an enormous bear who proves to be "an *unhuntable bear*" who, rather than being shot, "*died when his time come.*" At the conclusion of the Arkansan's tale, the frame narrator muses that the hunter is, like all "children of the woods," superstitious about the bear, and thus asserts his superiority over the Arkansas hunter. Similarly, the frame narrator of Twain's "Celebrated Jumping Frog" approaches "garralous old Simon Wheeler" for news about one Leonidas W. Smiley, and is treated instead to the tale of Jim Smiley and his frog. At the end, he makes his escape before Wheeler can regale him with a story about Jim Smiley's cow.

The contrast between the frame narrator and the teller of the tall tale, like that between the crackerbox philosopher and *New Yorker* humor, is similar, of course, to the contrast, developed in the colonial period, between European cultures and that of the emerging nation. As the vast territories of the United States were settled, distinct regional and sectional differences became apparent: not just rural versus urban, but North versus South and West versus East. The frontier tall tale was not written for a frontier reader, but instead for those in the East who, like the frame narrator, would find the story amusing because it conveyed a different sensibility and set of manners. "The Big Bear of

Arkansas" was published in the New York *Spirit of the Times,* which for thirty years before the Civil War published numerous sketches about various parts of the country.

Americans were fascinated by their differences from one another, and in an era before electronic media could introduce people in different parts of the nation to one another, the printed story served this purpose. One predictable result was the development of a number of regional and ethnic stereotypes, some of which have not lost their force even today. Perhaps the height of regional humor was achieved by Irvin S. Cobb in his series of 1920s books describing the peculiarities of various states under the general title "Cobb's America Guyed Books." Inspired by such satiric travel books as Mark Twain's *Innocents Abroad* (1869), Cobb is very much in the tradition of the crackerbox philosopher as he observes of New York that "so far as I know, General U. S. Grant is the only permanent resident," and of his native Kentucky that "the state is shaped like a camel lying down." The tendency of humor to exaggerate and simplify made it a prime vehicle for furthering such stereotypes as the shrewd Yankee, the aristocratic Southerner, the drunken Irishman, the crude (or supremely brave) frontiersman, the gossiping woman, the childlike (or dangerous) African American.

Such stereotyping may have taken deep root in American humor for several reasons. The size and the diversity of the country magnified differences, and often allowed citizens to understand each other only in superficial ways. Successive waves of immigration from other countries continually increased the culture's ethnic diversity, and each new group, with its customs, language patterns, and values, seemed a fair target for joking and satire that seem to be one way that people assimilate that which is different or threatening (as the Catholicism of the Irish was perceived as a threat to the nation's largely Protestant beginnings). Yet another contributing factor to American humor has been the habit of self-criticism fostered by democratic principles. As we have seen, for example, the figure of the New England Yankee embodied both positive and negative traits—shrewdness could be a means of survival, but it could also tip over into dishonesty—so that pride and confession could go hand in hand. Dunne's Mr. Dooley provides another example, for in creating this bartender with a thick Irish brogue, Dunne furthered elements of the common Irish stereotype: the loquacious man fond of strong drink.

Southern humorists as well as those in the North helped to invent the mythologies and stereotypes of their region. The Virginian William

Byrd was one of the earliest to remark upon the characteristics of his Southern neighbors, and he was followed in the nineteenth century by dozens of others. As M. Thomas Inge has noted, these Southern humorists "wrote about matters of masculine interest and portrayed a world of violence and exaggeration through tall tales and expanded metaphor."[9] The humor of what has come to be called the "Old Southwest"—which includes the states of Tennessee, Georgia, Alabama, Louisiana, Mississippi, Arkansas, and Missouri—was created primarily by journalists who tapped into the rich oral tradition of a region that was developing several distinct subcultures. The humor that Walter Blair characterized as coming from the Old Southwest between 1830 and 1867 in his *Native American Humor* arose not from the plantation aristocracy, but instead from the mountains, woods, and bayous of these Southern states—areas only loosely bound by the laws and codes of more settled regions. It was here that "The Big Bear of Arkansas" and the iconoclastic Sut Lovingood emerged, to be joined by Johnson J. Hooper's character Simon Suggs, who in one sketch earns the title "Captain" when he organizes his townspeople to protect against a threatened Indian uprising. Suggs and his comrades spend their time drinking whiskey and playing cards, and succeed in shooting not Indians, but a pony, a yoke of oxen, and the "Widow Haycock." Old Southwest humor is filled with violence, animals, and off-color jokes; it joyously exposes the foibles and excesses of men who live by their wits.

If we are to judge by Roy Blount, Jr.'s, characterization of Southern humor in the introduction to his *Book of Southern Humor* (excerpted in Chapter 8) and many of the selections in his collection, there is considerable continuity between the humor of the Old Southwest and more recent Southern humor. Time may have curbed the lawlessness, but there is a similar tendency to render experience in hyperbole, animals and guns are still featured, and the Southerner is still portrayed as having more faith in the concrete, physical fact than in the abstract idea. It is this last characteristic that Blount captures in what he terms "the quintessential Southern Zen koan": asked whether he believes in infant baptism, the Southerner responds, "Believe in it? Hell, I've seen it done!" Also, although Blount does not put it quite this way, Southern humor is concerned with the local and the everyday experience. He lists (somewhat tongue-in-cheek) the " 'typical' concerns of the region . . . [as] dirt, chickens, defeat, family, religion, prejudice, collard greens, politics, and diddie wa diddie." Another characteristic of Southern humor, which ties it to an oral storytelling tradition, is a love of language, not only the extravagant "stretchers" of hyperbole, but a delight in playing with and piling up words, as Blount does himself when musing about split infinitives: "Hell, I have known infinitives to actually just, truth of the matter, near about evermore before God in broad daylight purely . . . To the point where the infinitive was scattered to the winds like an opened-up sack of feed, *and the person speaking didn't even necessarily know what an infinitive was.*"

Blount's collection of Southern humor reaches back to the nineteenth century for some of its selections—including work by Mark Twain, Johnson J. Hooper, and one of the earliest Southern humorists, A. B. Longstreet, author of *Georgia Scenes* (1835)—but far more are from the twentieth century. Some differences can be noted from what Inge describes as the "matters of masculine interest" (that is, white males) that dominated earlier Southern humor. While the humor of African Americans could be more or less silenced in earlier periods—not considered part of "literature," not included in anthologies, just plain ignored—the same is not true today, and Blount includes the folk tales of Joel Chandler Harris, selections from the work of Zora Neale Hurston and Alice Walker, and some of Alice Childress's sketches about a black domestic worker. Far from being merely an oppressed group, Blount maintains, blacks are and have been central to Southern culture, which he characterizes as "Africo-Celtic," the second term referring to the original white settlers, "wild, oral, whiskey-loving, unfastidious, tribal, horse-racing, government-hating, Wasp-scorned Irish and Welsh and pre-Presbyterian Scots." Harris's "Br'er Rabbit," always outwitting larger, fiercer animals, represents the survival of an enslaved race, so it is not surprising that the same character shows up in the tales collected by anthropologist and fiction writer Hurston and published in her book *Mules and Men* (1935). The white men of the nineteenth-century tall tale hunted animals; African-American storytellers wove them into stories about coping craftily with oppression.

Female Southern humorists of the twentieth century have demonstrated their own coping mechanisms, responding to the stereotypes and mythologies that have developed around them. For the black Alice Childress, the domestic servant has to be reclaimed from the perception that she is dirty and dishonest; when the employer of Childress's character Mildred in *Like One of the Family* (1956) holds onto her purse whenever Mildred is in the apartment, Mildred is driven to tell her, "If I paid anybody as little as you pay me, I'd hold my pocketbook, too!" White Southern women have often used humor as a way of stepping down from the pedestals that traditional notions of ideal Southern womanhood have erected for them. Florence King's *Confessions of a Failed Southern Lady* (1985) records her grandmother's earnest but only partially successful attempts to make her a true Southern lady, the result of which she summarizes in the memorable line, "No matter which sex I went to bed with, I never smoked on the street." The humor of Southern women shares with that of Southern men a fondness for animals, the oddities of families, and language. Bailey White, who, like Garrison Keillor, comes to us through both printed stories and National Public Radio, writes frequently of life with her somewhat eccentric mother, and animals are often a part of the story. In "Toot and Teat," for example, Mama makes scrapple from the head of a female pig, and takes care of the sow's orphaned piglets by putting them in a box with a dog who periodically thinks she is pregnant. That the dog's name is Helen of Troy is no surprise in a region where many things are larger than life. Pointing to real rather than fictional absurdities is the business of Molly Ivins, who continues the long American tradition of the newspaper columnist writing humorously about politics. Ivins, a Texan, revels in the earthy, concrete language we associate with Old Southwest humor, and her work has some of the qualities of the tall tale. Writing of a congressional candidate who "thinks you get AIDS through your feet," she comments that he is "smarter than a box of rocks" for wearing shower caps on his feet while showering in a San Francisco hotel.

While a number of twentieth-century women humorists (not just in the South) have worked actively against stereotypes that have caused them to be seen in simplistic and discriminatory ways, many earlier women have seemed to be complicit in the furthering of such stereotypes. The early nineteenth-century writer Frances Whitcher, for example, published sketches describing small-town women as gossipy, competitive husband-hunters. Writing in rural New York State in the 1830s and 1840s, in the dialect humor then popular in most parts of the country, Whitcher portrayed women caught in the development of social-class struggle in the United States, vying with the quality of their homemade bread and hand-adorned bonnets for secure places on a community social ladder. Such struggles, like the pretensions of the urbanites in Royall Tyler's *The Contrast,* invite satire, and thus Whitcher presents Miss Sampson Savage, who "know'd she wa'n't a lady by natur nor by eddication, but she thought mabby other folks would be fools enough to think she was if she made a great parade." The speaker, Aunt Maguire, chatters on about Miss Savage while at the same time criticizing her for talking "without cessation." Another of Whitcher's characters, Priscilla Bedott, talks around and around her subject, digressing frequently, and when she tells us that her nickname is "Silly," we may be tempted to take the word in its literal sense as an adjective. Yet in providing satiric portraits of these women's behavior, Whitcher can also be seen as critiquing the origins of such behavior in the rise of genteel culture in the early nineteenth century, which increasingly stressed the separation of men's and women's spheres of influence and women's economic dependence on men. Thus, "Miss" (actually Mrs.) Sampson Savage, married to the wealthiest—if hardly the most respected—man in town, achieves authority in the only way available to her: a display of the material wealth made possible by her marriage.

By the latter decades of the century, both the "cult of gentility" and feminist protests against its restrictions had gained force, and both are central to Marietta Holley's first book, *My Opinions and Betsey Bobbet's* (1873). While Holley's character Samantha is amusing in her role as the sage philosopher, her friend Betsey is sharply satirized as the apotheosis of the dependent woman, who seeks the social approval that can be hers only if she marries. In the metaphor of the day, she is a "clinging vine" looking for a "sturdy oak" to which she can attach herself. Samantha and Betsey engage in comic debate about woman's role throughout the book, with Betsey maintaining in her affected manner of speech that it is "woman's greatest privilege, her crowning blessing, . . . to be a sort of poultice to the noble, manly breast when it is torn with the cares of life," to which the busy homemaker Samantha responds testily, "What has my sect done . . . that they have got to be lacerator soothers, when they have got everything else under the sun to do?" The contrast that Holley draws between Betsey's affectations and Samantha's common sense is one that had persisted in American humor since the colonial period, and the popularity of Holley's work over a period of four decades suggests that readers were drawn to Samantha's rustic appeal even if not all of them were sympathetic to her continual insistence that women be given the right to vote.

When Dorothy Parker began her career about the time that Holley's was concluding (the last Samantha book was published in 1914), dialect humor had lost much of its popularity in favor of sophisticated wit, but relationships between the sexes continued as predominant theme in women's humor. Indeed, some of the unhappy female personae in Parker's verses and sketches have more than a passing kinship with Betsey Bobbet in the sense that personal fulfillment is contingent upon male devotion that seems maddeningly elusive. Parker's "General Review of the Sex Situation," collected in her 1927 book *Enough Rope,* provides a succinct assessment of the dilemma in its first four lines:

> Woman wants monogamy;
> Man delights in novelty.
> Love is woman's moon and sun;
> Man has other forms of fun.

At the same time that Parker depicted women as losers in the unequal "battle of the sexes," however, her work, like that of Whitcher and Holley, shows that she understood such inequity to be the result of social structures rather than inherent in men and women. Her sketch "The Waltz" portrays male-female relationships as a culturally mandated dance which women could resist only privately, while acquiescing to it in public. The narrator's two voices represent these responses, as she says to her partner, "It's the loveliest waltz, isn't it?" but thinks to herself, "must this obscene travesty of a dance go on until hell burns out?"

By the middle of the twentieth century the most popular form of humor written by women depicted the life of the suburban homemaker as a comically chaotic experience involving the antics of children, the malfunction of household appliances, and partially successful attempts at cooking, dieting, and entertaining. Critically dubbed the "housewife humorists" by Betty Friedan in her 1963 book *The Feminine Mystique,* such writers as Phyllis McGinley, Jean Kerr, Peg Bracken, Margaret Halsey, and Shirley Jackson can be seen, as Friedan saw them, as contributing to an image of women as illogical and inept, pursuing perfection in a set of repetitive, trivial tasks. Halsey's narrator in *This Demi-Paradise: A Westchester Diary* (1960) admits her fear that she will not come up with the right amount of money at the conclusion of her daughter's Girl Scout cookie sale; Jackson's persona in *Life Among the Savages* (1953) tells of putting her husband's cup and saucer in the oven and an egg in his fruit-juice glass as she goes into labor with their third child; and Bracken, in her 1960 *I Hate to Cook Book,* acknowledges that many women do not want to deal with leftovers at all, much less do something creative with them. Friedan charged that such humor served to trivialize women's real discontents with their domestic role by making light of them. At the same time, we can see such humor as having a subversive force, much as Parker's "The Waltz" employs a second voice. Jackson's persona, for example, erupts angrily against male presumption when her doctor remarks while she is in labor, "I know *just* how you feel." And Bracken's book makes it clear that in cooking, as in other household duties, women are measured against impossibly high standards, which for Halsey were embodied in an "invisible critic" that hovered over her.

In their introduction to *Redressing the Balance: American Women's Literary Humor from Colonial Times to the 1980s* (excerpted in Chapter 9), Nancy Walker and Zita Dresner outline several characteristics of women's humor that may already be apparent in this brief overview. First, and most obviously, women—like anyone else, for that matter—have created humor about what they know best and what concerns them most. Rather than tall tales about outrageous frontiersmen, they have written about neighbors, relationships, sewing circles, and children. When their humor has been political, as it often has, it has tended to focus on women's rights—suffrage until 1920, and other forms of equality since women won the right to vote. Second, women's humor has been less aggressive and hostile than has that of men. The formulation of the "lady" that Florence King writes about so amusingly in her *Confessions* does not include these qualities, and even today's female stand-up comics acknowledge that they must be careful not to hit their targets too hard lest they turn audiences off. A third difference is that because of their unequal position in society, women may be even more conscious than men of what Louis Rubin calls "the great American joke": the incongruity between promise and reality, things as they should be and as they are. It is this kind of incongruity that Holley's Samantha Allen points to when her friend Betsey announces that woman's role should be to "soothe" the "lacerations" of the masculine ego. The busy Samantha suggests instead that men "soothe" each other, since they have more time than do women: "They might jest as well be a soothin' each other as to be a hangin' round grocery stores, or settin' by the fire whittlin'.". A much more recent example of women's humor of incongruity is Gloria Steinem's speculation about the socio-political changes that would result if men rather than women menstruated—including the prediction that "sanitary supplies would be federally funded and free."

The fact that the humor of American women has often used subversive methods to convey its messages, while appearing on the surface to further certain negative stereotypes of women, allies it closely to the humor of America's many ethnic groups. In their essay "Ethnic Humor: Subversion and Survival" (Chapter 12), Joseph Boskin and Joseph Dorinson point out the process by which such groups took the very tools used to denigrate them and used them to their own advantage: "Derisive stereotypes were adapted by their targets in mocking self-description, and then, triumphantly, adopted by the victims of stereotyping themselves as a means of revenge against their more powerful detractors." One way in which this works, Boskin and Dorinson argue, is by a kind of "first strike" method, in which members of an ethnic group make fun of themselves before someone else can do it, and they cite the kind of joke (actually, a riddle) that some Polish-Americans told when the Polish John Paul II became Pope: "Why doesn't the Pope let any dogs into the Vatican? Because they pee on poles." The authors acknowledge that a group using this kind of humor—that is, telling jokes with themselves as the target—is subject to various interpretations. It could suggest that members of the group accept the low status accorded them by others, and consider themselves worthy of being the targets of such humor. However, it seems far more likely, as Boskin and Dorinson assert, that members of ethnic groups "readily employed their own wits to criticize American values and peculiarities, and maintained thereby a measure of self-respect." If this is the case, then insisting on those characteristics that mark them as "different"—such as Mr. Dooley's Irish brogue—becomes a way of asserting a group identity and solidarity against a majority culture and its values.

In fact, by insisting in some ways on their "outsider" status as a position from which to critique American institutions and values, members of ethnic groups have participated in one of the central functions of American humor—to operate as a cultural corrective. Boskin and Dorinson point to Dunne's Mr. Dooley as a prime example of this participation. Among the targets of Mr. Dooley's humor is American materialism; when listing the wonderful technological advancements that Americans enjoy, such as the steam engine, the cotton gin, and the airplane, he identifies as the "crownin' wur-ruk iv our civilization—th'cash raygisther." The Jews had been dealing with discrimination for centuries in Europe, and had a comic tradition long before emigrating here that had some of the same purposes that developed in American humor: deflating the wealthy and pretentious, and promoting the interests of the common man. Boskin and Dorinson suggest that one of the reasons why Jews in such great numbers became prominent as humorists and comic performers in America was that their humorous traditions so closely paralleled those of American culture; they list Groucho Marx, Sid Caesar, Lenny Bruce, Jackie Mason, Don Rickles, and Mel Brooks, and to this list of performers could be added the writers Milt Gross, S. J. Perelman, Leo Rosten, and Max Shulman, among many others.

The enslavement of African Americans and subsequent cultural racism gave rise to numerous stereotypes of them in mainstream American culture, and largely hid from the view of white Americans the ways in which blacks used humor to resist oppression. Practicing comic traditions within their own communities, blacks, as Boskin and Dorinson point out, developed codes of language and character that allowed them to be outwardly subservient while communicating to each other visions of revenge and reversal of authority. The figure of "John" represented the slave against the "Master" in verbal renditions of out-witting the slaveowner, whereas the rabbit figure of black folktales plays tricks on the larger and more powerful animal characters, eluding their power. Both John and the rabbit break rules and wear masks, as do some of their counterparts in America's dominant humorous tra-dition, but not for the same reasons. Whereas the crafty Yankee ped-dler and such figures as Sut Lovingood practiced the native wit of the common man within a culture of which they were acknowledged to be a part and whose institutions they could affect, slaves stood outside that culture—denied citizenship and even full humanity. One result was the contrast between the triumphant characters of black folktales and the degrading stereotypical masks that African Americans were forced to wear in public: the subservient Uncle Tom, the smiling cook Aunt Jemima, the slow-witted Sambo—all figures of fun to white Americans, but hardly representing the real values of black culture.

Many Americans became familiar with comic stereotypes of blacks, the Irish, and other groups not on the printed page but in theatrical per-formance. Beginning soon after the Revolutionary War, drama celebrating American life and character—whether fundamentally serious or comic— often featured minor characters representing the nation's identifiable ethnic and national groups, and usually served as comic relief. In *An Emerging Entertainment,* Walter J. Meserve points out that the wave of Irish immigration following the War of 1812 prompted the emergence of the "stage Irishman," who "became a comic character . . . almost equal in popularity to the Yankee," and joining similar figures of the Indian, the Negro, and the Dutchman. Before 1828, Meserve notes, "Negroes invariably had speaking parts only as servants," and the Irish were also frequently portrayed in the same role.[10] As American dramatists looked for appropriate subject matter during the nineteenth century, they sometimes found it in novels written by their contemporaries, and in an effort to create appealing theatrical experiences for their audiences, they introduced comic stereotypes into the cast of characters. Thus, for example, when James Fenimore Cooper's 1821 novel *The Spy* was dramatized by Charles Powell Clinch in 1822, the plot included a humorous Negro servant. The most widely popular and enduring dramatization of an American novel was that created by George L. Aiken of Harriet Beecher Stowe's 1852 anti-slavery novel *Uncle Tom's Cabin*. The play made the most of Stowe's novel's great potential for sentimental scenes, but wholly invented its comic elements, making the black orphan girl Topsy and the long-suffering slave Uncle Tom into comic figures to which audiences responded enthusiastically. Although Stowe's novel was a best-seller, Blair and Hill, in *America's Humor,* propose that "the characters and scenes that the public came to know weren't, as a rule, those of the book but those in the six-act drama." Fulfilling audience expectations by then established by the minstrel show, Topsy sang and danced—"a minstrel show darky chucked into a drama"—and between acts Tom performed "minstrel-show hoedowns, songs, and Brother Bones monologues" (251–52).

If ethnic figures such as Mr. Dooley stood just sufficiently apart from mainstream American culture to critique its ideals and practices, the black figures popularized in the minstrel show from the 1830s through the rest of the century instead represented white America's anxieties about and appropriation of African-American culture. As Boskin and Dorinson suggest, the minstrel show served the purposes of whites, not blacks, who had little part in its creation: "The white performer who put on his blackface minstrel mask was performing a rite of exorcism . . . . The black persona he portrayed—indolent, inept, indulgent— embodied the anti-self and objectified the distance between social norms and man's instincts." In other words, by creating the benevolent Mammy and the foolish black male, whites tamed otherwise threatening presences in the culture and attempted to laugh away their own guilt. The format of the minstrel show reflected the opposition—by this time traditional in American humor—between the pretentious and the innocent, the well educated and the bumpkin. Exchanges between the master of ceremonies, known as the "interlocutor," and the blackface characters, who cracked jokes in dialect, created much of the humor in this popular form of performance. A similar format carried over into radio comedy, especially in the *Amos 'n' Andy* show, which premiered in 1928 and featured the supercilious Andy and the earnest but somewhat backward Amos. This program, like the minstrel show, was humor in blackface: the black characters were played by the white actors Freeman Gosden and Charles Correll.

A type of comic performance intervening historically between the minstrel show and radio (and effectively killed by the latter, which allowed audiences to stay home and laugh) was vaudeville, which had important influences on early radio and film comedy. Arthur Frank Wertheim estimates that in 1900 there were two thousand vaudeville theaters in America's cities, a number that had dwindled to fewer than a hundred by 1930, when many of them had been converted to movie theaters. Before its demise, however, vaudeville reflected more than any other humorous mode the ethnic diversity of urban America. As Wertheim notes, "vaudeville comedy routines were far different from the homespun humor of the comic Yankee and country yokel, major character stage types in the eighteenth and nineteenth century. With its slapstick, stooges, he-she jokes, punch-line monologues, and ethnic characterizations, vaudeville revolutionized stage comedy."[11] Vaudeville, which in addition to influencing radio and film can also be seen as a forerunner of stand-up comedy and television programs such as *Saturday Night Live,* no doubt perpetuated some ethnic stereotypes into the twentieth century. But unlike the minstrel show, which used stereotypes of African Americans to render the "other" harmless to whites, the ethnic portrayals of vaudeville could help with the assimilation process. As Lawrence E. Mintz has written of more recent ethnic stand-up comics, they may be laughed at for their distance from an American ideal, but they could also be "laughed with for their street-wise insistence on survival and their ironic exposure of injustices."[12]

Opposition between rural and urban values was at fever pitch around the turn of the twentieth century, having been crystallized in the presidential race of 1896, which pitted William Jennings Bryan, a Democrat committed to the interests of the common people of the West and the South, against Republican William McKinley, who had the backing of bankers and big business. McKinley's victory was one evidence of the power of the urban, industrial North, and many people felt that America was losing touch with its agrarian origins. Changes in American humor reflected these tensions. As has already been noted, the dialect humor that had for more than a century represented various parts of the American countryside fell out of favor, and the decline of the vaudeville show was in part due to a sense that its broad, rather crude humor belonged to an earlier, less sophisticated era. Such a transition was not without its paradoxes, of course. For example, nowhere were there more dialects spoken than in America's urban centers; Dunne's Mr. Dooley was only one instance of this. But these were, by and large, the dialects of Irish, Polish, German, and other immigrants who were eager to become "Americanized" and move up the socioeconomic ladder. Several of radio's earliest comic personalities typify this desire in the professional names they adopted: Isaiah Edwin Leopold became Ed Wynn, Benjamin Kubelsky became Jack Benny, and Nathan Birnbaum became George Burns. Thus, even as members of ethnic groups continued to be involved in humorous performance, the average radio listener might have been largely unaware of that fact.

The rapid development of film and radio in the early decades of the twentieth century and then of television in the 1950s not only provided new outlets for humorous expression but also emphasized the national over the regional experience. As millions of people watched the same movies and listened to the same radio programs (and, not incidentally, the same advertisements for products), they shared common cultural experiences that could mold tastes and attitudes across thousands of miles of the American landscape. However, electronic media were not solely responsible for what some have termed the "homogenization" of American culture. As Blair and Hill point out, the development of book and magazine publishing by the end of the nineteenth century also played a part in obscuring regional differences and altering the nature of American humor. "When our society became urbanized and cultural centers were formed, bookstores to a large extent could replace the newspaper, the popular subscription book hawked by agents, and the lecture platform" as outlets for humor, "and that streak of inferiority that had deliberately called hyperbolic attention to itself in earlier humor tended, at the turn of the century, to become an embarrassment" (369). The "streak of inferiority" to which Blair and Hill refer was associated with the rustic, crackerbox image that had been a source of national pride in earlier periods but that did not seem appropriate to a nation that had become a world power by the time of World War I.

Another factor causing changes in American humor at the turn of the century was what we might call the "professionalization" of American literature in general. Before the late nineteenth century, colleges and universities did not offer courses in American literature; not only did many people believe there was not enough indigenous literature to be worthy of such study, but college curricula tended to emphasize the classical literature of Greece and Rome rather than that produced closer to home. At the time that H. R. Haweis delivered his lectures on "American Humorists" to an English audience in 1881, his topic was of interest partly because it was an exotic curiosity, not because his listeners had been schooled in an American literary tradition, and much the same was true in America. In the late 1880s, Edmund Clarence Stedman and E. M. Hutchinson compiled the *Library of American Literature,* an eleven-volume project that represented one of the first attempts to define a distinct national body of literature (and did so by identifying predominantly New England male authors). As late as 1909, a student at Columbia University commented that although he was fond of reading Emerson, Whitman, and Thoreau, his "professors seldom refer to them."[13] By the 1920s, something of a revolution had occurred, and American literature was a fit subject to teach and to write about. It is no accident, then, that the real beginnings of the formal, academic study of American humor, in the work of Tandy, Rourke, and Blair, took place in the 1920s and 1930s. It is also no accident that each of these scholars felt that she or he could safely characterize an American humor that had its origins in a pre-urban, pre-industrial America, for that now seemed to belong to the past.

Three comic periodicals that spanned the turn-of-the-century period represent the mixture of elements that marked American humor in its transition from the rustic sage and minstrel-show racism to the clever urbanity of *The New Yorker. Puck* (1877–1918), *Judge* (1881–1937), and *Life* (1883–1936) were all consciously urban magazines, not only in their publishing location (New York), but also in the talents that they drew upon and the types of humor that they published. All three relied heavily upon comic art, including political cartoons, reflecting the growing popularity of visual humor as the technical means to reproduce it developed. The ethnic humor that grew out of metropolitan life mingled with the more sophisticated wit of the upper classes—*Puck* began as a magazine published in German by an immigrant from Vienna, and *Life* was an offshoot of the *Harvard Lampoon,* the most venerable of the university humor magazines (1876 to the present day). Aimed primarily at the literate, middle-class reader, these magazines tended to view urban ethnic conflict from somewhat above the fray; a comic dialogue between Irish laborers from a 1900 issue of *Judge* goes as follows:

> *Sucey:* Th' men shtruck fer an increase at twinty cints a day.
>
> *Callahan:* An' did yez git it?
>
> *Ducey:* We did. Th' boss put in twinty dagoes wid scints that wud knock ye down.

Judge also honored the American oral tradition by publishing proverbs, which owed much to the aphorisms of *Poor Richard's Almanac*. At the same time, however, these periodicals reflected the sophistication of their founders and editors. *Puck*'s motto was a quotation from Shakespeare's *A Midsummer Night's Dream*, "Oh what fools these mortals be!"; *Life* featured the illustrations of Charles Dana Gibson, which depicted high society, and whose drawings of the "Gibson Girl" set the standard for female beauty in the 1890s; and each issue of *Judge* included a drawing of "The Judge," who presided over human foolishness in black judicial robes.

While the image of "The Judge" is in some ways similar to *The New Yorker*'s Eustace Tilley, peering through his monocle, important distinctions can be drawn to represent the differences between these earlier magazines of humor and the one which would supplant them. Whereas a court judge is directly involved in the nation's political institutions, Tilley is portrayed as a dandy, scrutinizing nothing more significant than a butterfly; *The New Yorker* in its early days was distinctly apolitical, concentrating instead on the arts and the social life of New York, but *Judge, Puck,* and *Life* became directly involved in partisan politics, as American newspapers had been since the colonial period. *Judge* was for a time officially affiliated with the Republican Party, and during the 1896 presidential campaign the magazine openly backed McKinley, publishing caricatures of his opponent, William Jennings Bryan. *Puck,* on the other hand, was distinctly Democratic in its political leanings, championing the interests of labor against big business and monopolies, and *Life,* while claiming to be independent, tended to follow suit, especially during major political campaigns. All three magazines were quick to pounce upon political scandals and corruption on both the local and national levels, ridiculing those responsible with both words and comic art.

Despite their overt political stances, the turn-of-the-century humor magazines published a great deal of material intended solely to amuse readers. *Judge,* for example, reprinted material from college humor magazines, and by the early 1920s acknowledged the urban presence of large numbers of single women in its "Mabel and Madge" cartoons, which featured, in the words of Thomas Grant, "a pair of dim-witted urban single girls, who . . . fell comically into malapropisms."[14] A fairly typical cartoon showed Mabel and Madge looking at a passing young man; to Mabel's question, "Is he on the football team?" Madge responds, "Oh, yes! He's some kind of a drawback." The malapropism, or comic misuse of a word, had its origins in sophisticated comedy; named for Mrs. Malaprop in Richard Brinsley Sheridan's 1775 play *The Rivals,* it differs from the misspellings and mispronunciations of American dialect humor.

Another humorous form with a long history that became popular at the turn of the century was the parody—especially the literary parody—and one of the most well-known parodists of the first two decades of the twentieth century was Carolyn Wells, who wrote for *Judge.* Wells, who was an editor of collections of humorous writing as well as a humorist, wrote parodies of Hamlet's "To be or not to be" soliloquy, and created fanciful creatures such as the "Clothes Horse" and the "Golf Lynx." Wells was particularly fond of poking fun at stereotypical images of women. In "To a Milkmaid," she writes of "thy impossible milkpail and thy improbable bodice," and in "The Trailing Skirt" she addresses the early-century fashion dictate that women's skirts sweep the floor:

> Thou trundling, trailing skirt!
> Smearing thyself with dirt,
> Forever catching in the swinging doors
> As we go in and out of stores.

In addition to fashions, the comic magazines included regular features that appealed to other interests of the upwardly mobile urbanite, such as the popularity of golf and of that new invention, the automobile.

As America's pride in its own literature increased in the early years of the twentieth century, many writers and editors felt the need for a "new" American humor, which such magazines as *Puck, Judge,* and *Life* had begun to fulfill. John Kendrick Bangs, who helped to found *Life* and wrote for both *Puck* and *Judge,* announced in 1900 that, "it is not necessary nowadays to be vulgar to be amusing." Bangs, who also wrote for the prestigious *Harper's Magazine,* was well-versed in literature, and peppered his humor with literary references and allusions. His 1896 book *The House-Boat on the Styx* features conversations among such luminaries as Diogenes, Shakespeare, Napoleon, Alfred, Lord Tennyson, Artemus Ward, and Samuel Johnson. Yet Bangs was no pedant; his humor is zany, whimsical, and filled with imaginative reversals of everyday reality, as when he proposed to start a newspaper that reported what had not happened—for example, "George Bronson, colored, aged twenty-nine, a resident of Thompson Street, was caught cheating at poker last night. He was not murdered." An extreme version of such whimsical humor emerged on the West Coast in *The Lark,* which published monthly issues between 1895 and 1897 in San Francisco. Considered by some to be inspired nonsense and by others childish self-indulgence, *The Lark*'s humor was certainly not vulgar, but instead had a dreamlike quality, typified by *Lark* founder Gelett Burgess's verse "The Purple Cow":

> I never Saw a Purple Cow;
> I never Hope to See One;
> But I can Tell you, Anyhow,
> I'd rather See than Be One.

The element of the humor of Bangs and Burgess that was particularly "new" in the American humorous tradition was its almost complete lack of reference to social reality. From its earliest days, American humor had largely been a response to the practical realities of settling a wilderness, experimenting with a democratic political system, and negotiating the needs of different groups of people within a common national experience. Seldom had our humor been merely for fun, without serving some sociopolitical purpose, and what we might call the humor of reality—as opposed to the humor of fantasy—has maintained its dominance throughout American literary history. One reason for this trend is that the humor of wit and whimsy, the literary parody, and other forms requiring education and sophisticated tastes necessarily appeal to a small audience. Conscious of this limitation, the editors of *The Lark* and its Chicago cousin *The Chap-Book* took pride in being magazines for a small elite; Gelett Burgess wrote in the last issue of *The Lark* that "it has never been 'popular,' but something in the quality of its friends gave it repute. *The Lark* was received by the few who had 'discovered' it with indulgence."

The New Yorker began publication in 1925 with a similar stance of exclusivity. The magazine's founding publisher, Harold Ross, started with a sort of manifesto that decreed that *The New Yorker* was not for "the old lady in Dubuque," and such geographical snobbery extended even to the magazine's definition of New York as only Manhattan. Yet a combination of factors caused *The New Yorker* to take its place as America's premier periodical publishing humor—a status it has now enjoyed for more than seventy years. One of these factors, as everyone who writes about *The New Yorker* seems to agree, was Ross's sheer luck in staffing the magazine with extremely talented writers and artists. The list of early contributors reads like a *Who's Who* of the best comic writers and illustrators of the first half of the century: E. B. White, James Thurber, Wolcott Gibbs, Peter Arno, Dorothy Parker, Robert Benchley, Helen Hokinson, and many more. Another reason for *The New Yorker*'s success was its innovations in humor, of which perhaps the most important was the single-frame cartoon with a caption in which the visual and the verbal depend upon each other for humorous effect. One of the most famous cartoons, created by James Thurber, shows a man and woman in bed while a seal looks over the headboard behind them; in the caption, the woman says, "All Right, Have It Your Way— You Heard a Seal Bark!" Another innovation was the "Talk of the Town" section at the beginning of each issue—a series of observations of New York life, first written by E. B. White. Announcing this section in his 1924 prospectus for the magazine, Harold Ross described it as "a personal mention column—a jotting down in the small-town newspaper style of the comings, goings and doings in the village of New York. This will contain some josh and some news value."

It was precisely *The New Yorker*'s treatment of the city as a "village" that gave the magazine wide appeal beyond Manhattan. While the subjects of the "Talk of the Town" pieces were people, places, and events of a single New York borough, the column resembled those in small-town newspapers that told who had visited relatives there, who had celebrated birthdays and anniversaries, and who had won prizes at the county fair. As Steven H. Gale writes, "the flavor" is "that of a small-town newspaper reporting on current events in a folksy way that implies that the writer and reader know each other, share the same beliefs, and are on familiar terms."[15] Such an approach, Ross's manifesto notwithstanding, allowed "the old lady in Dubuque" to feel at home in the magazine's pages.

Although *The New Yorker* regularly published reviews of plays and books, and reported what was happening at upper-middle-class locations such as art museums, nightclubs, and the racetrack, the stance most writers adopted was far from snobbish; they were sophisticated, but not pretentious, worldly, but not effete. Something of this attitude can be seen in the poem titled "Bohemia" by Dorothy Parker, published in the September 17, 1927, issue of the magazine:

Authors and actors and artists and such
Never know nothing, and never know much.
Sculptors and singers and those of their kidney
Tell their affairs from Seattle to Sydney.

Playwrights and poets and such horses' necks
Start off from anywhere and end up at sex.
Diarists, critics, and similar roe
Never say nothing, and never say no.
People Who Do Things exceed my endurance;
God, for a man who solicits insurance!

The sense of shared problems and concerns conveyed in *New Yorker* humor was often contained in its cartoons as well. The anonymity of the American suburb was embodied in one of Robert Day's cartoons, which pictured, in the midst of row upon row of identical houses, a woman saying to a postman, "I'm Mrs. Edward M. Barnes. Where do I live?"

The first generation of *New Yorker* humorists—especially Thurber, Benchley, White, and Perelman—contributed to what has been termed the humor of the "little man" that flourished in the period between the two World Wars. The technological advancement and urbanization that drew American readers to more sophisticated types of humor during the era also created feelings of anonymity and bewilderment, as large corporations, mass advertising, high-rise apartment buildings, and rapid change became facts of life. The little man shared with the Jonathan figure of earlier years a sense of being overwhelmed by social complexities, but for him there was no return to rural simplicity—no "territory" to "light out to," as Huck Finn declares he will do at the end of Twain's novel. James Thurber, in his preface to *My Life and Hard Times* (1933), offered perhaps the most cogent description of the little man that he helped to create. His gestures are "the ludicrous reflexes of the maladjusted; his repose is the momentary inertia of the nonplussed." The little man's sense of ineffectuality may be largely caused by global disorders, but he locates the real problems within himself: "He knows vaguely that the nation is not much good anymore; he has read that the crust of the earth is shrinking alarmingly and that the universe is growing steadily colder, but he does not believe that any of the three is in half as bad shape as he is." For Thurber, the quintessential little man of the twentieth century was the humorist himself, who sat "on the edge of the chair of Literature," and "the wheels of [whose] invention are set in motion by the damp hand of melancholy." In *The American Humorist: Conscience of the Twentieth Century,* Norris W. Yates compares the little man to the typical persona of nineteenth-century American humor. Whereas the earlier figure was "self-made, self-employed, and self-reliant," the little man was "a consumer, both of goods and of pro-paganda."[16] The typical recourse of the little man is to retreat into his own imagination, as do the central characters of Thurber's "The Unicorn in the Garden" and "The Secret Life of Walter Mitty."

Thurber often represented the pressures of contemporary life in the form of animal fables. In "The Shrike and the Chipmunks," for example, a male chipmunk with artistic tendencies would rather arrange the nuts he gathers in attractive patterns than see how many he can accumulate, but his wife wants him to become "the wealthiest chipmunk in the woods." When the female chipmunk goes away for a few days, her husband's sloth protects him from the deadly attacks of the shrike, who cannot get in because "the doorway was clogged up with soiled laundry and dirty dishes." Restored to regular habits upon his wife's return, the chipmunk is killed by the shrike while taking a walk. The moral of Thurber's fable is a parody of one of Benjamin Franklin's Poor Richard aphorisms: "Early to rise and early to bed makes a male healthy and wealthy and dead."

The little man feels himself to be at the mercy of the media as well as of ambitious wives. E. B. White's "Dusk in Fierce Pajamas" is the fantasy of a man who realizes after reading *Vogue* and *Harper's Bazaar* that his "own life is by contrast an unlovely thing, with its disease, its banalities, its uncertainties, its toil, its single-breasted suits, and its wine from lesser years." His imagination takes him to a series of social settings suggested by the magazines, which whimsy makes increasingly bizarre, until he is "in the modern penthouse of Monsieur Charles de Bastagui. The staircase is entirely of cement, spreading at the hemline and trimmed with padded satin tubing caught at the neck with a bar of milk chocolate." Of all the writers who addressed the dilemmas of the little man, S. J. Perelman most frequently allowed whimsy to spin into absurdity, especially when his persona is confronted with modern technology. In "To Sleep, Perchance to Steam," Perelman is introduced to his first electric blanket, called by its manufacturer an "Electric Comforter," which leads him to speculate that he "could pass through a room containing the Electric Comforter in the original gift box and emerge with a third-degree burn." Reading, but not reassured by, the instruction booklet, Perelman "experienced a distinct tingling sensation which could only have emanated from the booklet itself. Luckily, I had the presence of mind to plunge it into a pail of water and yell for help."

When scholars began to rediscover women's contributions to American humor, it became clear that the "little man" had been accompanied by a "little woman" during the interwar period. But whereas the little man is haunted by a universe that seems insane and/or dangerous, the little woman's concerns are more local and immediate—especially the culture's expectations of her performance in her assigned role. Instead of the fantasies of White's and Perelman's characters, her head is filled with the voices of etiquette manuals, homemaking guides, and popular magazines; in little man humor, women (such as the female chipmunk) nagged him, but in little woman humor, women were themselves beset with advice and standards from all quarters. The speaker in Dorothy Parker's "The Waltz" is an example of the little woman, fulfilling the social expectation that she be an amiable dancing partner against her will. Cornelia Otis Skinner's persona is another example. The speaker in Skinner's *Soap Behind the Ears* (1941) is subject to behavioral expectations when shopping for her son's clothes; the clerks "seem to expect the average mother to act and talk as if she's stepped off the front page of *Good Housekeeping*. And what's worse, I do." In *Dithers and Jitters* (1939), Skinner's speaker confesses that she lacks the supposedly innate female talent for flower-arranging, "one of those tenderly becoming gestures expected of us women—like mending socks or crying at weddings." Women writers also pushed the little woman to two different extremes. One, exemplified by Parker's story "Big Blonde," is desperation: Hazel Morse has learned a set of skills that are supposed to please men; when these fail, she attempts suicide. At the other end of the spectrum are characters such as Anita Loos's Lorelei Lee, in *Gentlemen Prefer Blondes* (1925). Sometimes wrongly seen as the stereotypical "dumb blonde," Lorelei is actually the supreme *eiron,* pretending ignorance of the world but telling readers, in her comically ungrammatical style, how she flatters the egos of men in order to maintain a comfortable way of life.

If the humorous little man and little woman were intended to represent the anxieties of the average American in the decades following World War I, the medium through which humor reached that American was increasingly the radio, which continued the American oral tradition in a particularly intimate form: individuals and families listened to comic sketches and dialogues that seemed performed especially for them in the privacy of their own homes. As one author has said, "A successful radio performer sounded as if he or she spoke to each individual on a one-to-one basis. Millions came to feel that they knew such radio 'personalities' intimately."[17] In the mid-1920s, about 20 percent of American homes had radios; by the time the nation entered World War II in 1941, the number was close to 90 percent. As radio networks developed during the 1930s, listeners in all parts of the country could simultaneously experience the same comedy broadcasts, which made possible a sharing of an American sense of humor that had never before been possible. Both direct listener responses and the sales of products that sponsored radio programs provided fairly quick indications of what the American public found amusing.

Radio humor began by borrowing from earlier forms, notably the vaudeville show. The two-man "song and patter" team was a direct carryover from the vaudeville stage, alternating musical numbers with comic dialogue. The vaudeville emphasis on ethnic humor also made the transition to radio; the German-Jewish dialect comedy team of Weber and Fields performed during the inaugural broadcast of the National Broadcasting Company in 1926. Some of the most enduring radio comedians had begun their careers in vaudeville: Ed Wynn, Fred Allen, Jack Benny, and George Burns and Gracie Allen. For the performer, this change from one comic medium to another was not always easy. As Arthur Frank Wertheim points out in *Radio Comedy*, several crucial differences could be obstacles to success. The costumes and props used by a stage performer were clearly of no use when an audience could not see the act, and the absence of a responsive audience meant that comedians had to develop a sense of timing without hearing laughter or applause.

Perhaps most important for the development of American humor, appealing to a diverse, invisible audience put certain restraints on comic subject matter. A radio comic who was broadcast regularly had to have new material for each show, in contrast to the vaudeville performer who went from town to town telling the same jokes. A radio humorist also could not risk alienating a segment of the faceless audience; Wertheim quotes a vaudeville performer who commented on this fact in 1926: "[the radio performer] can not tell stories that hold a race, a class or a religion up to ridicule, he cannot jest of things which are not familiar to the every day life of his hearers." And because radio was from the start perceived as "family home entertainment," "lewd jokes and double entendres were taboo" (14–15). Ed Wynn, who was particularly popular in his program *The Fire Chief* in the 1930s, solved the audience dilemma by pioneering the concept of the studio audience at his broadcasts, and he continued to wear the outlandish costumes of his vaudeville days.

Much early radio humor was, as Wertheim says, "inane and corny," depending upon puns and other wordplay. One of Wynn's stories concerned a boy whose father tells him to write a ten-page essay on milk, but the boy decides he can get by with one page by writing about condensed milk. If radio comics, bowing to a diverse audience, avoided humor that ridiculed races and creeds, apparently women were expected to go along with joking at their expense. One of Wynn's routines involved fictitious letters from listeners, and when one of these asked the significance of a married man dreaming he was a bachelor, the reply was, "it's a sign that he's going to meet with a great disappointment when he wakes up." Radio comics typically worked with one or more "straight men," who set the comedian up for his comic lines. Similar to the interlocutor of the minstrel show, the straight man adopted a pose of seriousness or innocence that allowed the comic to deliver the punch line. As advertising became increasingly important to the radio industry, the announcer who delivered the commercial message often became a straight man. When *The Fire Chief*'s announcer accidentally mispronounced "gasoline" as "gasoloon" during one broadcast, Wynn's teasing him about his slip became a regular feature of the show. Rather than resisting such interplay between announcer and performer, advertisers quickly realized the publicity value of such joking. As Roland Marchand notes, "Program stars such as Ed Wynn, Heywood Broun, and Jack Benny were induced to 'kid' the sponsor's product during their comedy skits and routines, thus associating the product with their own personalities" (109). Thus, radio humor, in addition to amusing its audiences, was used to further the interests of American business.

The *Amos 'n' Andy* program, which borrowed from the minstrel show the device of white men impersonating blacks, had far less racist intentions than its predecessor. While it did perpetuate certain stereotypes of African Americans, it appealed to black listeners as well as white ones, in large part because its creators, Gosden and Correll, based the shows on material gathered on research trips to Harlem. So great was their commitment to realism, Wertheim points out, that "dots on a map of Harlem in their office indicated the exact location of important places in the show" (57). Also, *Amos 'n' Andy* played upon a different version of the little man than did the humor of Thurber and White: when the stock market crashed just two months after the program began to be broadcast over NBC, Gosden and Correll immediately made the economic depression part of the show, indicating how the resulting hardships affected working people of any race. Part of the program that aired the day after the crash both plays upon the ignorance of the character Lightnin' (who is similar in some ways to Jonathan in Tyler's *The Contrast*) and shows how a troubled economy would affect the average hardworking American. The following exchange takes place when Lightnin'—whose name suggests the very quickness of understanding he does not have—approaches Andy for a job with his taxi company:

> *Andy:* Is you been keepin' yo' eye on de stock market?
> *Lightnin':* Nosah, I ain't never seed it.
> *Andy:* Well, the stock market crashed.
> *Lightnin':* Anybody git hurt?
> *Andy:* Well, 'course Lightnin', when de stock market crashes, it hurts us bizness men. Dat's what puts de repression on things.

Listeners could be amused by Lightnin's misapprehension that the stock market was a building that had fallen down, and at the same time comforted by the idea that we were all in this together.

A great deal of the appeal of the comic characters that populated American radio in its heyday of the 1930s and 1940s was due to characteristics with which millions of Americans could identify. Jack Benny, who helped radio comedy emerge from its dependence on vaudeville slapstick and concentrate instead on memorable characters, said of his program that it was "built on a foundation of real people. . . . We try to have things happen to us that would happen to anyone. Things that will be interesting and, above all, funny. I'd be willing to bet you that there are very few who don't know people like Mary Livingstone, Phil Harris, and Rochester. Therefore, we feel that we represent, to a certain extent, the audience."[18] Benny played a stingy egotist who was continually deflated by the other characters in the show, including his black servant, Rochester. One running joke, which was popular in an increasingly youth-conscious society, was Benny's refusal to pass the age of thirty-nine. Bob Hope created a wiseguy persona, which Wertheim describes as "the nation's favorite court jester." Although Hope readily needled public figures, he was not a political satirist, but instead "represented the successful, patriotic, charitable, and virtuous All-American to radio listeners in the 1940s" (304), the period of World War II and a heightened sense of nationalism.

Other radio characters recalled earlier traditions of American humor. The popular *Fibber McGee and Molly* program was set in the fictional Midwestern town of "Wistful Vista," thus playing upon America's former agrarian innocence. Jim Jordan's character Fibber drew upon the little man, with his fantasies of power and adventure, and the bragging hero of the nineteenth-century tall tale. His "fibs" were grandiose accounts of piloting a hot-air balloon, deep-sea fishing, and bare-handed combat with bears, told in a folksy dialect: "I'll never forget the time I rid acrost Africa on a huntin' trip on a bicycle. Yes sir, Toots, that was in 1897. Capetown to Tripoli. Made it in twenty-two days exactly." In contrast to these imagined exploits, Fibber McGee was a household bungler, unable to accomplish a simple repair without a disaster, and one of the running jokes on the program was the McGees' overstuffed hall closet, which tumbled its contents on anyone who opened the door, which made use of radio's great potential for sound effects.

One of radio's most enduring comic couples was George Burns and Gracie Allen, whose dialogues featured Gracie as the scatterbrained innocent with a paradoxical air of self-assurance. The pair's routines frequently turned on wordplay, as in the following excerpt:

George: You're absolutely brilliant. I'm beginning to think you are a wizard.

Gracie: I'm a wizard?

George: Yes. You know what a wizard is.

Gracie: Yes, a snowstorm.

George: Well, if that's a snowstorm, then what's a blizzard?

Gracie: A blizzard is the inside of a chicken. Anybody knows that.

George Burns and Gracie Allen were among the relatively few performers who made a successful transition from vaudeville to radio and then to television. Each medium demanded different comic skills and a different relationship to the audience, which by the 1950s was increasingly fascinated by the box that brought both pictures and sound into their living rooms. In 1948 there were fewer than two hundred thousand television sets in American homes, but by 1952 this number had climbed to seventeen million. Advertisers quickly saw the potential for bringing visual representations of their products into the household, and many abandoned radio programs they had sponsored for years in order to take advantage of the new medium. Other factors played a role in diminishing the importance of radio as a medium for humor. Listeners had become less tolerant of the ethnic and racial stereotypes on which much radio comedy depended; blacks had never been as accepting of Jack Benny's servant Rochester (with his single name suggesting the days of slavery) as they had been of the more independent Amos and Andy, and with the civil rights movement of the 1950s, such characters seemed dangerous anachronisms. Also, as college attendance burgeoned following World War II, Americans demanded a more sophisticated humor than that provided by radio's jokes and sound effects.

Whether television actually provided more sophisticated humor than had radio is a debatable point, although it certainly has presented more types of comic expression than radio was capable of doing—including quiz-show banter, visual slapstick, stand-up comics, and situation comedies—and the combination of sound and visual image made possible a more complex audience experience. What is perhaps most striking, however, is that with few exceptions, television humor in its early decades, particularly in its most enduring form, the situation comedy, portrayed a world in which, as David Marc says in *Demographic Vistas* (excerpted in Chapter 14), the "family was white and had a name that bespoke Anglo-Saxon ancestry and Protestant religious affiliation." In the 1950s and 1960s, even as Americans were becoming aware of the need to respect rather than make fun of racial and ethnic diversity, television conveyed a white, middle-class world. *Amos 'n' Andy* made the transition from radio to television for a brief period in the early 1950s (with black actors instead of whites in blackface), but the protests of civil rights leaders forced it off the air despite its largely sympathetic portrayals of blacks. The popular media of the postwar period welcomed peace by showcasing an ideal America of nuclear families in suburban settings, handling whatever minor problems they might have with common-sense morality and good humor.

In "Television Is Funny," David Marc argues that television occupies the role of "jester" in American life, in the sense that whether we are offended by some of the messages it conveys or insulted by the attempts of the "boob tube" to manipulate us, the medium is both popular and profitable, and humor has always been integral to its success. Those who would snobbishly dismiss television as culturally insignificant, Marc proposes, fail to recognize how deeply rooted it is in other art forms. For example, the physical antics and racial and ethnic stereotypes of early televised wrestling recalled vaudeville and minstrel performances. But even more pervasive, he notes, has been television's appropriation of the conventions of the theater, especially in the situation comedy: each episode resembles "a short, self-contained play . . . complete with laughter and applause." The subject of the situation comedy, Marc asserts, is nothing less than American culture: "It dramatizes national types, styles, customs, issues, and language." That it does so conservatively, avoiding controversial issues until they can be perceived as safely comic, should not be surprising, given advertisers' reluctance to alienate potential consumers of their products. Marc points to the fact that *All in the Family,* which dealt with 1960s issues such as race, alternative lifestyles, and challenges to the status quo, did not appear until 1971. Situation comedies of the previous two decades—including *Father Knows Best, The Donna Reed Show, The Trouble with Father,* and *Make Room for Daddy*—presented a stable culture in which minor disruptions of ethics or propriety were put to rights within half an hour. And one could also observe that the centrality of fatherhood represented in this list of titles suggests a stable, patriarchal order.

Lawrence E. Mintz, in his essay "Ideology in the Television Situation Comedy" (Chapter 15), agrees with Marc about this form of humor as a certain kind of reflection of American culture—or, perhaps more accurately, of American culture as it might like to be. Mintz goes beyond Marc, however, by analyzing how the sitcom conveys its ideology through its "structure, premises, characterizations, plot-themes, and semiotic elements." Mintz points out that in its structure, the sitcom has a yearning for the "normalcy" that Americans wanted to return to following World War II. Each episode begins with life running in its familiar grooves for the characters, and once the comic disruption of the plot has been resolved, a state of normality is restored. This resistance to change, Mintz notes, is at odds with the American dream of "achievement, opportunity, growth, mobility," and he posits that perhaps the sitcom conveys the more realistic message that "vertical mobility is a dream unlikely to be realized." Happiness is to be found in the family rather than in the realization of the little man's fantasies, and Mintz argues that even in sitcoms with workplace (*The Mary Tyler Moore Show*) or military (*Hogan's Heroes*) settings, the characters' familial relationships with each other take center stage.

Character types provide another evidence of the essential conservatism of the sitcom. Mintz notes that while these television comedies employ a wide range of comic types, one of the most enduring is that descendant of the Jonathan figure, the "average guy"—nonintellectual, sometimes bigoted (Archie Bunker in *All in the Family*) or foolish (Ralph Cramden in *The Honeymooners*), but admirable as the "common man" of democratic ideals. Since the 1970s, sitcoms increasingly have dealt with issues such as racism and sexuality, but because of the need to appeal to a mass audience, the shows have provided only shallow or superficial ways of handling them. Mintz concludes that the television situation comedy may be contemporary America's "most effective form" of conveying ideologies that reflect the audience's "values, attitudes, dispositions, fears, and hopes."

David Marc characterizes the television situation comedy as a "representational" form of humor in that it replicates, with some degree of realism, everyday life. Television's other major form of humor, the comedy-variety show, he terms "presentational"—various artists present their songs, skits, monologues, and dialogues to the audience. Such a format has an obvious ancestor in vaudeville, in which singers, dancers, and comics took their places on the stage one after another, and the format was also used in the early days of radio. *The Ed Sullivan Show* was one of the longest-running variety shows on television, although it featured more musical numbers than it did stand-up comics, which Marc considers one of the most appropriate as well as the most challenging forms of television humor. Indeed, Marc's vivid description of the stand-up comic applies equally well to live performance:

> Stand-up comedy, as developed in the American nightclub, is one of the most intense and compelling of modern performance arts. Eschewing the protection of narrative superstructure and continuity, the stand-up comedian nakedly faces the audience. He truly works in the first person, making no distinction between persona and self. When successful, the monologist offers an awesome display of charismatic power: the lone individual controlling the imaginative and physical responses of millions. By the same token, nowhere is failure more pathetic or painful.

The risk taken by the stand-up comic is that he (and, less often, she) is alone, not part of a group or an element in a story, and gambles that what he believes to be funny will be shared by the audience.

In "Stand-up Comedy as Social and Cultural Mediation" (Chapter 11), Lawrence Mintz argues that this form of humor long predates the vaudeville show—that it is, in fact, "the oldest, most universal, basic, and deeply significant form of humorous expression. . . . the purest public comic communication." Using the insights of sociologists and anthropologists, Mintz locates the origin of modern stand-up comedy in ancient "rites, rituals, and dramatic experiences" that include "the tradition of fools, jesters, clowns, and comics, which can be traced back at least as far as the Middle Ages." In the history of American culture specifically, Mintz defines the stand-up tradition to include the circus clown, the minstrel show, and the humorous lecture-circuit performer of the nineteenth century, such as Mark Twain and Artemus Ward. It is the function of stand-up comedy within a culture that is of most interest to Mintz in this essay; as he alternately affirms and subverts commonly accepted cultural values, the comedian serves as our "comic spokesman," allowed a freedom of expression not permitted the ordinary individual. The stand-up comic thus gives voice to what the audience might secretly feel but not dare say, and often does so by using the guise of a socially unacceptable persona—"the grotesque, the buffoon, the fool, the simpleton, the scoundrel, the drunkard, the liar, the coward, the effete, the tightwad, the boor, the egoist, the cuckold, the shrew, the weakling, the neurotic"—whose views we can superficially reject. Mintz draws his examples from the world of performance art— for example, the egotistical pennypincher Jack Benny, the socially inept Woody Allen, the self-deprecating Phyllis Diller, the promiscuous and provocative Richard Pryor. We can also find instances of the use of such guises in America's humorous literary tradition—the mock-innocent Jonathan, Huck Finn, and Lorelei Lee; the renegade Sut Lovingood; the victimized Dorothy Parker; the bewildered S. J. Perelman. On paper, however, such figures lack an important dimension that Mintz ascribes to the comic performance, that is, the interplay between comic and audience in which a degree of community is established so that humor can do its work of cultural mediation.

The sense of community between stand-up comic and audience is similar to what Gerald Mast calls the "comic climate" of film. That is, just as the comic performer must establish what Mintz terms the "license of comedy" so that certain things can happen that could not if the situation were perceived as "serious," so the filmmaker provides one or more signals that "the action is taking place in a comic world." Mast's *The Comic Mind: Comedy and the Movies* (excerpted in Chapter 13) does not deal exclusively with the American film comedy, and with good reason: more than most forms of humor, film, perhaps because of the universality of the visual image, has been an international phenomenon. While Americans today may identify movies with the giant film industries of Hollywood, in the early decades of the twentieth century most American films were made on the East Coast. The quintessential little man of silent film, Charlie Chaplin, was an Englishman by birth; and European and American producers, directors, and actors have influenced each others' work over the years. In describing the eight comic plots he distinguishes, then, Mast uses examples from both European and American films and also from the plays of Shakespeare and classical dramatists.

American comic films have frequently drawn upon the traditions and values that already have been encountered in this overview. In *America's Humor,* Blair and Hill cite the Yankee peddler and the character of Colonel Sellers in Mark Twain's 1873 novel *The Gilded Age* as forerunners of the "blustering buffoonery" of the great film comic W. C. Fields. Despite his masterful use of gesture, facial expressions, and timing, Fields's humor was largely verbal, often in the tradition of the tall tale. When, for example, a friend of Fields's character in *The Bank Dick* is about to swat a fly on a bar, Fields launches into a tale worthy of Twain's Simon Wheeler: "Don't hurt that fly—that's Old Tom—they named a gin after him. That fly followed me out here from the show. . . . He used to drive the chariot races in the flea circus. One afternoon in a small town outside of Hoosic Falls, when I was ignominiously dragged off to the local Bastille and placed in durance vile at the behest of a blackguard reporting the loss of his silver timepiece, Old Tom . . . stuck his left hind leg in the Governor's inkwell, dragged it above the dotted line, forging the Governor's signature [on a letter of pardon] . . . I love that fly."

Such verbal excesses were matched, especially in the silent film comedy, by elaborate physical pantomime that also seemed to express America's larger-than-life experience. In his classic essay "Comedy's Greatest Era," writer James Agee celebrates the physicality of the silent-film actor: "Startled by a cop, this . . . comedian might grab his hatbrim with both hands and mash it down over his ears, jump high in the air, come to earth in a split violent enough to telescope his spine, spring thence into a coattail-flattening sprint and dwindle at rocket speed to the size of a gnat along the grand, forlorn perspective of some lazy back boulevard."[19] Part of Agee's fondness for the silent film stems from the actor's skill in the expressive use of his body, but another part, implied though not stated in his essay, has to do with the silent film's appeal to ordinary, working-class people. Some silent film actors, like some early radio personalities, came from vaudeville, which many sophisticated Americans considered beneath them. Writing of the silent comedies created by Mack Sennett, "the father of American screen comedy," between 1912 and 1930, Agee recalls that "'nice' people, who shunned all movies in the early days, condemned the Sennett comedies as vulgar and naive. But millions of less pretentious people loved their sincerity and sweetness, their wild-animal innocence and glorious vitality. . . . [movie audiences were] unrespectable people having a hell of a fine time" (6–7).

Changes in American film comedy during the twentieth century continued to reflect alterations in both technology and cultural reality. In an essay on film comedy, Wes D. Gehring divides the genre into three historical periods: the silent films of the early decades of the century, the "studio era," and films of the post-World War II period. Three major factors influenced film comedy beginning in the early 1930s. The widespread use of sound in motion pictures allowed filmmakers to add music and witty dialogue to the visual clowning of the silent film, resulting in a more sophisticated comedy that reflected the taste of the times. Indeed, *New Yorker* writers such as Dorothy Parker and Robert Benchley went to Hollywood during the 1930s to contribute their wit to screenplays. A second factor was the economic depression of the decade, which increased the American appetite for comedy as a momentary escape from hard times. The Depression also created a fascination with the upper classes, and wealthy people were portrayed in film comedy as either "eccentrically and/or incompetently endearing" or objects of ridicule, such as the "stuffy mountain of a dowager named Margaret Dumont in the Marx Brothers movies."[20] The third important development of the period was the implementation of film censorship in the form of the Motion Picture Production Code, established in 1930. Promoted primarily by the Catholic Legion of Decency, the code represented an attempt to regulate the films' moral messages, preventing them from glorifying crime and toning down sexual explicitness. One of the victims of the code, as Gehring points out, was the near-bawdy comedy of Mae West, who, in her first film, *Night After Night* (1932), responded to the compliment "Goodness, what beautiful diamonds!" with the line "Goodness had nothing to do with it, dearie." A combination of such censorship and a renewed sense of nationalism in the years before and during World War II brought to film comedy the rustic Yankee figure who uses common sense to address national problems, most notably in Frank Capra films such as *Mr. Deeds Goes to Town* (1936) and *Mr. Smith Goes to Washington* (1939). The war itself spawned a number of patriotic comedies, many of them featuring the zany comedy teams Abbott and Costello and Laurel and Hardy.

Gehring identifies five types of film comedy in the years following World War II, most of them having origins in other forms of humor both on and off the screen: personality comedies, populist cracker barrel comedy, screwball comedy, parody, and black comedy (75). In personality comedy, a single actor dominates the film, employing a comic persona that becomes familiar from one film to another. Bob Hope was the first major such film personality, beginning in the 1940s; he has been followed by Jerry Lewis, Red Skelton, Eddie Murphy, Steve Martin, and Woody Allen, among others. This focus on a single personality recalls the vaudeville comedy routine, with its stereotypical tendencies, and is also similar to stand-up comedy. The most recognizable cracker-barrel comedies of the postwar period featured the rustic couple Ma and Pa Kettle, based on characters in Betty MacDonald's best-selling 1945 novel *The Egg and I,* a humorous account of an urban couple's attempt to raise chickens in the rural Northwest. The screwball comedy of the 1930s, essentially a boy-meets-girl story with comic plot twists and clever dialogue, moved to the postwar suburbs, as did a large part of the American middle class. The parody film is a self-conscious genre in which films make fun of other films or types of films, often deflating the ideals of heroism. The movie Western has been a common target, from Bob Hope's *The Paleface* in 1948 through Mel Brooks's *Blazing Saddles* in 1974. Like literary parody, film parody depends for its effects on the audience's familiarity with the original, and the success of film parody in America testifies to a nation of moviegoers. The final category that Gehring lists has fewer precedents in American humor, although a parallel development in literature began in the 1930s with such works as Nathanael West's *Miss Lonelyhearts* (1933) and *A Cool Million* (1934). Black comedy— the literary counterpart is often called "black humor"—is not named for an association with race; the term "black" refers to the grim nature of the film's subject matter, from totalitarianism in Chaplin's *The Great Dictator* (1940) to nuclear threat in *Dr. Strangelove* (1964) and the realities of warfare in *M*A*S*H* (1970). While we can see elements of this dark humor in the undeniable violence of the tall tale and in portions of *Huck Finn,* its presence in film and literature of the mid- to late-twentieth century seems a response to the particular horrors of this century.

If Americans have been enthusiastic movie audiences, the form of visual humor that has the most daily impact upon us is the comic strip. The fact that comic strips may do more than amuse us was given eloquent testimony in 1975 by then-President Gerald Ford, who commented in a speech that "there are only three major vehicles to keep us informed as to what is going on in Washington: the electronic media, the print media, and *Doonesbury . . .* not necessarily in that order."[21] Comic strips may, like *Doonesbury,* feature political satire; they may, like *Blondie,* show amusing vignettes of domestic life; they may deal with the antics of children, like *Dennis the Menace,* or use children to mirror the adult world, like *Peanuts.* Some "comic" strips are not funny at all, (e.g., adventure stories such as *Steve Canyon* or dramas such as *Mary Worth*) but the several-panel format puts them in the same category as humorous ones. So popular have comic strips been in their century of existence that comic-strip characters have been used to advertise products; a *Li'l Abner* strip promoted Cream of Wheat cereal in American magazines in the 1940s, for example.

In his introduction to *Comics as Culture* (Chapter 10), M. Thomas Inge asserts that comic strips "serve as revealing reflectors of popular attitudes, tastes, and mores." One reason that we can be so certain that the comics reflect mainstream American values, Inge points out, is precisely because they appear in daily newspapers, so that "the syndicates, editors, and publishers submit strips to the severest kind of scrutiny and control to be sure that no parent, political bloc, or advertiser whose support they court will take offense." As a result of this pressure to appeal to the widest possible audience, individual newspapers sometimes cancel sequences of comics they fear might offend readers, as happened with a sequence in Lynn Johnston's *For Better or For Worse* that dealt with homosexuality; and some papers print such strips as *Doonesbury* on the editorial page instead of the comics page.

Inge notes that in addition to drawing upon major themes and character types of Western culture and promoting such values as family life, courage, and fair play, comic strips have influenced American language and popular culture, so that we associate spinach with Popeye and speak of "Dagwood sandwiches," named for that character's ability to get most of the contents of a refrigerator between slices of bread. Further, the comic strip is one of the few truly indigenous art forms (Inge elsewhere mentions jazz music as the other primary form) to have exerted an influence on other cultures. Inge points to the impact of the comics on some of Pablo Picasso's art early in this century, and on the pop art movement of the 1960s. What we so far lack, Inge believes, is a way of analyzing the comics as an art form in and of itself without relying on the vocabulary we use to speak of other art forms, including narrative and drama. The first step he urges readers to take is to recognize the comics as a "form of legitimate culture, quite capable of confronting the major questions of mankind, but . . . with a gentler spirit that leads to laughter at the moment of recognition."

The daily comic strip provides a good example of how American humor has been subject to both continuity and change. Some currently syndicated strips have been running for decades with their basic premises essentially unaltered. *Mary Worth,* whose title character Inge has called "the matronly Miss Lonelyhearts of the Geritol set," began in the 1930s[22] ; Dagwood and Blondie and their children have not aged for years, and although Blondie now works outside the home in a catering business, Dagwood still collides with the mailman and naps on the couch. *Dilbert,* on the other hand, is a product of the computer age, addressing the cubicled world of the corporate programmer while at the same time continuing the tradition of the little man overwhelmed by a crazy world. In books and periodicals as well as other media, America's humorists have kept alive certain themes and issues while adapting them to contemporary life. The nation's diversity is still reflected in a variety of racial and ethnic voices. The urban sophisticate still counterpoints the folksy philosopher, and we still observe what Rubin called "the great American joke"—the disparity between the promised ideal and the less-than-perfect realities with which we live.

As a group to whom the ideal has seldom been promised, Native-American writers of the twentieth century have expressed their anger at several centuries of European oppression and genocide, but they have also displayed a remarkably resilient humor when addressing cultural encounters. Louise Erdrich and Michael Dorris's *The Crown of Columbus* (1991) is a modern retelling of Christopher Columbus's "discovery" of America that takes decidedly satiric stabs at presumptions of European superiority. Poet Paula Gunn Allen has a keen sense of the ironies of contemporary Native American life in a culture in which native heritage has become a commodity. In her poem "Taking a Visitor to See the Ruins," Allen describes taking a tourist to New Mexico to see, not the "pueblos/once home to vanished people" that he had expected to see, but instead her mother and grandmother living in a high-rise apartment:

> the two who still live pueblo style in high security dwellings
> way up there where the enemy can't reach them
> just like in the olden times.

And Louise Erdrich shares this sense of irony in her poem "Dear John Wayne," in which she recounts the experience of Native American young people at a drive-in movie watching the American Western hero encounter a group of Indians "arranged like SAC missiles,/their feathers bristling in the meaningful sunset."

Among America's comic novelists, Philip Roth has most consistently mined the possibilities of American Jewish humor, beginning with *Portnoy's Complaint* (1969), which abounds in jokes about overbearing Jewish mothers. Roth's work demonstrates the extent to which, for a century, Jewish comics and humorists have been central to the American humorous tradition. Not only has their humor featured the resilient underdog that shares similarities with the American "common man," but Roth in particular has drawn upon a number of humorous forms in his work, including vaudeville, political satire, and the tradition of oral storytelling. Roth's *The Great American Novel* (1972) not only deals with that great American pastime, baseball, but also has many of the qualities of the tall tale, including, in the form of its "Prologue," what Blair and Hill call "proportionately one of the lengthiest 'frames' for a boxed narrative in the history of our humor" (477). The story that this narrator has to tell is one of a peculiarly American persecution: the suppression of the history of a major baseball league.

Langston Hughes's character Jesse B. Semple (whose ironic nickname is "Simple"), from the 1940s into the 1960s, recalls Seba Smith's Jack Downing in his mock-naive questioning of institutions, but there is an edge to Semple's voice that is missing from Downing's: whereas the politics that fascinate Downing do not necessarily affect his own fate, Semple, as a black man, is not so fortunate. Through Semple, who first appeared in Hughes's *Chicago Defender* newspaper column in 1943, Hughes attacked the injustice of racial segregation and America's slowness to achieve true racial equality. In one Semple sketch, for example, Hughes's character finds himself in a whites-only waiting room but is unable to leave because, a policeman tells him, the single door is for whites-only use. Semple also pointed to the failure of those considered black leaders to speak directly to the needs of their people, as he does in the following mock-innocent address to one "Dr. Butts": "Dr. Butts, I am glad to read that you writ an article in *The New York Times,* but also sometime I wish you would write one in the colored papers and let me know how to get out from behind all these *buts* that are staring me in the face. I know America is a great country *but*—and it is that *but* that has been keeping me where I is all these years. I can't get over it, I can't get under it, and I can't get around it, so what am I supposed to do?"

The absurdity of a social system that continually shoved "buts" in front of African Americans (pun no doubt intended) has been a constant source of humor, evident particularly in jokes that circulate among blacks. One of the most extended discussions of this humor is the chapter "Black Laughter" in Lawrence W. Levine's book *Black Culture and Black Consciousness*. Levine includes a joke that indicates that blacks were not confident that even legal integration would solve their problems: a black woman goes to a posh restaurant and asks for foods stereotypically associated with blacks, such as black-eyed peas, hamhocks, and collard greens, and when the waiter informs her that none of these items is available, she responds, "Honey, I knowed you-all wasn't ready for integration."[23] Late in his career, Langston Hughes collected numerous examples of such humor in his *The Book of Negro Humor* (1966).

In addition to ethnic diversity, a difference between rural and urban humor—perhaps better expressed as folksy versus sophisticated, or the humor of the common man versus the humor of an educated elite—persists in late twentieth-century America. One difference from a century ago, however, is that because of the wide circulation of both print and electronic media, many Americans are able to experience and appreciate both kinds of humor. Roy Blount, Jr., who is from Georgia and lives in New York City, makes a similar point in a recent essay when he writes that "surely every American should aspire to jokes so inclusive and yet so multi-directional . . . as to leave no one entirely cold and no one wholly cozy." Identifying his own humorous "affinity group" as "literate Southerners," Blount uses his own sense of humor to bridge the former gap between the two types of humor, "[L]iterate Southerners [are] people who would appreciate a joke . . . involving Kafka and a palmetto bug. Or let's say Proust and a hushpuppy. Such a person wouldn't have to have read Proust; I haven't, for example; but he or she would have to know (a) that—as I understand it—Proust bit into a *madeleine* and started remembering things, and (b) that a *madeleine* is a baked good of some sort. Come to think of it, a hushpuppy is a fried good, but there must be some way in which a hushpuppy and a *madeleine* are analogous. They're both made of batter."[24]

The oral storytelling tradition that we associate with the cracker box and agrarian life is today carried on by Garrison Keillor, whose tales of life in the mythical Minnesota community of Lake Wobegon, where "all the women are strong and all the men are good looking and all the children are above average," are conveyed by radio and also by the even older medium of live stage performance, which recalls the traveling performances of Mark Twain and Will Rogers. The sound effects that were so much a part of early radio comedy are featured in Keillor's *Prairie Home Companion,* and his stories of small-town life in the upper Midwest promote the values of innocence, common sense, and fair play that Americans like to associate with an idyllic agrarian past. But at the same time, a number of Keillor's stories have been published in *The New Yorker,* which underscores the fact that it is no longer possible to categorize American humor as purely "rural" or "urban," with entirely different audiences.

Another evidence of the endurance of the oral tradition in America is the circulation of what Jan Harold Brunvand (represented in Chapter 7) calls "urban legends." Although the stories to which this term refers are sometimes conveyed in the electronic or print media, they usually pass through the culture by word of mouth, accepted as true by most tellers and listeners, though they describe bizarre events or circumstances. Although many urban legends are not comic in substance, they share with the nineteenth-century tall tale the quality of exaggeration, but are commonly set in urban or suburban areas rather than the backwoods. Some urban legends, such as "The Solid Concrete Car," in which a jealous husband or boyfriend fills his rival's car with concrete, may actually have occurred one or more times, but such a story assumes the status of urban legend when large numbers of people claim it happened to what Brunvand calls a "FOAF"—a friend of a friend. A number of urban legends are intrinsically comic, involving misunderstandings, mistaken identity, and slapstick antics. An example is the story of the golfer who, frustrated by continually hitting his ball into water hazards, throws his golf bag into a pond and leaves, only to return a few minutes later to retrieve his car keys from its pocket. College campuses have produced their share of urban legends, including the story that one of the campus buildings was intended for another university but was erected at this one by mistake, and the widely held belief that the length of time a class must wait for a late professor depends upon his or her academic rank.

The pervasiveness of urban legends, contemporary radio and television humor, and jokes that circulate on the Internet should not suggest that all of modern American humor appeals or is intended to appeal to everyone. We began with the premise that humor requires a reader, listener, or viewer who is sufficiently familiar with the subject matter and perspective of humor to relate to it—to, as we say, "get it." Cartoons in *The New Yorker,* for example, may have fairly universal appeal, but they often refer to trends, fads, or personalities so specific as to perplex readers who are out of touch with them. The title of one of Fran Lebowitz's books, *Metropolitan Life* (1978), suggests that she writes specifically for an urban reader—more particularly, a New York reader—who can relate to her account of looking for a city apartment that actually has a complete bathroom, the habits of New York taxi drivers, and references to streets and stores in Manhattan. Similarly, Garry Trudeau (creator of *Doonesbury*) parodies *New York Times* classified advertisements in his 1993 "Advt.," with results designed to amuse the urban-literate reader:

> SUCCESSFUL, PROFESSIONAL, QUALITY-time couple seeks 24-hour, seven-day, live-in nanny to care for our two little miracles, 3 and 5, teach them manners, values, Spanish, etc. $110 wk. Call secretary at (315) 999-1515.
>
> ⎯⎯⎯⎯⎯
>
> WILL TRADE PORK bellies for Hampton time share. Call beeper number (914) 777-1588.

While television, film, and other mass media have helped to familiarize contemporary Americans with ways of life far different than their own everyday experience, some of our humor seeks quite specific audiences.

In 1931, Thomas L. Masson called upon humorists to help correct society's wrongs—to "show us the utter folly of so much that we accede to." In 1994, Moshe Waldoks, editor of *The Best American Humor, 1994,* found American life so full of absurdities that a humorist would find it difficult to create material that could match the daily news in comic potential. Declaring that "we live in an age that defies parody," Waldoks provides a list of current events that reads in part as follows:

> I am writing in a week when Olympic skater Tonya Harding was under suspicion for conspiring to break Nancy Kerrigan's knee; Lorena Bobbitt was found temporarily insane when she sliced off her husband's penis; . . . afternoon talk shows were devoted to body-piercing for teenagers and s/m marriage ceremonies; . . . Dan Quayle appeared in a Lay's potato(e?) chip commercial; Staten Island was thinking of seceding from New York City; Bill Clinton made a Reaganesque State of the Union speech, leaving the Republicans not quite speechless; and did I mention that Tonya

Harding was still under suspicion of conspiring to break Nancy Kerrigan's knee?

Now try to be funny after all that.[25]

In order to "be funny after all that," contemporary humorists—especially in such quick responsive forms as the comic strip and stand-up comedy—need only work slight exaggerations on what already seems absurd. Trudeau's mock classified ads are only a short step away from the actual ones, and his comic strip *Doonesbury* often pushes a potentially absurd political or social controversy to its logical extreme. During the recent controversy about whether "ebonics" is an actual language spoken by some African Americans, for example, a *Doonesbury* strip featured a black educator who identified the utterance "Ain't no way. Nobody jivin' 'bout nothin' " as a "quadruple negative . . . an ancient Egyptian idiom." In addition to referring to a cultural argument about education, Trudeau's strip also reminds us that African Americans have traditionally had to speak two languages, with the public speech of acquiescence obscuring the voice of the crafty, powerful rabbit.

The gap between the ideal and the real, which has been the source of so much of America's humorous expression, has been pointed out by an increasing variety of people and in a number of forms. For example, while lack of social, political, and economic equality has been a subject of women's humor for well over a hundred years, its literary expression has been augmented in the performance of stand-up comics and in visual media such as the comic strip. Much of this feminist humor has challenged traditional notions of social class surrounding the ideal "lady." Roseanne Barr's comic persona is a working-class wife and mother who openly rejects the standards for perfection in the role of homemaker: "I will clean house when Sears comes out with a riding vacuum cleaner." Judith Martin's *Miss Manners' Guide to Excruciatingly Correct Behavior* (1982), while offering real advice on social etiquette, parodies the supercilious tone of most such manuals. Nicole Hollander's comic-strip character "Sylvia" is deliberately created to violate norms of ideal femininity; she is middle-aged and irreverent, and is often pictured dressed in robe and slippers, drinking beer and smoking cigarettes. A common format in the strip has Sylvia resisting the messages of mass media by talking back to the voice from her television set. When an advertisement intones, "With men or boys at home, your bathroom needs cleaning every day," she responds, "Not if you bolt the door." Korean-American stand-up comic Margaret Cho often addresses racial stereotypes in her act. When following a comedian who had joked about Asian taxi drivers, for example, she introduced herself by saying, "Hi, my name is Margaret Cho, and I drive very well." And like other groups that have been subject to discrimination in American culture, gays and lesbians use humor as a platform from which to address their status. An example is Gail Sausser, whose book *Lesbian Etiquette* (1986) displays a common-sense humor not that far removed from Holley's Samantha Allen. Bemused by questions about why people "choose" to be gay, Sausser quips, "As if one morning each of us stood in front of the mirror and said, 'I think I'll become a persecuted minority today.'"

———

While it is clear that no single definition of American humor can adequately capture and explain such diversity of issues, forms, and styles, some general conclusions can be drawn about its nature and purposes. Humorous expression has always been integral to the American experience. Since the beginnings of nationhood in the late eighteenth century, the existence of freedom of speech and a free press has allowed and encouraged people to openly circulate their views about institutions, policies, values, groups, and individuals. Assisting this circulation, especially in the twentieth century, has been a rapid expansion of technology, so that humor can be found in automobile bumper stickers, on the Internet, and in film as well as in newspapers, magazines, and novels. A second general observation is that America's geographical and ethnic diversity has had a decided effect on the nation's humor. While such forms as the ethnic joke and the minstrel show reveal anxieties about differences, members of minority groups have used humor as a means of survival, group identification, and protest against discrimination. It could be argued, in fact, that humor's capacity to relieve tension and render acceptable that which is potentially threatening has helped in the process of assimilating various groups into American culture. While the concept of a single "national character" has been wisely abandoned, it is nonetheless true that certain widely shared values, such as the freedoms put forth in the Bill of Rights, stand in contrast to our many differences, and this leads to a final conclusion about American humor: the paradox that while humor declares nothing to be sacred, Americans have used it to press for those ideals of equality, opportunity, and freedom that often seem to gleam elusively in the distance.

NOTES

1. E. B. White and Katharine S. White, eds., *A Subtreasury of American Humor* (New York: Modern Library, 1941), xiii. Subsequent references will be page numbers in the text.

2. Sigmund Freud, "Humor," in *The Complete Psychological Works of Sigmund Freud,* trans. James Strachey, 24 vols. (London: The Hogarth Press, 1961), 21:162.

3. Thomas L. Masson, foreword to *Our American Humorists* (1931; reprinted ed. Freeport, NY: Books for Libraries Press, 1966).

4. Walter Blair, " 'A Man's Voice, Speaking': A Continuum in American Humor," in *Essays on American Humor: Blair Through the Ages,* ed. Hamlin Hill (Madison: University of Wisconsin Press, 1993), 40.

5. For an analysis of John Smith as an unwitting early American humorist, see Thomas J. Haslam, "Absentee Government, the Absurd Frontier, and the Laughable Origins of American Identity; or, the Twice-Told Fish Tale of Captain John Smith," *Studies in American Humor* 7 (1989): 58–66.

6. Carl Holliday, *The Wit and Humor of Colonial Days (1607–1800)* (Philadelphia: J. B. Lippincott, 1912), 91.

7. Cameron Nickels, *New England Humor: From the Revolutionary War to the Civil War* (Knoxville: University of Tennessee Press, 1993), 8. Subsequent references will be page numbers in the text.

8. Jennette Tandy, *Crackerbox Philosophers in American Humor and Satire* (New York: Columbia University Press, 1925), ix.

9. M. Thomas Inge, *Perspectives on American Culture: Essays on Humor, Literature, and the Popular Arts* (West Cornwall, CT: Locust Hill Press, 1994), 7.

10. Walter J. Meserve, *An Emerging Entertainment: The Drama of the American People to 1828* (Bloomington: Indiana University Press, 1977), 240–41.

11. Arthur Frank Wertheim, *Radio Comedy* (New York: Oxford University Press, 1979), 88. Subsequent references will be page numbers in the text.

12. Lawrence E. Mintz, "The 'New Wave' of Standup Comics: An Introduction," *American Humor* 4 (Fall 1977): 1.

13. Randolph Bourne, quoted in the introduction to Max J. Herzberg, *The Reader's Encyclopedia of American Literature* (New York: Thomas Y. Crowell, 1962), v.

14. Thomas Grant, "Judge," in *American Humor Magazines and Comic Periodicals,* ed. David E. E. Sloane (New York: Greenwood Press, 1987), 186.

15. Steven H. Gale, "The New Yorker," in *American Humor Magazines and Comic Periodicals,* 186.

16. Norris W. Yates, *The American Humorist: Conscience of the Twentieth Century* (Ames: Iowa State University Press, 1964), 39.

17. Roland Marchand, *Advertising the American Dream: Making Way for Modernity, 1920–1940* (Berkeley: University of California Press, 1985,) 108.

18. Jack Gauer and Dave Stanley, *There's Laughter in the Air!: Radio's Top Comedians and Their Best Shows* (New York, 1945), 75.

19. James Agee, "Comedy's Greatest Era," in *Agee on Film: Reviews and Comments by James Agee* (New York: McDowell, Obolensky, 1958), 3.

20. Wes D. Gehring, "Film Comedy," in *Humor in America: A Research Guide to Genres and Topics,* ed. Lawrence E. Mintz (New York: Greenwood Press, 1988), 73–74.

21. Quoted in Blair and Hill, *America's Humor*, 511.
22. M. Thomas Inge, "The Comics," in *Humor in America: A Research Guide to Genres and Topics*, 38.
23. Lawrence W. Levine, *Black Culture and Black Consciousness: Afro-American Folk Thought From Slavery To Freedom* (New York: Oxford University Press, 1977), 319–20.
24. Roy Blount, Jr., "Why You Calling Little Pork Chop?" *Oxford American* (January/February 1997): 94.
25. Moshe Waldoks, introduction to *The Best American Humor, 1994* (New York: Simon and Schuster, 1994), 11.

Suggestions for Further Reading

This list of resources for the study of American humor is subdivided into the following categories: Bibliographical Materials includes critical works on humor, biographical dictionaries of humorists, and guides to research on topics and genres; Critical Studies includes books about types of humor, humorous media, and individual humorists; and Anthologies includes collections of humorous writing published since the late nineteenth century—those no longer in print will be found in many libraries. This list does not include the many articles on American humor to be found in scholarly journals. However, journals to see for additional criticism include *Studies in American Humor, Studies in Popular Culture, Thalia: Studies in Literary Humor, American Quarterly, American Studies,* and *American Literature.*

BIBLIOGRAPHICAL MATERIALS

Mintz, Lawrence E., ed. *Humor in America: A Research Guide to Genres and Topics.* New York: Greenwood Press, 1988.

This volume consists of nine bibliographic essays on types of American humor, including media such as radio, film, and the comics, political humor, women's humor, and racial and ethnic humor. The work concludes with an essay on the use of folklore methodology in studying American humor.

Nilsen, Don L. F., ed. *Humor in American Literature: A Selected Annotated Bibliography*. New York: Garland. 1992.

Compiled by the foremost bibliographer of American humorous writing, this guide is indispensable to research in American humor. Including both books and articles, the entries on individual authors are arranged chronologically from 1575 to the late twentieth century, and subsequent sections list studies of genres, regions, and historical periods in American humor.

Sloane. David E. E., ed. *American Humor Magazines and Comic Periodicals*. New York: Greenwood Press, 1987.

An indispensable resource for the study of American comic periodicals, this comprehensive, 600-page volume provides histories and descriptions of hundreds of magazines featuring humor that were published between 1757 and the 1980s. The work also includes essays on college humor magazines, scholarly humor magazines, and humor in American almanacs and is well indexed for easy use.

Trachtenberg, Stanley, ed. *American Humorists, 1800–1950*. 2 vols. Detroit: Gale Research, 1982.

Part of the *Dictionary of Literary Biography* series, these two volumes provide biographical/critical entries on dozens of humorous writers, each including a listing of the writer's published work and a brief bibliography of other sources of information. Appendices to Volume 2 provide an historical overview of American humor and essays on book illustration and humor in newspapers and magazines.

CRITICAL STUDIES

Agee, James. "Comedy's Greatest Era." In *Agee on Film: Reviews and Comments by James Agee,* 3–19. New York: McDowell, Obolensky, 1958.

In an essay originally published in *Life* magazine in 1949, Agee argues that silent film comedies produced between 1912 and 1930 were unsurpassed in the film medium for true comic effect, particularly in the work of their "most eminent masters": Charlie Chaplin, Harold Lloyd, Harry Langdon, and Buster Keaton.

Bier, Jesse. *The Rise and Fall of American Humor*. New York: Holt, Rinehart, and Winston, 1968.

Bier argues that genuine American humor is "skeptical, cynical, pessimistic" in its truth-telling. He finds these attributes to be positive until the middle years of the twentieth century, when "black" humor, "sick" humor, and obscenity turned laughter into "hysteric humor that screams."

Blair, Walter. *Essays on American Humor: Blair Through the Ages,* ed. Hamlin Hill. Madison: University of Wisconsin Press, 1993.

Compiled as a tribute to one of America's leading scholars of American humor, this volume includes essays by Blair on American humor written from the 1920s through the 1980s. The third section of the book contains eight essays on the work of Mark Twain.

———. *Horse Sense in American Humor: From Benjamin Franklin to Ogden Nash.* New York: Russell and Russell, 1942.

Defining "horse sense" as common sense or "mother wit" that develops through practical experience rather than education, Blair argues that it is the source of much of American humor, typically expressed in the colloquial style deriving from the oral tradition.

———, and Hamlin Hill. *America's Humor: From Poor Richard to Doonesbury.* New York: Oxford University Press, 1978.

Blair and Hill's study comes the closest of any published work to being a comprehensive history of American humor, although women's contributions are almost completely ignored and the authors pay most of their attention to pre-twentieth-century humor.

———, and Raven I. McDavid, Jr., eds. *The Mirth of a Nation: America's Great Dialect Humor.* Minneapolis: University of Minnesota Press, 1983.

The essays in this collection attest to the popularity of dialect humor in the nineteenth century, including the rustic philosophers of New England, the frontier boasters, the efforts of local-color writers to render the speech patterns of various regions, ethnic humor such as the Irish character Mr. Dooley, and Mark Twain's extensive use of American dialects.

Brown, Carolyn S. *The Tall Tale in American Folklore and Literature.* Knoxville: University of Tennessee Press, 1987.

Brown analyzes the origins of the tall tale as an oral storytelling form and the various forms it may take, including its incorporation into written literature, paying particular attention to Harris's character Sut Lovingood and the work of Mark Twain and Garrison Keillor.

Clark, William Bedford, and W. Craig Turner, eds. *Critical Essays on American Humor.* Boston: G. K. Hall, 1984.

This wide-ranging collection serves as a partial history of the study of American humor, including essays on the subject originally published between the 1870s and the 1950s as well as some written especially for this volume.

Cohen, Sarah Blacher, ed. *Comic Relief: Humor in Contemporary American Literature.* Urbana: University of Illinois Press, 1978.

The essays in this volume concur that humor alleviates the pain of difficult times. The works deal with the use of comic elements in otherwise serious literature, including the work of Vladimir Nabokov, Mary McCarthy, Philip Roth, and midcentury poets.

Collier, Denise, and Kathleen Beckett. *Spare Ribs: Women in the Humor Biz.* New York: St. Martin's Press, 1980.

By "humor biz" the authors mean comic performance, both live and on the screen, and the book consists of interviews with stand-up comics, television and film actresses, and comedy writers and producers. The volume opens with statements by Phyllis Diller and Joan Rivers about their experiences as pioneers in female comic performance.

Friedman, Bruce J. *Black Humor.* New York: Bantam, 1965.

The essays in this collection deal with mid-twentieth-century authors, including Edward Albee, John Barth, Joseph Heller, and Terry Southern, who create a grim humor as a response to a world that seems increasingly absurd and fragmented.

Granger, Bruce Ingham. *Political Satire in the American Revolution, 1763–1783.* Ithaca: Cornell University Press, 1960.

By focusing on the dominant form of American humor during the Revolutionary War period and quoting extensively from satiric pieces that appeared in newspapers, magazines, and pamphlets, Granger is able to show how humor functioned as a weapon in the struggle for American independence.

Habegger, Alfred. "Male and Female Humor." In *Gender, Fantasy, and Realism in American Literature,* 115–95. New York: Columbia University Press, 1982.

In this second part of his study of the American novel from the 1850s to the 1880s, Habegger argues that a central basis of American humor is the contrast between ideal gender roles, the masculine given to play and fooling and the feminine devoted to upholding standards of decorum.

Haweis, H[ugh] R[eginald]. *American Humorists.* New York: Funk and Wagnalls, 1882.

This early study is based on a series of lectures that Haweis, an Anglican clergyman, delivered at the Royal Institution in London in 1881. The six chapters, which include biographical data as well as discussions of humorous writing, are devoted to Washington Irving, Oliver Wendell Holmes, James Russell Lowell, Artemus Ward, Mark Twain, and Bret Harte.

Holliday, Carl. *The Wit and Humor of Colonial Days (1607–1800).* Philadelphia: J. B. Lippincott, 1912.

An early, fairly comprehensive study of American humorous expression in its first two centuries, Holliday's readable text is particularly valuable for its copious use of examples of colonial wit and humor.

Inge, M. Thomas. *Comics as Culture.* Jackson: University Press of Mississippi, 1990.

In a profusely illustrated study of comic strips and comic books, Inge demonstrates how these forms are woven into other aspects of American culture, serving as an influence on both Charlie Chaplin and William Faulkner, augmenting American language, and reflecting developments in technology.

———. *Perspectives on American Culture: Essays on Humor, Literature, and the Popular Arts.* West Cornwall, CT: Locust Hill Press, 1994.

Taken together, the essays in this volume argue that "popular" culture cannot be separated from the rest of American culture. In addition to examining the humor of Thoreau and Hawthorne, Inge traces the adaptation of Mark Twain's work to the comic-book format, assesses Walt Disney's role in the American Dream, and, in the final section of the book, analyzes the impact of American culture on writers in other countries.

Keough, William. *Punchlines: The Violence of American Humor*. New York: Paragon House, 1990.

Arguing that violence is a central element of American humor, Keough traces different kinds of violence in the writings of Twain, Bierce, Lardner, and Vonnegut, and also in film, stand-up comedy, political humor, and television.

Levine, Lawrence W. "Black Laughter." In *Black Culture and Black Consciousness: Afro-American Folk Thought From Slavery To Freedom*, 298–366. New York: Oxford University Press, 1977.

Levine analyzes the nature and function of humor within the African-American community from its largely oral forms of protest humor during slavery to its role in fostering black group solidarity in the twentieth century, liberally illustrating his analysis with examples of jokes and stories.

Marc, David. *Demographic Vistas: Television in American Culture*. Philadelphia: University of Pennsylvania Press, 1984.

Believing that American television is essentially a "comic medium," Marc analyzes what he feels to be representative genres and personalities, including Jackie Gleason, the crime show, the situation comedy, and late-night comedy programs.

Masson, Thomas L. *Our American Humorists*. 1931. Reprint, Freeport, NY: Books for Libraries Press, 1966.

Masson, the literary and managing editor of the comic magazine *Life* during the early decades of the twentieth century, devotes short chapters of analysis to the work of thirty-two individuals who contributed work to that periodical and seven chapters to groups of humorists such as "The Younger Set" and "The Comic Poets."

Mast, Gerald. *The Comic Mind: Comedy and the Movies*, 2d ed. Chicago: University of Chicago Press, 1979.

Following a discussion of types of comic films, Mast provides a history of film comedy from the silent films of Mack Sennett to the comedies of Woody Allen. An appendix lists distributors of comic films.

Morris, Linda A., ed. *American Women Humorists: Critical Essays*. New York: Garland, 1994.

Morris's collection makes available many of the essential writings on American women's humor to date. The first section consists of introductions to anthologies of women's humor published between 1885 and 1988; the second includes essays surveying the tradition of women's humor; and the third is composed of essays on individual humorists from the early eighteenth century to the present.

Nickels, Cameron. *New England Humor: From the Revolutionary War to the Civil War*. Knoxville: University of Tennessee Press, 1993.

In the most comprehensive study to date of New England humor from the late-eighteenth to the mid-nineteenth century, Nickels analyzes the development of the Yankee/Uncle Sam figure and representations of New England values on stage, in print, and in illustrations. He concludes with a chapter on the New England version of the "cracker-barrel philosopher."

Rourke, Constance. *American Humor: A Study of the National Character.* Garden City, NY: Doubleday and Co., 1931.

Rourke, an anthropologist who specialized in the study of American popular culture, drew upon almanacs, jokebooks, stage comedy, tall tales, and poetry from the eighteenth through the early twentieth century to support her argument that the American "comic spirit" sprang from a need to reinvent the self and experience.

Rubin, Louis D., Jr., ed. *The Comic Imagination in American Literature.* New Brunswick, NJ: Rutgers University Press, 1973.

This collection of thirty essays explores such diverse topics as the uses of humor by writers ranging from Benjamin Franklin to William Faulkner, and the types of humor such as Yankee humor and light verse. This volume is most useful for essays on topics not given much treatment elsewhere, such as Erskine Caldwell, Chicago humor, and the humor of the Harlem Renaissance.

Schmitz, Neil. *Of Huck and Alice: Humorous Writing in American Literature.* Minneapolis: University of Minnesota Press, 1983.

Using Huckleberry Finn and Gertrude Stein as leading figures, Schmitz argues that humor originates in a use of language that undermines authority and speaks from the margins of reality rather than from its center.

Sheppard, Alice. *Cartooning for Suffrage.* Albuquerque: University of New Mexico Press, 1994.

In this profusely illustrated book, Sheppard demonstrates that women in early twentieth-century America made frequent use of comic art to press for the right to vote.

Sloane, David E. E., ed. *American Humor: New Studies, New Directions.* Tuscaloosa: University of Alabama Press, 1998.

Designed to indicate the state of research in American humor at the end of the twentieth century, this collection of essays focuses on popular culture, including television and film; gender issues in literature and the comic strip; new appraisals of the humor of Edith Wharton, Mark Twain, and Edgar Allan Poe; foreign languages and American humor; and issues in the teaching of American humor.

Sochen, June, ed. *Women's Comic Visions.* Detroit: Wayne State University Press, 1991.

The essays in this collection are grouped into three categories: theories of women's humor; women's written humor, including the comic art of Helen Hokinson and Nicole Hollander; and a particularly useful group of essays on women as comic performers, including Lucille Ball, Moms Mabley, Lily Tomlin, and Kate Clinton.

Tandy, Jennette. *Crackerbox Philosophers in American Humor and Satire.* New York: Columbia University Press, 1925.

Tandy's pioneering study identified as central to the American humorous tradition the voice of the "common American," which used humor to represent the perspective of the unsophisticated but wise observer of American culture from 1830 to the 1920s.

Thurber, James. *The Years with Ross.* Boston: Little, Brown and Co., 1959.

An account of the first several decades of *The New Yorker* magazine and its founder, Harold Ross (1892–1951), written by a frequent contributor of humorous prose and drawings, Thurber's account is filled with anecdotes about the magazine and its editors and writers.

Walker, Nancy A. *"A Very Serious Thing": Women's Humor and American Culture.* Minneapolis: University of Minnesota Press, 1988.

The first full-length study of American women's humor, Walker's book discusses obstacles to women's humorous expression posed by ideal concepts of the "feminine" and describes a female tradition of humor that frequently conveyed its messages in subversive ways.

Wallace, Ronald. *The Last Laugh: Form and Affirmation in the Contemporary American Comic Novel.* Columbia: University of Missouri Press, 1979.

Arguing that humor is the novelist's response to the absurd and tragic in mid-twentieth-century American life, Wallace examines the comic elements in otherwise bleak novels by John Barth, John Hawkes, Vladimir Nabokov, Ken Kesey, and Robert Coover.

Wertheim, Arthur Frank. *Radio Comedy.* New York: Oxford University Press, 1979.

In the best single-volume study of American radio comedy, Wertheim surveys the development of radio humor from its origins in the 1920s until the competition of television caused its decline in the 1950s. The work focuses on both specific comedy programs and the careers of major comic performers.

Yates, Norris W. *The American Humorist: Conscience of the Twentieth Century.* Ames: Iowa State University Press, 1964.

Examining humorous writers from 1900 to 1950, Yates proposes that American humorists of this period, including many who wrote for *The New Yorker* and other urban periodicals, provided profound commentary on man's relationship to society.

ANTHOLOGIES

Blair, Walter, ed. *Native American Humor.* 1937. San Francisco: Chandler Publishing Co., 1960.

In a series of introductory essays, Blair identifies several types of humor that flourished between 1830 and the end of the nineteenth century as "native" to American culture: Down East humor, humor of the Old Southwest, literary comedians, local colorists, and the work of Mark Twain. The selections that comprise the bulk of the volume are organized according to these categories.

Blount. Roy, Jr., ed. *Roy Blount's Book of Southern Humor.* New York: W. W. Norton, 1994.

Convinced that there is something special, if difficult to define, about the humor of the American South, Blount, himself a humorous writer, has arranged thematically nearly 150 selections primarily from the twentieth century, including excerpts from novels and plays, stories, poems, folktales, and song lyrics.

Bruère, Martha Bensley, and Mary Ritter Beard, eds. *Laughing Their Way: Women's Humor in America*. New York: Macmillan and Co., 1934.

Acknowledging Kate Sanborn's 1885 *The Wit of Women* as the predecessor to their own collection, the editors assume that the question of whether women have a sense of humor has been settled. The volume includes work primarily by early twentieth-century women, arranged by both genre (for example, "versifiers") and subject matter (for example, "feminists").

Carlinsky, Dan, ed. *College Humor*. New York: Harper and Row, 1982.

The college humor magazine has served as a training ground for a number of people who have become well-known humorists, including Robert Benchley, James Thurber, S. J. Perelman. and Art Buchwald. Carlinsky's volume provides a sampling of cartoons, stories, light verse, and jokes from more than ninety college magazines from the 1870s to the 1980s.

Cerf, Bennett, ed. *An Encyclopedia of Modern American Humor*. Garden City, NY: Doubleday and Co., 1954.

Compiled by publisher, humorist, and television personality Bennett Cerf, this "encyclopedia" is actually a collection of prose and poetry by prominent humorists of the first half of the twentieth century. The volume is useful for the selections on regional humor, light verse, theatrical comedy, and radio humor.

Clemens, Samuel Langhorne, William Dean Howells, and Charles Hopkins Clark, eds. *Mark Twain's Library of Humor*. New York: Charles L. Webster and Co., 1888.

Containing a generous sampling of nineteenth-century American humor, including some by women writers such as Marietta Holley and Harriet Beecher Stowe, this volume is especially valuable for its large number of illustrations from the original publications.

Cohen, Hennig, and William B. Dillingham, eds. *Humor of the Old Southwest*, 3d ed. Athens: University of Georgia Press, 1994.

Cohen and Dillingham have put together the most comprehensive collection available of the frontier humor that flourished particularly between 1835 and 1861 in such Old Southwest states as Kentucky, Tennessee, Arkansas, Georgia, and Mississippi. Each author is identified in a headnote, most authors are represented by more than one selection, and the volume contains an extensive bibliography.

Dodge, Robert K., ed. *Early American Almanac Humor*. Bowling Green, OH: Bowling Green State University Popular Press, 1987.

Dodge has compiled comic selections from American almanacs published between 1776 and 1800, grouping them in chapters such as "The Yankee," "Ethnic and Racial Humor," "Men, Women, Marriage, and Sex," and "Soldiers and Sailors."

The Editors of *Reader's Digest*. *The* Reader's Digest *Treasury of American Humor*. New York: McGraw-Hill, 1972.

Although largely composed of anonymous jokes, epigrams, and anecdotes printed in the *Reader's Digest* over a fifty-year period, this collection, because of the magazine's wide circulation, affords insight into America's taste in humor between 1920 and 1970.

Hughes, Langston, ed. *The Book of Negro Humor*. New York: Dodd, Mead, 1966.

Defining humor as "laughing at what you haven't got when you ought to have it," Hughes collected jokes, excerpts from autobiographies, song lyrics, sketches, poems, and commentary from his own character "Simple" to demonstrate how African Americans had used humor to battle racism and foster a sense of community.

Richler, Mordecai, ed. *The Best of Modern Humor*. New York: Alfred A. Knopf, 1983.

Richler, an author of comic novels, includes selections of literary humor primarily from the mid-to-late twentieth century, including a number of excerpts from novels.

Sanborn, Kate, ed. *The Wit of Women*. New York: Funk and Wagnalls, 1885.

Sanborn's volume represents the first full-scale effort to prove that women (both European and American) do create humor. Although Sanborn tended to include snippets of humorous work rather than complete selections, her book has been the starting point for contemporary scholars of American women's humor.

Shalit, Gene, ed. *Laughing Matters: A Celebration of American Humor*. Garden City, NY: Doubleday and Co., 1987.

Compiled by an editor and television personality, this anthology includes a wide range of twentieth-century humor, including scripts of radio programs, comic films, and comic strips.

Walker, Nancy A., and Zita Dresner, eds. *Redressing the Balance: American Women's Literary Humor from Colonial Times to the 1980s*. Jackson: University Press of Mississippi, 1988.

This chronologically arranged collection demonstrates the evolving themes and issues of the women's tradition of American humor beginning with the wit of colonial poet Anne Bradstreet and concluding with the work of Native American poet Paula Gunn Allen and the lesbian wit Gail Sausser.

White, E. B., and Katharine S. White, eds. *A Subtreasury of American Humor*. New York: Modern Library, 1941.

The editors, both of whom worked for *The New Yorker* magazine in its early decades, include selections from the nineteenth and early twentieth centuries, arranged according to both themes and forms, including "Parodies and Burlesques," "The Critics at Work," and "Folklore and Tall Stories."

II

H. R. HAWEIS

1 American Humorists in 1882

Several decades before American literature was the subject of formal study in American colleges and universities, many readers on both sides of the Atlantic believed that the nation's humorous writers had created the most distinctively "American" literary expression. Hugh Reginald Haweis (1838–1901), an Anglican clergyman who lectured frequently on music and literature as well as religion, represented this view in his 1882 book *American Humorists.* Based on a series of lectures he had delivered in London the previous year, the book deals with six nineteenth-century writers (Washington Irving, Oliver Wendell Holmes, James Russell Lowell, Artemus Ward, Mark Twain, and Bret Harte) whose work seemed to embody to Haweis the "national character" of "our American cousins." In his introduction to the chapter on Washington Irving, he identifies the three "shocks," or contrasts, in the American experience that he believed created the "peculiarities" of American humor. Haweis proved to be an astute observer; later commentators on American humor also have pointed to incongruity as one of its hallmarks.

American wit has three main roots. These roots seem part and parcel of the national character, and are inseparably connected with the early history of our American cousins.

First, I notice the shock between Business and Piety. That is always a fruitful source of comedy to outsiders. Those famous Pilgrim

From H. R. Haweis, *American Humorists* (New York: Funk and Wagnalls, 1882), 10–13.

Fathers who went over in the *Mayflower,* to create a new civilization and conquer a new world, were singularly wide awake as well as pious. They were martyrs to a religious idea, but they were keenly alive to the practical interests of real life.

I have nothing to say against religion and business going hand in hand. The two occupy parallel but not necessarily antagonistic planes, and have, or ought to have, frequent side-channels of communication; but the habits and instincts developed by each are too often practically irreconcilable, and sometimes flagrantly inconsistent.

"John," said the pious grocer, "have you sanded the sugar?" "Yes, sir." "Larded the butter?" "Yes, sir." "Floured the ginger?" "Yes, sir." "Then come in to prayers."

The brisk competition between business and piety, together with the various cross lines of thought and feeling which it begets—derived no doubt from the thrift and 'cuteness of the early settlers—underlies a good deal of the modern American wit.

The Pilgrims were far too grim and grave to joke; but their descendants, who are fully alive to their peculiarities and weaknesses, while inheriting a full share of both, are not so particular.

Washington Irving's skit on the Yankee lawyer who became a converted man upon seeing a ghost, and after that never cheated—"except when it was to his own advantage"—is a fair thrust at that spirit which has the "form of godliness, denying the power thereof," and which, however morally deplorable, has an irresistibly comic side to it.

Another deep undertone of American humor is the forcible and national contrast forever present to the American mind between the Yankee and the poor Red Man whom he has supplanted.

Washington Irving and Aretemus Ward have both made great play with this element. The picture in "Knickerbocker" of the wily Dutch trader sitting down opposite the red man, and smoking gravely with him "the calumet of peace," listening to the poetical savage's interminable tirades of oratory *à la* Fenimore Cooper, and puffing away gravely without understanding a word of it, but never omitting to put in a "Yah! mein Herr!" at each pause, with a stolid and Batavian gravity—that is a feature quite peculiar to and inseparable from the national life and humor.

Lastly, the contrast between the vastness of American nature and the smallness of man, especially European man, seems to be a never-failing source of amusement to Yankee humorists.

Their general ability to "whip creation" turns largely upon the bigness of their rivers, mountains, and prairies, and the superior enterprise generated by these immensities.

By one wit, Niagara is valued because it could put out "our" Vesuvius in "ten minutes." Our biggest rivers are to the Mississippi and Missouri as babbling streams, our lakes are mere ponds; even the Alps and Pyrenees begin to look puny; and as to fields and woods, they are as paddocks and shrubberies to the virgin forests and boundless prairies of yon mighty Transatlantic continent.

The American visitor who was asked how he liked the Isle of Wight, is said to have replied, "It was well enough, but so dangerous"; and when asked to explain, he said the fact was the island was so small that when he got out of bed in the morning, he found himself in danger of tumbling into the sea!

To sum up the peculiarities of American humor: First, there is the shock between Business and Piety. Secondly, the shock of contrast between the Aboriginal and the Yankee. Lastly, the shock of contrast between the bigness of American nature and the smallness of European nature, or, as for the matter of that, Human Nature itself outside America.

You will notice that I have only selected a certain number of American humorists; and when I published my list, people at the Royal Institution asked me, "Why do you omit James, and Cable, and Leland, and Howells, and so forth!"

I have noticed in life that whenever a man sets himself to do one thing, his friends always ask him why he did not do something else.

In this case my reply was:

"I select those men, without prejudice to any others, who in my opinion suffice to embody the genius of American humor, as far as it has got."

Then I was asked:

"Why begin with Washington Irving?"

"Simply because Washington Irving was the first considerable American writer."

"But why call him a humorist?"

"Because he *was* a humorist. He was a great deal more, but he was *that*. Shakespeare and Scott were a great deal more, but they were humorists. I might deal with Irving as an historian or a biographer or an essayist, but I leave these varied and important aspects on one side in order to deal with him as a humorist—the first humorist, the father of American humor."

2 The Yankee

American anthropologist Constance Rourke was one
of a small number of scholars who helped to define
the field of American humor during the 1920s and
1930s. As an anthropologist rather than a literary
scholar, Rourke was as interested in folk tales and legends as she was in written texts. In the depiction of
the "Yankee" in her 1931 book *American Humor: A
Study of the National Character* she relied in part on
an oral tradition to define this "presiding genius," the
"symbolic American." The portrait of the Yankee that
emerges is a man with an infinite capacity to adapt
to changing circumstances, representing America's relatively rapid evolution from a group of European
colonies to a sovereign nation. Among Rourke's other
books was a 1934 biography of Davy Crockett, whose
actual life and accomplishments have been obscured
by the many legends that he and others created about
him, and in 1942 she published *The Roots of American
Culture and Other Essays.*

As a people the Americans are said to have had no
childhood, and the circumstance has been shown
to contain pathos as well as loss. But the Yankee stepped out of a darkness that seems antediluvian. Even the name Yankee abides in a thick
early dusk, though a passionate research has been devoted to its origin, and numberless theories formed to fit private notions of the
Yankee character. The air of "Yankee Doodle" may have come from
Galway, Germany, Spain, Hungary, Persia; it may have been a twelfth-
century church chant; in one stage it was probably a nursery rhyme.
No one knows the lineage of the early words. In the matter of racial origins no greater stability has been reached. For many years in England
the Yankee was compared with the yeoman of Yorkshire, who was also

From Constance Rourke, *American Humor: A Study of the National Character*
(Garden City, NY: Doubleday and Co., 1931), 19–26. © 1931 by Harcourt Brace
and 1959 by Alice P. Fore. Reprinted by permission of Harcourt Brace.

a wanderer, given to swapping. This ancient and inveterate practice among the northern Saxons was said to have driven hordes of invaders from the country. Many of the original Pilgrims came from Yorkshire, but the strain cannot be proved as determining the Yankee character, for numbers of others came from the south of England; and Ulster, France, Scotland, and Wales added their elements. Racial strains in the Yankee were well mixed.

As the texture of early Puritan life is examined, sources of Yankee strength become apparent, but not of Yankee humor: for humor is a matter of fantasy, and the fantasies of the Puritan, viewed with the most genial eye, remain sufficiently dark. After the abysses revealed by Cotton Mather had been skirted the New England imagination still ran boldly to witches and ghosts. Whittier said that some Irish immigrants settled in New Hampshire about 1820, bringing with them potatoes and fairies; the potatoes flourished, but the fairies died out. The native mind was not prosaic, but it perceived supernatural creatures of a large mold. Whittier wrote of an old strolling woman known as a witch through the valley of the Piscataqua, who once came to his grandfather's house and fell into a deep sleep of several hours. During this time wild gusts of wind swept over the valley and down the river, upsetting wherries and market-boats on the way back from Portsmouth, and the old woman was thought to have cast a vengeful wind-breathing spell. Whittier also pictured a grotesque and hideous phantasm that appeared more than once on the white shore of a little lake that mirrored spray and leaf of pine and maple, and was fringed with orchards. A woman standing at a crossroad nearby saw a horse and cart of a style used in New England a century before drive rapidly down a steep hillside and pass over a stone wall a few yards in front of her. The driver's countenance was fierce; behind the cart and lashed to it was a struggling woman of gigantic size, her face contorted by agony and fear, her arms and feet bare, her gray hair streaming. At the edge of the pond the noiseless cavalcade vanished.

Between these many shadows and the persistent humor of the Yankee the gulf seems wide. But humor bears the closest relation to emotion, either bubbling up as from a deep and happy wellspring, or in an opposite fashion rising like a rebirth of feeling from dead levels after turmoil. An emotional man may possess no humor, but a humorous man usually has deep pockets of emotion, sometimes tucked away or forgotten. If there were no index beyond these haunting shapes it would be clear that emotion was pervasive in New England. The exactions of pioneer life had deepened, yet suppressed, emotion. Again, emotion was stirred by the terror of the prevailing faith, yet caught within the meshwork of its tenets. Such compression with such power was bound to result in escapes and explosions. The result was a rebound; and frequently enough this occurred in New England, from the time of the revelers at Merrymount onward. A consultant opposition existed between the dark emotions and an earthy humor.

The Revolution, with its cutting of ties, its movement, its impulses toward freedom, seemed to set one portion of the scant population free from its narrow matrix. The obscure dweller in the villages or on the farms—the Yankee—bounded up with his irreverent tune, ready to move over the continent or to the ends of the earth, springing clean away from the traditional faith, at least so far as any outward sign appeared in his growing portrait. He could even take the Revolution as a joke; most of his songs about it streamed nonsense. He had left the deeper emotions behind or had buried them.

Proof of his anterior experiences remained in his use of the mask. The mask was a portable heirloom handed down by the pioneer. In a primitive world crowded with pitfalls the unchanging, unaverted countenance had been a safeguard, preventing revelations of surprise, anger, or dismay. The mask had otherwise become habitual among the older Puritans as their more expressive or risible feelings were sunk beneath the surface. Governor Bradford had encouraged its use on a considerable scale, urging certain gay spirits to enjoy themselves in secret, if they must be convivial. No doubt the mask would prove useful in a country where the Puritan was still a power and the risks of pioneering by no means over. The Yankee retained it.

Bostonians were and were not Yankees for many years. Sooner or later most New Englanders acknowledged themselves to be Yankees. Abroad, all Americans, even those from the South, were promptly dubbed Yankee. By the end of the Revolution the small United States had emerged as Brother Jonathan, an out-at-elbows New England country boy with short coat-sleeves, shrunken trousers, and a blank countenance. In the following years of inflated triumph the quiet, uncouth Yankee lad was often innocently put forward as a national sym-bol. The image was adopted in another of those half-lighted transitions which belong to Yankee history. No one can be sure how or when it was chosen. The name has been thought to derive from Washington's friend, Jonathan Trumbull of Connecticut, but that dignified figure hardly embodied the Yankee. Out of a past crowded with many dark passages, out of the travail of the Revolution, by a sudden, still agreement the unformed American nation pictured itself as homely and comic.

"The comic," says Bergson, "comes into being just when society and the individual, freed from the worry of self-preservation, begin to regard themselves as works of art." With his triumphs fresh and his mind noticeably free, by 1815 the American seemed to regard himself as a work of art, and began that embellished self-portraiture which nations as well as individuals may undertake. No one can say where or how these efforts might have ended if the American had been left to himself. He was not. Foreign artists insisted upon producing *their* portraits. After a few tours of observation the French, carrying the amiable light luggage of preconceptions derived from Rousseau, declared him to be a child of nature. The phrase gained a considerable popularity and had a long life, but it was difficult to graft the florid idea upon a Yankee base. The British schooling was more constant, and went deeper.

Notebooks in hand, British travelers poured across the sea; and while the onset was flattering the results were not, as these appeared in volumes that rose through many obscure writers to Captain Hall and the famous Mrs. Trollope and finally to Dickens and were echoed in British pulpits or in the august pages of the *Quarterly Review*. Perhaps the conscious or unconscious sense of an enduring tie between the two nations prompted this marked freedom of utterance. Accustomed to self-criticism of a quantity and stringency which the Americans and possibly no other people have ever attained, the British focused this talent without reserve upon the United States. In the intimate history of relations between the two countries these utterances played an important part; they were full of emotion and aroused emotion in return. The harsh accusations need not be repeated. Many of them were true. But the tacit sense of an alliance did not always make for British understanding. Irving, who surely cannot be accused of lack of sympathy for the British, discussed their extreme credulity in viewing American affairs. At the same time he indicated an essential flaw in the American armor. "Why are we so exquisitely alive to the aspersions of England?" he asked. He found the Americans "morbidly sensitive to the most trifling collision," and feared that the resultant sarcastic habit might ruin the national temper.

Irving's friend Paulding expressed the sarcasm and revealed the hurt in his *John Bull in America,* a highly popular allegory published in 1825 and many times reprinted. Paulding was acutely aware of a natural alliance between the two nations. With the familiar homely approach he said that Brother Jonathan "always wore a linsey-woolsey coat that did not above half cover his breech, and the sleeves of which were so short that his hand and wrist came out beyond them, looking like a shoulder of mutton . . . . He was a rather odd-looking chap, and had many queer ways: but everybody that had seen John Bull saw a great likeness between them, and swore that he was John's own boy, and a true chip off the old block. Like the squire he was likely to be blustering and saucy, but in the main he was a peaceable sort of careless fellow, that would quarrel with nobody if you would only let him alone." Because of his sense of a bond, British criticism stung Paulding sharply. Though he took many a neat potshot at the American character and scene he lapsed into confused and bitter anger when he saw shots coming thick from the British side. The outcome, however, was that he laughed, and turned his allegory into a trenchant broad burlesque of the British traveler in America, which had points of perennial application. The laughter spread, loud and confused, sensitive and satirical. A little sheaf of allegories similar to Paulding's were written, which made a running accompaniment for a wider more emphatic assertion.

During the Revolution a fable had appeared on the stage called *The Contrast,* by Royall Tyler, whose theme was suggested by the exhortations and queries of its prologue—

Exult, each patriot heart!—this night is shewn
A piece, which we may fairly call our own;
Where the proud titles of "My Lord! Your Grace!"
To humble *Mr.* and plain *Sir* give place.
Our Author pictures not from foreign climes
The fashions or the follies of the times. . . .
On native themes his Muse displays her pow'rs;
If ours the faults, the virtues too are ours.
Why should our thoughts to distant countries roam,
When each refinement may be found at home?
Who travels now to ape the rich or great,
To deck an equipage and roll in state;
To court the graces, or to dance with ease,
Or by hypocrisy to strive to please?
Our free-born ancestors such arts despis'd;
Genuine sincerity alone they priz'd;
Their minds, with honest emulation fir'd,
To solid good—not ornament—aspir'd. . . .

Thus the prologue attacked a question referred to many years later in the title of Mrs. Trollope's famous book—the manners of the Americans, a subject, indeed, which was often to engage British attention.

The new American rejoinder was double: first that all refinements might be found at home; then that they didn't matter. On the whole the second view prevailed in the play and perhaps elsewhere. The contrast lay between an honest plain American and a silly, foppish, infamous Englishman. But it was a third character, the Yankee Jonathan, who gave savor to the notion that only a rough sincerity was of consequence in America. Introduced for the purpose of comic relief, he might easily have become a puppet; but his author hailed from Vermont, and Jonathan drew the breath of life. Astute and simple, gross and rambling, rural to the core, he talked "nat'r'l"—talked his way through the scenes, and became a presiding genius.

His appearance was dynamic. For a generation or more the fable and the portrait were worked over by many hands, until at last, from 1825 onward, when the British commentaries were in full swing, Yankee plays began to appear on the American stage all over the country.

Neat, small, and brightly colored, they repeated the original fable with a naive and belligerent charm; each was sharply different from the others in scene and thread of story; in each the Yankee was a looming figure. He might be a peddler, a sailor, a Vermont wool-dealer, or merely a Green Mountain boy who traded and drawled and upset calculations; he was Lot Sapsago or Jedediah Homebred or Jerusalem Dutiful; sometimes he was a sailor. But he was always the symbolic American. Unless he appeared as a tar his costume hardly varied: he wore a white bell-crowned hat, a coat with long tails that was usually blue, eccentric red and white trousers, and long boot-straps. Brother Jonathan had in fact turned into Uncle Sam. Half bravado, half cock-alorum, this Yankee revealed the traits considered deplorable by the British travelers; he was indefatigably rural, sharp, uncouth, witty. Here were the manners of the Americans! Peddling, swapping, practical joking, might have been national preoccupations. He burst periodically into song, with variations of "Yankee Doodle," with local ballads celebrating Yankee exploits, or chanteys. Some of the plays verged upon the operatic, and the prevailing high national pitch was repeated by casual allusions. A tavern was called "The Sign of the Spread Eagle." Beneath this aegis roamed the Briton, still wicked, still mannered and over-polished, either rich or nefariously seeking riches, and always defeated by simple rural folk to the accompaniment of loud laughter.

Once indeed there was no contrast; rather the wistful contention of an alliance was repeated, and a gawky Yankee lad proved to be the son of an English nobleman.

This wry triumphant portrait was repeated again and again, up and down the Atlantic coast, over and over in the newly opened West, where its popularity had a quirk of oddity. Sectionalism had become rampant in the late 1820's; the western almanacs and papers were full of stories disparaging the Yankee. But of all portions of the country the West was smarting most acutely from British criticism; the emblematical Yankee was boisterously applauded there. He also traveled to England, where he was viewed with disapproval, not because of his derision of the British, which seems to have been received with equanimity, but because the character was genuinely disliked. Still, the Yankee was a novelty, and the Americans a favorite subject. With a sturdy disregard of pleasure London audiences continued to attend the Yankee plays.

Phantasmal conceptions may have sprung from this simple early stem, at home and abroad. Other national types had developed slowly, even through centuries, without close definition by themselves or by others. The American stepped full-length into the public glare, and steadily heightened the early yellow light. He gazed at himself in the Yankee plays as in a bright mirror, and developed the habit of self-scrutiny, which may have its dangers for the infant or youth, whether the creature be national or human.

WALTER BLAIR

3 The Requisites for American Humor

In a career that spanned more than sixty years, Walter
Blair did more than any other single individual to
legitimize the study of American humor. From the
beginning of his academic work in the 1920s, when
American literature in general was just beginning to
be regarded as worthy of serious study, until his
death in 1992, he remained the foremost scholar of
nineteenth-century American humor, particularly of
its leading figure, Mark Twain. Only a handful of book-
length studies of American humor preceded his 1937
Native American Humor, which, as both critical commentary and anthology, influenced the field for
decades to come. Among Blair's many other books are
Horse Sense in American Humor (1942) and, edited
with Raven I. McDavid, Jr., *The Mirth of a Nation:
America's Great Dialect Humor* (1983). For Blair, the
"requisites" of a true American humor were not in
place until 1830, when Americans had achieved sufficient detachment to see and consciously exploit
the comic aspects of their experiences, and when they
had developed forms and styles of expression that
were not simply borrowed from England and Europe.

The term, "American humor," like many another
term in general use, is more easily understood than
defined. As it is usually employed, it does not mean all humor produced
in America, since much humor originating in this country is not in any
way marked by its place of origin. Nor does it mean humor with characteristics discoverable in the comedy of no other land, since apparently

From Walter Blair, ed., *Native American Humor* (1937; reprint ed., San Francisco:
Chandler Publishing Co., 1960), 3–16.

there is no such humor. It means humor which is *American* in that it has an emphatic "native quality"[1]—a quality imparted by its subject matter and its technique. Its subject matter is national in the sense indicated in 1838 by a writer who was hailing the beginnings of this type of writing. Said this writer, an English critic:

> Humour is national when it is impregnated with the convictions, customs, and associations of a nation. . . . National American humour must be all this transferred into shapes which produce laughter. The humour of a people is their institutions, laws, customs, manners, habits, characters, convictions,—their scenery whether of the sea, the city, or the hills,—expressed in the language of the ludicrous. . . .[2]

Its technique, which will be characterized hereafter, is of a sort which develops effectively such subject matter. The phrase, "native American humor," suggests as well as any the usual implication of the term.

American humor—in this sense of the term—did not come into widespread existence until about 1830, more than two hundred years after John Smith wrote the first American book. In other words, though the colonists were more prolific of humor than is generally supposed,[3] the beginnings of this type of writing came late. And they were long coming because most American authors failed for a long time to perceive the richest comedy about them or to discover a technique which revealed that comedy.

In part, of course, the perception of comedy depended upon the attitude of the writers. Many details in the native scene which seemed comic to the people of the nineteenth century belonged to the seventeenth and eighteenth centuries as well. Furthermore, quite early, some of the colonists saw and recorded some of these details. One is forced to conclude—not very profoundly, perhaps—that many early writers failed to develop American humor because they were too earnest, too serious about subjects which later proved amusing.

Proof of this is discoverable in the writings of two colonial authors, Francis Higginson and John Smith, who were so serious in their treatment of typical details that, though their works now provoke laughter, they themselves did not realize that their materials were amusing. By contrast, two rare frivolous souls of colonial times, Sarah Kemble Knight and William Byrd, in their treatment of typical details, foreshadowed American humor.

Undoubtedly comedy unperceived by the author is implicit in *New England's Plantation* (1630) by Francis Higginson. In his rhapsodic account of newly opened territory, similar to those produced by writers on every American frontier, eager to share with others the blessings of a land of milk and honey, Higginson wrote enthusiastically of New England's fertility, its plentiful game and fish, its salubrious climate. Corn, he said, grew amazingly: "Thirty, forty, fifty, sixty [fold increases] are abundant here. Yea, Joseph's increase in Egypt are outstript. . . . Our planters hope to have more than a hundredfold this year." Root vegetables flourish astonishingly, "both bigger and sweeter than ordinarily is found in England." And the wild beasts—"bears, and they say some lions also . . . several sorts of deer, some whereof bring three or four young ones at once, which is not ordinary in England . . . wolves, foxes, beavers, otters, martens, great wild cats, and a beast called a molke, as big as an ox"—furnish food a-plenty and precious furs. Even the fish in the sea are plentiful "almost beyond believing . . . our fishermen take many hundreds together . . . their nets take more than they are able to haul to land . . . they fill two boats at a time. . . ."

But the climax is Higginson's enthusiasm for the climate of New England, concerning which most people today are likely to have some reservations. ". . . there is hardly," he exclaims, rapturously, "a more healthful place in the world. . . ."

> Many that have been weak and sickly in old England, by coming hither have been thoroughly healed, and grown healthful and strong. None can more truly speak hereof . . . than myself. . . . My friends that knew me can well tell how very sickly I have been, and continually in physic, being much troubled with tormenting pain . . . and abundance of melancholic humors. But since I came hither . . . I thank God I have had perfect health, and freed from pain . . . and whereas beforetime I clothed myself with double clothes and thick waistcoats to keep me warm, even in the summer time, I do now go as thin clad as any. . . . a sup of New-England's air is better than a whole draught of Old England's ale.[4]

To us, though not to Higginson, this is amusing. The unconscious comedy of the ecstatic passage was effectively demonstrated by Higginson himself, however, when, during the very year his moving tribute to the healthfulness of New England appeared, the poor man sickened and died.[5] His demise conveniently and irrefutably proves that his unconscious humor was the humor of exaggeration, often called typically American.[6] In early writings of colonists who, like Higginson, whistled to keep up their spirits or sought to persuade other settlers to join them by reporting the richness of the new world—in natural resources, in the spiritual grace and the bravery of its inhabitants— time after time comedy was missed by similarly narrow margins.[7]

Later Americans, more sympathetic to comedy, more detached, and hence more perceptive of incongruities, were to discover the comic possibilities of such an attitude as the booster's enthusiasm displayed by Higginson.[8] Here, for example, is how an Arkansan, in 1845, made capital of subject matter akin to Higginson's:

> Strangers, if you'd asked me how we got our meat in Arkansaw, I'd a . . . given you a list of varmints that would make a caravan, beginning with the bar, and ending off with the cat . . . a bird . . . is too trifling. I never did shoot at but one, and I'd never forgive myself for that, had it weighed less than forty pounds. . . . You see, the thing was so fat that it couldn't fly far; and when he fell out of the tree, after I shot him, on striking the ground he bust open behind, and the way the pound gobs of tallow rolled out of the opening was perfectly beautiful.
>
> . . . Arkansaw . . . the creation state, the finishing-up country —a state where the *sile* runs down to the centre of the 'arth, and government gives you title to every inch of it. Then its airs—just breathe them, and they will make you snort like a horse. It's a state without a fault, it is.[9]

Other writers in the nineteenth century were to find comedy in harrowing adventures similar to those which, from the time of Captain John Smith, had been celebrated by colonists and frontiersmen. As Henry Adams has shown, Smith, like Higginson, was an unconscious creator of comedy. When that blustering, mustachioed Elizabethan soldier of fortune retold his tale of captivity, the number and the ferocity of his Indian captors provide comedy of exaggeration not unlike that in Falstaff's famous yarn to Prince Hal. Hence, when one compares the first version of Smith's yarn with the second, laughter, unforeseen by the bold captain, results:

> Eight guards, which had been sufficient in 1608, were multiplied into thirty or forty tall fellows in 1624. What was enough for ten men at the earlier time would feed twenty according to the later version . . . a few months after the event, a people was

described, savage, but neither cruel nor bloodthirsty . . . kind and even magnanimous toward their captive . . . . Yet in 1624, throughout his long imprisonment, he was . . . expecting every hour to be put to one death or another.[10]

But two centuries were to pass before a perception of the outlandish and grotesque qualities of American wilderness adventures made possible the display of their fantastic comedy in a whole series of sketches consciously, not unconsciously, humorous.[11]

Two colonial authors came nearer than Higginson and Smith, however, to cultivating the most fertile field for nineteenth century American humor—American character. From the seventeenth century, comedy had lurked in the mingling of people of many civilizations, of many classes, on one sparsely settled continent; and the attempts of these people to adjust themselves to totally new ways of living and the sensing by every man of the amazing differences between himself and his neighbors had provided the stuff of rich comedy.[12] But though some colonial writers were stern with their neighbors for differing from them,[13] and though some interestedly recorded the fact that many races lived in America, effective comic portraiture did not evolve in America, with minor exceptions,[14] until the eighteenth century. Then, two authors contemptuous of folk they saw on their travels, Madam Knight, a light-hearted lady traveling from Boston to New York, and William Byrd, a sophisticated Southern aristocrat on a surveying party, partially, at least, developed the comedy of American character.

The sprightly Sarah Kemble Knight, recording some of her adventures in her *Private Journal of a Journey from Boston to New York* (1704–1705),[15] is frivolous enough, amused enough, to limn an admirable picture of a gawky Connecticut Yankee and his awkward Joan whom she saw in a merchant's house. The man was

a tall country fellow, w*th* his alfogeos full of Tobacco; for they seldom Loose their Cudd, but keep Chewing and Spitting as long as they'r eyes are open,—he advanc't to the middle of the Room, makes an Awkward Nodd, and spitting a Large deal of Aromatick Tincture, he gave a scrape with his shovel like shoo . . . Hugging his own pretty Body with his hands under his arms, Stood staring rown'd him, like a Catt let out of a Baskett. At last, . . . he opened his mouth and said: have You any Ribinen for Hatbands to sell I pray? The Questions and Answers about pay being past,

the Ribin is bro't and opened. Bumpkin Simpers, cryes its con-
founded Gay I vow; and beckoning to the door, in comes Jone
Tawdry, dropping about 50 curtsees, and stands by him: hee
shows her the Ribin.

Law you, sais shee, *its right Gent,* do You, take it, *tis dreadfull
pretty.*

The vividly pictured Jonathan and Joan, the backgrounds of their
lives, their peculiarities of gesture, of manner, and particularly of
speech, foreshadowed what was to be the stuff of America's favorite
comedy a century after they were created. Similarly, William Byrd, in
his *History of the Dividing Line betwixt Virginia and North Carolina*
(1728),[16] hinted at the sort of humor later to be popular when he pictured the poor whites of Lubberland:

> The Men, for their Parts, just like the Indians, impose all the Work
> upon the poor Women. They make their Wives rise out of their Beds
> early in the Morning, at the same time they lye and Snore, till the
> Sun has run one third of his course, and disperst all the unwhole-
> some Damps. Then, after Stretching and Yawning for half an Hour,
> they light their Pipes, and, under the protection of a cloud of
> Smoak, venture out into the open Air; tho', if it happens to be never
> so little cold, they quickly return Shivering into the Chimney
> corner. When the Weather is mild, they stand leaning with both
> their arms upon the corn-field fence, and gravely consider whether
> they had best go and take a small Heat at the Hough [hoe]: but gen-
> erally find reasons to put it off till another time.

Such passages look forward to the myriad picturings in detail of
the Jonathans and Lubbers of their country which were to be a leading source of humor in the coming century. The varied men and
women whose characters, whose very accents, were molded by the
country and the times, and the social and political backgrounds of those
men and women, were, as S. S. Cox noted in 1875, when he tried to
summarize American humor, endlessly amusing:

> we have in America specific objects of humor—the scheming
> Yankee, the big, bragging brave Kentuckian, and the first fam-
> ily Virginian. We have lawyers on the circuit . . . ; loafers on a
> spree . . . ; politicians in caucus; legislators in session; travelers
> on cars and steamers; indeed the history of every American's life
> is humorous.[17]

But passages like Byrd's and Madam Knight's were unusual because, of the vast majority of the colonists, at least of the serious men and women who wrote, one might say what a French scholar of English humor said of the Anglo-Saxons:

> Their mental equipment was such as rather to promise future fitness [for humorous writing], than to secure actual ability. Like most early races, they would be handicapped for humorous thinking by the violence of their passions, and by their general incapacity to be detached from the urgency of their feelings and ideas.[18]

Detachment was needed before many could follow the lead of Byrd and Madam Knight. The detachment was likely at first, as in the writings of these two authors, to be colored with contempt. Later, it was to be more tolerant. But detachment and a certain amount of frivolity were requisites for the development of native American humor.

These were not the only requisites, however. Before this humor could become at all pervasive, two other things were needful—(1) a general perception of the elements in the American scene which Higginson and Smith saw but did not consciously exploit, and of the elements of American character which the Southern gentleman and the New England lady observed and wrought into brief passages of comedy,[19] and (2) the development of a technique which allowed effective and extensive comic treatments of these materials. How needful these powers of perception and this technique were is revealed by writers of the latter part of the eighteenth century and the early part of the nineteenth century—writers sufficiently detached and appropriately frivolous who were eager to produce comic writings but who did not articulate American humor.

These authors failed largely because, lighthearted and eager to amuse as they were, they looked to eighteenth-century English models to learn how to write.[20] And their models did not reveal to them the necessary methods of finding American comedy or of reporting it.

Suppose, for example, American writers turned to the simplest models for the simplest type of humor—the English jest books. In these they would find anecdotes beginning, "When Sidney Smith's physician. . ." or "Ben Jonson, owing a man some money. . ." or "A shrewish wife. . ." From these they would, as a rule, get enough inspiration to copy the ancient English wheezes.[21] And even jest books which made an occasional attempt to develop American humor consistently retold mossy anecdotes which had nothing to do with the native scene or native life.[22]

Equally unproductive of a stimulus to national humor, it appears, were the neoclassical models of comic or fictional treatment which Americans followed more consistently than any others.[23] A glance at the newspapers published in every part of the country between 1800 and 1830 will show that, as in an earlier period,[24] the Addisonian essay was predominant. In nearly all these papers, columns or quadrangles at the ends of columns which were not filled by records of congressional debates, stories of national happenings, and foreign news were filled with essays by English or American authors who were steeped in the *Spectator* tradition.[25] Two compilations of newspaper humor, one English, one American, reveal the predominance of this type of humor on both sides of the Atlantic in the early years of the century.[26] And since only the data concerning publication on the title page, a few scattered references to localities, and a paltry number of jests which are vaguely national, distinguish the American book from the contemporary volume published in London, it is evident that the copying of these models did not stimulate humor with much of an American flavor. Essays on the ancient subjects, "Duelling," "City Manners" and "Fashion"[27] in the American volume are just as localized as the character sketches which introduce us to shadowy figures named "Scepticus," "Frothy," "Pedanticus" or the like,[28] or limn a vague "Uncle Jonathan" and "Cousin Peter."[29]

Not only these portions of the newspapers but also the periodicals devoted largely to humor were American—though scarcely Americanized—versions of the *Spectator* and the *Bee*. Composed "in every city of importance" by "a band of young lawyers without cases, or young beaux with a taste for letters and some claim to wit,"[30] these might have been written by "Oliver Oldschool, Esq." of London as easily as by "Oliver Oldschool, Esq." of Philadelphia.[31] Hudson, N.Y., for example, had *The Wasp* (1801–1803), edited by Robert Rusticoat; Philadelphia had its *Tickler,* edited by Toby Scratch 'em; Boston had Roderick Rover's *The Thistle* (1807) and Tim Touchstone's *Scourge* (1811), while in the South, Baltimore produced *The Observer* and the *Scourge* (Titus Tickler, Esq., ed.), and the Richmond Literary Club held forth in *The Rainbow.*

Most of these transplanted English periodicals, quite properly, have managed to fall into obscurity. The association of John Pendleton Kennedy of Baltimore with *The Red Book* (1818–1819) gave that

Addisonian publication whatever lasting importance it had—and that importance did not derive from the fact that it published native humor.[32] Washington Irving's association with the New York *Salmagundi Papers* (1807–1808) gave them a certain biographical interest and Irving's genius and the skill of his associates gave them qualities which make these papers still enjoyable; but they, like Irving's earlier "open imitations of the *Spectator* and the *Tatler*,"[33] Jonathan Oldstyle Papers (1802), were too much in the English tradition to be much concerned with American scenes, life, or character. Except here and there,[34] the subjects incessantly developed were the frail sex, fashions, assemblies, theatrical productions, and highly generalized characters.

A typical characterization is that of Pindar Cockloft, who might as well have been English as American:

> He is now in his fifty-eighth year—is a bachelor . . . and an oddity of the first water. Half his life has been employed in writing odes, sonnets, epigrams, and elegies. . . .
>
> In his younger days he figured as a dashing blade in the great world; and no young fellow of the town wore a longer pig-tail, or carried more buckram in his skirts. From sixteen to thirty he was continually in love. . . . The evening of his thirtieth birthday . . . he was seized with a whim-wham that he was an old fool to be in love at this time of life . . . . From that time he gave up all particular attention to the ladies.[35]

It was characters such as these—characters portrayed in a generalized style, with no particular background in place or time—which were likely to emerge in imitations of eighteenth century English writings.[36] Actually, the imitation of neoclassical writers caused most American humorous authors to fail to see that this country as well as England had its comic types. Hugh H. Brackenridge, who wrote, in *Modern Chivalry,* what Henry Adams called "a more thoroughly American book than any written before 1833,"[37] in 1805 admitted that when he looked around in America to find a comic figure, he had had to be satisfied with an Irish clown. He could not portray an English clown or a Scotch clown well, he said; hence he had made use of an Irishman. An American did not seem a comic possibility to him because:

> The American has, in fact, yet no character; neither the clown nor the gentleman; so that I could not take one from our country, which I would much rather have done as the scene lay there.[38]

Brackenridge had learned to portray an Irishman, he implies, because the English stage had shown him such a character. But no English work had suggested to him the qualities of a Yankee, a Pennsylvania Dutchman, a Virginian, or a Kentuckian.[39]

But even when a disciple of neoclassicism had better luck than Brackenridge in discovering distinctively American comedy before 1830, he employed a technique which, admirable though it was, differed from that of typical American humor.[40] Irving's portrayals of Yankees, Kentuckians, and Virginians in *Knickerbocker's History of New York* (1809),[41] presented in the delightful style he had "formed upon the prose of Goldsmith, Sterne, Swift, Steele, and Addison, with romantic coloring from Mrs. Radcliffe,"[42] were as amusing and as effective as any master of an eighteenth-century style could have made them. But, since he employed an eighteenth-century style, his portrayals were generalized, unlocalized, relatively unconcerned with individualizing details.[43]

Its effect is about the same as the effect of Byrd's passage about the Lubbers, cited above, or of Barlowe's pleasant presentation of a typical American scene, a cornhusking:

> For now, the corn-house fill'd, the harvest home,
> Th' invited neighbours to the *Husking* come;
> A frolic scene, where work, and mirth, and play,
> Unite their charms, to chace the hours away.
>   Where the huge heap lies center'd in the hall,
> The lamp suspended from the cheerful wall,
> Brown corn-fed nymphs, and strong hard-handed beaux,
> Alternate rang'd, extend in circling rows,
> Assume their seats, the solid mass attack;
> The dry husks rustle, and the corn-cobs crack;
> The song, the laugh, alternate notes resound,
> And the sweet-cider trips in silence round.
>   The laws of Husking ev'ry wight can tell;
> And sure no laws he ever keeps so well:
> For each red ear a general kiss he gains,
> With each smut ear she smuts the luckless swains;
> But when to some sweet maid the prize is cast,
> Red as her lips, and taper as her waist,
> She walks the round, and culls one favor'd beau
> Who leaps, the luscious tribute to bestow.

Various the sport, as are the wits and brains
Of well pleas'd lasses and contending swains;
Till the vast mound of corn is swept away,
And he that gets the last ear, wins the day.[44]

This admirable sketch deals with a scene of the sort a nineteenth-century humorist would be delighted to treat; it is vivid, and it is written in high good spirits. But a typical American humorist, writing in the style of the century which produced American humor, would be pretty sure to use even more details than does this unusually detailed eighteenth-century description—details about the farmer who held the husking, about the barn where the husking was held, about the gathering of the huskers, about individual "lasses" and "swains"—their faces, figures, costumes, actions. Some of these might not receive attention, but the later humorist would be pretty sure to record much conversation, catching the dialect, the intonations, the characteristics which revealed themselves in speech.[45] The elegant style would probably suffer, but such details as these would in part atone for the loss.[46]

Even after the writers of America became sufficiently detached, sufficiently jocose, then, before the characteristic writings of American humorists could appear, two developments were necessary: the development of perception of the comic possibilities of the American scene and American character, and the development of a fictional technique which would reveal them. Somehow, American authors had to become aware of native materials for humorous literature; somehow they had to learn to exploit them.

NOTES

1. The phrase is that of Will D. Howe, in *The Cambridge History of American Literature*, vol. 2 (New York, 1918), 150.
2. H. W., "Slick, Downing, Crockett, Etc.," *The London and Westminster Review* 32 (December 1838), 138–39.
3. For studies of humorous writings during the years before 1800, see Carl Holliday's book, *The Wit and Humor of Colonial Days, 1607–1800* (Philadelphia, 1912); the same author's article, "Colonial Laughter," *English Journal* 24 (February 1935), 125–36; Henry Clay Lukens, "American Literary Comedians," *Harper's* 80 (April 1890), 783–88; Stephen Leacock, *The Greatest Pages of American Humor* (Garden City, 1936), 1–24.
4. *New England's Plantation, or a short and true description of the Commodities of that Country,* reprinted in the *Massachusetts Historical Society Collections*, vol. I. Since similar passages might be cited from the writings of Alsop, Morton, Ward and half a dozen authors of the same period, it will be evident that Higginson is fairly representative.

5. Thomas Wentworth Higginson, *Life of Francis Higginson* (New York, 1891), 128.

6. H. W., in the review cited (footnote 2), as early as 1838 said: "The curiosity of the public regarding the peculiar nature of American humour seems to have been easily satisfied with the application of the all-sufficing word exaggeration." Though American humor has other qualities as well, exaggeration is a device very frequently employed.

7. There are a few exceptions, notably Franklin's tales about prodigious American sheep and leaping whales and some passages in the writings of the Rev. Samuel Andrew Peters, which are embryonic American tall tales. Franklin's fanciful yarns are printed in his *Works,* vol. 7, ed. Jared Sparks (Boston, 1847), 289–90, and Peters' invention is displayed in *A General History of Connecticut . . .* (London, 1781).

8. Early in the nineteenth century, they are smiling at the Kentucky preacher who, describing eternal bliss, suggested that heaven was "a regular Kentuck of a place" or they were telling tales about game so plentiful that the hunter killed great numbers of animals with a single shot of his gun. Mark Twain's Beriáh Sellers is the greatest achievement in this type of humor, but during the twentieth century, Americans were still amused by the Californian who arose at a funeral "to say a few words about the climate of California," and in 1936, the rhymed boast of the Rotarian club about the glories of a small town amused those who viewed the picture, "Mr. Deeds Goes to Town."

9. *The Big Bear of Arkansas, and Other Tales, Illustrative of Characters and Incidents in the South and Southwest* (Philadelphia, 1845), 16–17.

10. Henry Adams, *Historical Essays* (New York, 1891), 53–54.

11. Indians much more ferocious than those who menaced Smith were the comic redmen who, in 1853, seized Sal Fink: ". . . she war captered in the most all-sneaken manner by about fifty Injuns, an' carried by 'em to Roast Flesh Hollow, whar the blood drinkin' wild varmints detarmined to skin her alive, sprinkle a leetle salt over her, an' devour her before her own eyes. . . ." *Crockett Almanac* (Philadelphia, New York, Boston, and Baltimore, 1852). For other fantastic yarns about the redmen or the beasts of the wilderness, see *The Spirit of the Times* of the forties and fifties, or read the chapter called "Hunters and Fishermen" in *Humor of the Old Deep South,* ed. Arthur Palmer Hudson (New York, 1936), 98–125.

12. As Andrew Lang says, in "Western Drolls," *Lost Leaders* (London, 1889), 186: "The contrasts, the energy, the mixture of races in America, the overflowing young life of the continent, doubtless give its humorists the richness of its vein." George Edward Woodberry makes the same point in *America in Literature* (New York, 1903), 157–58, as he considers Western humor, and F. L. Pattee, in *American Literature Since 1870* (New York, 1915), 24, points out: "The incongruities of the new world—the picturesque gathering of peoples like the Puritans, the Indians, the cavaliers, the Dutch, the negroes and the later immigrants; the makeshifts of the frontier, the vastness and the richness of the land, the levelling effects of democracy, the freedom of life, and the independence of spirit—all have tended to produce a laughing people."

13. Particularly were they stern about differences of religious belief. A famous example is Bradford's consideration of his neighbors led by Thomas Morton, in *History of Plymouth Plantation* (Boston, 1856), 236–43.

14. Perhaps more than a minor exception is Thomas Morton, who in his *New English Canaan* (1637) naughtily and frivolously derided the speech, the costumes, the religious attitudes of the Plymouth colonists. Compare Chapter 14 of his book with the passage by Bradford cited above.

15. First published by Theodore Dwight, in 1825, and more recently made available in reprints, ed. W. R. Deane (1858) and G. P. Winship (1920).

16. Printed first in German in 1737 and in English in 1841. The passage quoted below is from the definitive edition, ed. J. S. Bassett (1901). For comment on the passage dealing with Lubberland, see A. S. McIlwaine, *The Poor White in American Literature* (Unpublished University of Chicago Doctoral Dissertation, 1937).

17. "American Humor," *Harper's Magazine* 50 (April 1875), 700. A more detailed summary is that of V. L. O. Chittick, in *Thomas Chandler Haliburton* (New York, 1924), 533–34.

18. Louis Cazamian, *The Development of English Humour: Part I. From the Early Times to the Renaissance* (New York, 1930), 28–29.

19. It should be pointed out, perhaps, that the passages quoted are not representative of either volume as a whole. Such sketches were almost as unusual in the writings of both authors as they were in eighteenth-century American writings in general.

20. They failed, that is, to be "American" humorists. There is, of course, no need either to bewail or to commend this failure.

21. See, for example, *The American Jest-Book. Containing A curious Variety of Jests, Anecdotes, Bon Mots, Stories &c.* (Boston, 1796), in which few jests, despite the title, are American in any sense.

22. *The Chaplet of Comus; or Feast of Sentiment, and Festival of Wit* (Boston, 1811) boasts that "the reader will find in this collection more specimens of American humor than in any other publication," but, only six of the first twenty-five anecdotes are even vaguely connected with America. See also Constance Rourke, *American Humor, a Study of the National Character* (New York, 1931), 306: "In most of the joke-books before 1840 only the faintest traces of native humor can be discovered."

23. This dependence has been frequently noted by critics. See particularly V. F. Calverton's *The Liberation of American Literature* (New York, 1932).

24. Elizabeth Cook, *Literary Influences on Colonial Newspapers (1704–1750)* (New York, 1912). See also E. C. Coleman's *The Influences of the Addisonian Essay before 1810* (Urbana, 1936).

25. Smaller gaps were usually filled with English anecdotes or passages of poetry. Newspapers examined for this period represented New York, Washington, D.C., New England, the Middle States, and the Southwest.

26. *The Spirit of the Public Journales; or Beauties of the American Newspaper for 1805* [compiled by George Bourne] (Baltimore, 1806), which draws material from ninety-six newspapers of various parts of the country, and *The Spirit of the Public Journals for 1804* (London, 1805). Although these do not attempt exactly the same thing, they are comparable on points essential here. The American volume, at least, is representative.

27. There are two on this perennial favorite, one in heroic couplets.

28. See "Characteristics," 42–45, 64–70; "The Idler," 75–78; "Begin in Time," 92–95; "Honesty is the Best Policy," 109–13.

29. "Uncle Jonathan's Reflection," 20–24. The names alone are individualized.

30. John Bach McMasters, *A History of the People of the United States,* vol. 5 (New York, 1900), 296, treating the period 1790–1800, thus characterizes the editors. Remarking that "the list is too long to cite," he names seven such publications. See also Frank Luther Mott, *A History of American Magazines, 1741–1850* (New York, 1930), 170.

31. Oliver Oldschool happened to be Dennie, the editor of the Philadelphia *Port Folio,* which, as Professor Boynton has noted, typically indicated in the statement of its program that its contents were all to be composed "after the manner of" various English authors. See *Literature and American Life* (Boston, 1936), 215–16.

32. Edward M. Gwathmey, *John Pendleton Kennedy* (New York, 1931), 60–61. Like Irving's earlier *Salmagundi Papers,* the satire had certain local applications.

33. Charles Dudley Warner, *Washington Irving* (Boston, 1881), 30.

34. A few passages, notably those on American elections, on militia drills, and on travel books about America, gave the book a slightly national character.

35. *Salmagundi Papers,* no. 2, February 4, 1807.

36. Later Irving and Paulding, his collaborator, under a different stimulus, were to develop more particularized characters.

37. *History of the United States,* vol. 1 (New York, 1890), 124.

38. *Modern Chivalry,* Book 3, Chapter 17.

39. Complaint against another influence of English fictional methods in America is made by John Neal, in *The Down-Easters, &c.&c.&c.* (New York, 1833), v–vi: "To judge by our novel-writers, play-makers and poets, with here and there a partial exception . . . we have cottages and sky-larks in this country; pheasants and nightingales, first families, youth of 'gentle blood,' and a virtuous *peasantry;* moss-grown churches, curfews and ivy-mantled towers; with a plenty of hard-hearted fathers, runaway matches—to nobody knows whom, for nobody knows what; unfaithful wives, cruel step-mothers, treacherous brothers—any thing and every thing in short which goes to the ground-work of a third-rate English or Scotch novel, and nothing—absolutely nothing—whereby a stranger would be able to distinguish an *American* story from any other, or to obtain a glimpse of our peculiar institutions, or of the state of society here. . . ." This complaint, of course, has to do with the effects of Gothic romances upon American fiction.

40. Similarly, of course, most nineteenth-century fictional depictions differed from eighteenth-century depictions: the phenomenon is not discoverable in humor alone.

41. Book 3, Chapters 6–7; Book 4, Chapter 4.

42. Henry Seidel Canby, *Classic Americans* (New York, 1931), 70.

43. This statement remains true of the passages cited in spite of the fact that Irving pointed out in "The Author's Apology," which prefaced the 1848 edition, that his main purpose was "to embody the traditions of the city [of New York] in an amusing form; to illustrate its local humors, customs, and peculiarities; to clothe home scenes and places and familiar names with . . . imaginative and whimsical associations . . ." —in spite of the fact, in other words, that he was interested, like various romantic writers, in the local past. Scott understandably asserted that he "never read anything so closely resembling the style of Dean Swift."

44. *The Hasty Pudding* (1793), canto 3, lines 6–28. The text is from the first edition, published in 1796.

45. G. W. Harris's "The Knobs Dance" offers an illuminating comparison.
46. Irving's depiction of the quilting party in "The Legend of Sleepy Hollow," *The Sketch Book* (1819), written after Irving had adopted a more particularized style of writing than is apparent in his earlier works, employs something like the detail here suggested. Except for the fact that the conversation is practically unrecorded and the fact that Irving's style is more polished than is common, this is a characteristic piece of American humor.

LOUIS D. RUBIN, JR.

4 The Great American Joke

Louis Rubin is well known as a scholar of Southern literature. He served as editor of *The American South: Portrait of a Culture* (1979) and as general editor of *The History of Southern Literature* (1985). In the early 1970s, when Rubin edited the collection of essays titled *The Comic Imagination in American Literature,* scholars had written about American humor for nearly fifty years, and yet Rubin was correct when he wrote in his introduction that many were reluctant to take the message of humor seriously. In his convincing essay "The Great American Joke," Rubin claims that humor had long been a necessary component of American literature precisely because of the wide gap between the lofty ideals of a democracy and the mundane realities of everyday life. If pointing out such incongruity is, as Rubin believes, one of the major tasks of the writer in a democratic culture, humor arises from the contrast between "the formal, literary language of traditional culture and learning, and the informal, vernacular language of everyday life."

He took a pen and some paper. "Now—name of the elephant?"
"Hassan Ben Ali Selim Abdallah Mohammed Moise Alhammal Jamsetje-jeebhoy Dhuleep Sultan Ebu Bhudpoor."
"Very well. Given name?"
"Jumbo."

—Mark Twain, *The Stolen White Elephant*

From Louis D. Rubin, Jr., ed., *The Comic Imagination in American Literature* (New Brunswick, NJ: Rutgers University Press, 1973), 3–15. © Louis D. Rubin, Jr. Reprinted by permission of Louis D. Rubin, Jr.

The American literary imagination has from its earliest days been at least as much comic in nature as tragic. Perhaps this is only as might be expected; for while the national experience has involved sadness, disappointment, failure and even despair, it has also involved much joy, hopefulness, accomplishment. The tragic mode, therefore, could not of itself comprehend the full experience of the American people. From the moment that the colonists at Jamestown were assailed by the arrows of hostile Indians, and one Mr. Wynckfield "had one shott cleane through his bearde, yet scaped hurte," there has been too much to smile at. The type of society that has evolved in the northern portion of the western hemisphere bears no notable resemblance either to Eden or to Utopia, of course. From the start it has been inhabited by human beings who have remained most human and therefore most fallible. Even so, if one views American history as a whole it would be very difficult to pronounce it a tragedy, or to declare that the society of man would have been better off if it had never taken place (though Mark Twain once suggested as much).

Yet for all that, it is remarkable how comparatively little attention has been paid to American humor, and to the comic imagination in general, by those who have chronicled and interpreted American literature. Thalia, the muse of comedy, has always been something of a wallflower in critical circles, and the attention has gone principally to Melpomene and her more glamorous celebrants of tragedy. In large part, of course, this is because in the hierarchy of letters comedy has always occupied a position below and inferior to tragedy. We have tended to equate gravity with importance. The highest accolade we give to a humorist is when we say that even so he is a "serious" writer—which is to say that although he makes us laugh, his ultimate objective is to say something more about the human condition than merely that it is amusing. This implies that comedy is "un-serious"—we thus play a verbal trick, for we use "serious" to mean both "important" and "without humor," when the truth is that there is no reason at all why something cannot be at once very important and very comic.

In any event, more time and effort have been invested in attempting to study and to understand American tragedy than American comedy, and humorous writing is customarily relegated to a subordinate role. In so doing, we have been guilty of neglecting a valuable insight into the understanding of American society. For not only have many American writers been comic writers, but the very nature of comedy would seem to make it particularly useful in studying life in the United States. When Mark Twain speaks of "the calm confidence of a Christian holding four aces," he makes a joke and notes a human incongruity of interest to historians of American Protestantism. The essence of comedy is incongruity, the perception of the ridiculous. The seventeenth-century English critic Dennis's remark, that "the design of Comedy is to amend the follies of Mankind, by exposing them," points to the value of humor in searching out the shortcomings and the liabilities of society. In a democracy, the capacity for self-criticism would seem to be an essential function of the body politic, and surely this has been one of the chief tasks of the American writer. Thus H. L. Mencken, himself a newspaperman, rebukes the American press. The brain of the average journalist, he reports, "is a mass of trivialities and puerilities; to recite it would be to make even a barber beg for mercy." From colonial times onward, we have spent a great deal of time and effort criticizing ourselves, pointing out our shortcomings, exploring the incongruities and the contradictions within American society. As the novelist and poet Robert Penn Warren put it, "America was based on a big promise—a great big one: the Declaration of Independence. When you have to live with that in the house, that's quite a problem—particularly when you've got to make money and get ahead, open world markets, do all the things you have to, raise your children, and so forth. America is stuck with its self-definition put on paper in 1776, and that was just like putting a burr under the metaphysical saddle of America—you see, that saddle's going to jump now and then and it pricks." Literature has been one of the important ways whereby the American people have registered their discomfort at those pricks, and repeatedly the discomfort has been expressed in the form of humor—often enough through just such a homely metaphor as Warren used. For if we look at Warren's remark, what we will notice is that it makes use of a central motif of American humor—the contrast, the incongruity between the ideal and the real, in which a common, vernacular metaphor is used to put a somewhat abstract statement involving values—self-definition, metaphysical— into a homely context. The statement, in other words, makes its point through working an incongruity between two modes of language—the formal, literary language of traditional culture and learning, and the informal, vernacular language of everyday life.

This verbal incongruity lies at the heart of American experience. It is emblematic of the nature and the problem of democracy. On the one hand there are the ideals of freedom, equality, self-government, the conviction that ordinary people can evince the wisdom to vote wisely, and demonstrate the capacity for understanding and cherishing the highest human values through embodying them in their political and social institutions. On the other hand there is the *Congressional Record*—the daily exemplary reality of the fact that the individual citizens of a democracy are indeed ordinary people, who speak, think and act in ordinary terms, with a suspicion of abstract ideas and values. Thus, Senator Simon Cameron of Pennsylvania, after his Committee on Foreign Relations had rejected the nomination of Richard Henry Dana as U.S. Ambassador to England, could exult because his country would not be represented at the Court of St. James's by "another of those damned literary fellows." The problem of democracy and culture is one of how, in short, a democracy can reach down to include all its citizens in its decision-making, without at the same time cheapening and vulgarizing its highest social, cultural, and ethical ideals. Who, that is, will, in a democracy, commission the Esterhazy quartets? Confronting this problem, Thomas Jefferson called for an *aristoi*, an aristocracy of intellect; he believed that through public education the civilized values of truth, knowledge and culture that he cherished would be embodied and safeguarded in the democratic process so that leadership could be produced which would not be demagogic and debasing. His good friend John Adams was skeptical of this ever coming to pass, and Adams's great-grandson, Henry Adams, lived to chronicle and deplore a time when the workings of political and economic democracy made heroes of the vulgar and the greedy, and had no place in the spectrum of power, he thought, for an Adams who by virtue of inbred inheritance still believed in the disinterested morality, as he saw it, of the Founding Fathers. What Henry Adams could not fathom was why the public could nominate for the presidency of the United States a Ulysses Grant, a James A. Garfield, a James G. Blaine, and then vote for him. He could only conclude that "the moral law had expired—like the Constitution." "The progress of evolution from President Washington to President Grant," he concluded, "was alone evidence enough to upset Darwin."

The problem has been part of American experience from the start, and it is at least as crucial today as in the past. Though it is by no means purely or uniquely American, it is nevertheless distinctively so, and if we look at American literary history we will quickly recognize that the writers have been dealing with it all along the way. Herman Melville's famous invocation to the muses in *Moby-Dick* faces it squarely:

If, then, to meanest mariners, and renegades and castaways, I shall hereafter ascribe high qualities, though dark; weave round them tragic graces; if even the most mournful, perchance the most abased, among them all, shall at times lift himself to the exalted mounts; if I shall spread a rainbow over his disastrous set of sun; then against all mortal spirits bear me out in it, thou just Spirit of Equality, which hast spread one royal mantle of humanity over all my kind! Bear me out in it, thou great democratic God!

Melville wanted to create a tragedy along metaphysical lines, and yet he wanted to write about the Nantucket whaling fleet; his problem was how to render the everyday experience of life aboard a whaling vessel while creating a tragic protagonist, one who, in Aristotle's classic formula, could arouse pity and terror through his fall from eminence. Obviously such a protagonist, Aristotle declared, "must be one who is highly renowned and prosperous,—a personage like Oedipus, Thyestes, or other illustrious men of such families." How to give a whaling captain such heroic stature? Melville's solution was partly one of language. He separated the two elements. He used a literary, highly poetic, Shakespearean diction to chronicle Ahab, and a much more vernacular, colloquial diction to report on the activities of the crew. He made the language distance between tragic captain and motley crew serve his ultimate meaning.

In so doing, however, Melville was forced to distort and impoverish the experience of a whaling captain. He could not make (nor did he wish to make) Captain Ahab into a "typical" Nantucket whaling skipper. He had to leave out a great deal of what an ordinary whaling captain does and says and thinks. The Captain of the *Pequod* must not cuss out the cabin boy in approved Nantucket style. To achieve the magnificent tragedy of Ahab against the universe, Melville was forced to sacrifice much of what a whaling captain was *as a whaling captain*. The "realism" of *Moby-Dick* does not extend to the Captain of the *Pequod*. No one would lament the loss; *Moby-Dick* is worth whatever it cost to make it possible. But all the same, the problem remains. How does the writer evoke the civilized values—of language, religion, philosophy, culture in general—that have traditionally been used to give order and delineate meaning in society, while at the same time remaining faithful to the everyday texture of "low life" experience? How may a whaling captain grapple with the eternal verities and yet be shown doing it in the terms in which such things would confront a whaling captain, and in a mode of language that can reproduce his experience *as* a whaling captain? How many Nantucket whaling skippers, upon confronting their prey, would be heard declaring "Aye, breach your last to the sun, Moby Dick . . . thy hour and thy harpoon are at hand"? How to make a whaling captain into a tragic hero, in other words, without using as model the literary image of a Shakespearean tragedy? This has been the dilemma of the American writer from colonial times onward.

Henry James, in a famous passage about Nathaniel Hawthorne, expressed the cultural problem quite (I will not say succinctly, since that is no word for the style of even the early Henry James) appropriately. Taking his cue from something that Hawthorne himself wrote, James declared that:

> one might enumerate the forms of high civilization, as it exists in other countries, which are absent from the texture of American life, until it should be a wonder to know what was left. No State, in the European sense of the word, and indeed barely a specific national name. No sovereign, no court, no personal loyalty, no aristocracy, no church, no clergy, no army, no diplomatic service, no country gentlemen, no palaces, no castles, nor manors, nor old country-houses, nor parsonages, not thatched cottages nor ivied ruins; no cathedrals, nor abbeys, nor little Norman churches; no great Universities nor public schools—no Oxford, nor Eton, nor Harrow; no literature, no novels, no museums, no pictures, no political society, no sporting class—no Epsom nor Ascot! Some such list as that might be drawn up of the absent things in American life—especially in the American life of forty years ago, the effect of which, upon an English or a French imagination, would probably as a general thing be appalling.

But James does not stop there. "The American knows that a good deal remains," he continues; "what it is that remains—that is his secret, his joke, as one may say. It would be cruel, in this terrible denudation, to deny him the consolation of his national gift, that 'American humor' of which of late years we have heard so much." James's words are appropriately chosen, for so much of American literature has focused upon just that national "joke"—by which I take him to mean the fact that in a popular democracy the customary and characteristic institutions that have traditionally embodied cultural, social and ethical values are missing from the scene, and yet the values themselves, and the attitudes that derive from and serve to maintain them, remain very much part of the national experience. This is what Robert Penn Warren meant by the "burr under the metaphysical saddle of America," which pricks whenever the saddle jumps. Out of the incongruity between mundane circumstance and heroic ideal, material fact and spiritual hunger, democratic, middle-class society and desire for cultural definition, theory of equality and fact of social and economic inequality, the Declaration of Independence and the Mann Act, the Gettysburg Address and the Gross National Product, the "Battle Hymn of the Republic" and the Union Trust Company, the Horatio Alger ideal and the New York Social Register—between what men would be and must be, as acted out in American experience, has come much pathos, no small amount of tragedy, and also a great deal of humor. Both the pathos and the humor have been present from the start, and the writers have been busy pointing them out. This, then, has been what has been called "the great American joke," which comedy has explored and imaged.

One of the more amusing sketches in Joseph Glover Baldwin's *The Flush Times of Alabama and Mississippi* (1853) is that entitled "Simon Suggs, Jr., Esq: A Legal Biography." Baldwin took his character's name from that given to the old scoundrel in Johnson Jones Hooper's Simon Suggs stories. Like his father, Suggs, Jr., is semiliterate and a complete rogue. The sketch opens with some correspondence between Suggs, Jr., and the promoters of a New York biographical magazine, who write to inform him that he has been honored by having been chosen to have his biographical sketch appear in public print, and asking him to furnish biographical details and a suitable daguerreotype. The letter to Suggs, Jr., is couched in the most formal and flowery of terms, but its message is in effect a suggestion that by having his biography appear in the magazine suitably worded, Suggs, Jr., will perhaps be chosen to be a judge some day. To this elaborately worded invitation—"We know from experience, that the characteristic diffidence of the profession, in many instances, shrinks from the seeming, though falsely seeming, indelicacy of an egotistical parade of one's own talents and accomplishments . . ."—Suggs, Jr., responds with misspelled alacrity: "I'm obleeged to you for your perlite say so, and so forth. I got a friend to rite it—my own ritin being mostly perfeshunal. He done it—but he rites such a cussed bad hand I cant rede it: I reckon its all kerrect tho'." He doesn't have a daguerreotype available, but the engraving of his famous father appearing in Hooper's *Some Adventures of Simon Suggs* will do for him if retouched to make him look a bit younger. He then receives another letter from the publisher, thanking him for his sketch, "the description of a lawyer distinguished in the out-door labors of his profession, and directing great energies to the preparation of proof." In a postscript, however, the editor informs Suggs, Jr., that "our delicacy caused us to omit . . . to mention what we suppose was generally understood, viz., the fact that the cost to us of preparing engravings &c. &c., for the sketches or memoirs, is one hundred and fifty dollars, which sum it is expected, of course, the gentleman who is perpetuated in our work, will forward to us before the insertion of his biography. . . ."

Suggs, Jr., now realizes what is going on, and he writes, "*Dear Mr. Editor*—In your p.s. which seems to be the creem of your correspondents you say I can't get in your book without paying one hundred and fifty dollars—pretty tall entrants fee!" He tells them "I believe I will pass. I'll enter a nolly prossy q. O n-e-h-u-n-d-r-e-d-dollars and fifty better! Je-whellikens." He has begun "to see the pint of many things which was very vague and ondefinit before." And so on.

Following this exchange of correspondence, we then get the text of the biographical sketch which was prepared by Simon Suggs, Jr.'s friend for inclusion in the magazine. It is cast in the elegiac, flowery tone of such self-adulatory biographical sketches, and it makes the most of a very checkered career, putting the kindest construction possible on the events of that career. What is described is the story of various slick dealings by a consummate rogue and trickster, involving much swindling, knavery, and dishonesty, and couched throughout in the most formal and literary of tones. The humor consists of the self-important pomposity of the literary method of narration as it contrasts with the very undignified vernacular antics being described. To wit:

> Col. Suggs also extricated a client and his sureties from a forfeited recognizance, by having the defaulting defendant's obituary notice somewhat prematurely inserted in the newspapers; the solicitor, seeing which, discontinued proceedings; for which service, the deceased, immediately after the adjournment of court, returned to the officer his particular acknowledgements. . . .

The sketch concludes with Simon Suggs, Jr., in Washington attempting to settle claims on behalf of the Choctaw Indians, and with the suggestion that "may the Indians live to get their dividends of the arrears paid to their agent."

Now the humor of this sketch, like that of most of the writings of the humorists of the old nineteenth-century Southern frontier, comes out of the clash of language modes. Baldwin is perhaps the most extreme of all of them in this respect. A well-educated and highly literate man, he adopts the persona of a cultivated gentleman in order to describe the wild, untutored, catch-as-catch-can doings of the old frontier regions. The tone is that of condescension, and the humor arises out of the inappropriateness of the way in which vernacular and usually crass activities are described in quite ornate and pompous language. But although the author's spokesman is a man of culture and refinement who is amused by and somewhat contemptuous of the uninhibited, semicivilized crudeness of the frontier folk, there is also an element of respect for the way that the low-life characters can get right to the point and deal directly with experience. Suggs, Jr.'s shrewdness in spotting what the invitation to submit a sketch for the magazine really involves, his failure to be taken in by the flowery language and erudite circumlocutions of the thing, are, in the context, quite admirable. Suggs, Jr., is a rogue, to be sure, as his biographical sketch admirably demonstrates, but he does not pretend to be anything other than that. The New York entrepreneur, by contrast, is every bit as dishonest. Though his magazine is supposedly designed to supply "a desideratum in American literature, namely, the commemoration and perpetuation of the names, characters, and personal and professional traits and histories of American lawyers and jurists," and though he says that Simon, Jr., has been selected for inclusion by "many of the most prominent gentlemen in public and private life, who have the honor of your acquaintance," what he is really doing is selling self-advertisements in the guise of biographical sketches. Unlike Simon, Jr., however, he pretends to be doing so "from motives purely patriotic and disinterested," in order that "through our labors, the reputation of distinguished men of the country, constituting its moral treasure, may be preserved for the admiration and direction of mankind, not for a day, but for all time." Suggs, Jr., in brief, is a crude but honest rogue, and the editor of the magazine is a civilized but hypocritical confidence man.

Here, indeed, is the elementary, basic American humorous situation—the "great American joke," and in one very obvious form. The humor arises out of the gap between the cultural ideal and the everyday fact, with the ideal shown to be somewhat hollow and hypocritical, and the fact crude and disgusting.

The so-called frontier humor was admirably constituted to image the problems of meaning and existence in a society that was very much caught up in the process of formation. In the Old Southwest—Georgia, West Florida, Alabama, Mississippi—of the 1820's, 1830's, and 1840's, virgin wilderness was almost overnight being converted into farmland, and towns and cities coming into being where the forest trails crossed. New wealth was being created, and old fortunes either vastly augmented or lost overnight. Rich and poor flocked into the new lands, and the social distinctions brought from the older society of the Eastern seaboard were very much disordered and distorted by the new circumstance. The ability to parse a Latin verb or ride to the hounds would be less than completely useful in the fashionable parlors of Tuscaloosa, Alabama, and Columbus, Mississippi, for some time to come. Society, in other words, was being reordered, and former distinctions of class and caste rearranged in accordance with the realities of wealth and power in a changed community. Since language, education, culture are always ultimately grounded in social position, the social confusion of an open frontier society is reflected in a confusion of language and cultural modes and attitudes. It will take several generations for the descendants of a Simon Suggs, Jr., to acquire the social polish and cultural sophistication that educational advantages made possible by new wealth can ultimately afford them; and the effort to chronicle the checkered career of an opportunistic rascal in the sophisticated language appropriate to a biographical sketch in an Eastern magazine provides the rich incongruity that Baldwin could draw on for purposes of humor.

The clash between the ideal and the real, between value and fact, is of course not an exclusively American motif. Cervantes rang the changes on it in *Don Quixote,* and Aristophanes before him. But a society based theoretically upon the equality of all men, yet made up of human beings very unequal in individual endowment, and containing within it many striking social, economic and racial differences, is more than ordinarily blessed with such problems in human and social definition, and the incongruities are likely to be especially observable. The very conditions of a frontier society, with its absence of settled patterns and with its opportunities for freedom and individuality, are ideally suited for this kind of humor. One finds it already in flower long before the Declaration of Independence. Consider a work such as William Byrd II's *History of the Dividing Line.* An English-educated planter, trained for the law in the Middle Temple, member of the Royal Society, one accustomed to command and to receiving the deference due a wealthy planter, goes off with a surveying party to determine the boundary line between the Virginia and the North Carolina colonies. There in the Dismal Swamp he encounters rustics who are without culture, refinement, ambition, or wealth, and who moreover do not seem to feel the lack of such commodities very much. His response is to poke fun at them, to use ridicule to rebuke the failure of the vulgar fact to approximate the cultural and social ideal. So he adopts a mode of language that through its inappropriateness to the triviality of the occasion, makes the settlers appear ludicrous: they "stand leaning with both their arms upon the cornfield fence, and *gravely consider* whether they had best go and take a small heat at the hoe . . ." [italics mine]. Here again is the same clash of modes that Baldwin and the Southwestern Humorists would use to chronicle the New Men in the New Territory. In both instances the fact—the ordinary man, as he is, unregenerate and uncaring—is satirized by being described in a language mode customarily reserved for more elevated subject matter. But where in Byrd the satire is all directed at the low-life objects, in Baldwin it is not so one-sided. For though Baldwin is a Virginian and a Whig and a man of education and culture, he is enough of a democratic American to admire the independence and the practicality of his low-life characters just a little, and so he does not confine his ridicule to them. He turns the language mode, the elevated diction, back on itself. He is consciously over-elegant, overly genteel in his choice of phraseology, so that the formal diction, the language of Culture, is also being mocked. The Great American Joke thus works both ways, and the incongruity illuminates the shortcomings of both modes.

Neither Byrd's *History of the Dividing Line* nor Baldwin's *Flush Times of Alabama and Mississippi* is, strictly speaking, literature, so much as subliterature. The one is narrative history, the other humorous journalism. Neither was designed purely or primarily as full-fledged artistic statement. But the same kind of incongruity they offer, the clash of genteel and vulgar modes, has been incorporated into the comic art of many of America's best and most respected writers. A single example will suffice to illustrate. The twentieth-century novelist William Faulkner has not only written certain novels that are possibly the only genuine literary tragedy produced by an American author in this century, but he is also one of the finest comic writers in American literature. In his comic masterpiece, *The Hamlet,* Flem Snopes and a Texan bring a herd of wild Texas horses to Mississippi and offer them for sale at very low prices. They are snapped up by the inhabitants, who are then invited to claim the horses they have purchased. Before very long wild horses are being pursued all over the landscape; they jump fences, leap over people, run into houses, overturn wagons, until as nighttime comes they are scattered over miles of countryside. One hapless purchaser, felled by the stampeding Texas herd, is carried unconscious into a house by some of his friends. Afterwards they go outside:

> They went out; they didn't look back. They tiptoed up the hall and crossed the veranda and descended into the moonlight. Now that they could pay attention to it, the silver air seemed to be filled with faint and sourceless sounds—shouts, thin and distant, again a brief thunder of hooves on a wooden bridge, more shouts faint and thin and earnest and clear as bells; once they even distinguished the words: "Whooey. Head him."

Once again, both language modes are at work: the heightened literary diction, drawing on the full resources of cadenced prose and metaphor, and the vivid colloquial counterthrust. The haunting, beautiful description of the pursuit over the pastoral landscape is undercut by the broad vulgar comedy of the actual fact itself—the hoodwinked farmers vainly attempting to corral their untamable purchases. But Faulkner is not satirizing his characters; the human dignity he has given them as they go about the activities that are the plot of *The Hamlet* is such that, though they are "low-life," they are not thereby debased. Thus when, with the escape of the wild horses and their pursuit, he moves into the mode of formal literary diction and metaphor to describe what happens, the effect of incongruity does not produce satire and ridicule, so much as a delightful counterpoint of modes that plays them back and forth, against and around and along with each other. The shouting is "faint and thin and earnest and clear as bells," even as they *do* call out "Whooey. Head him." The contrast of literary language and poetic description with vernacular fact and colloquial speech is developed into as marvelously comic a scene as any in American literature. Both elements are at work, and in their juxtaposition each delineates the other. It is a masterful intensification of the same brand of humor as that of Byrd's *Dividing Line*, Baldwin's *Flush Times*, Irving's *Knickerbocker History*, Longstreet's *Georgia Scenes*, Clemens's *Connecticut Yankee*, Hemingway's *Torrents of Spring*, Barth's *Sot-Weed Factor*, and many another works of American comedy. It is the interplay of the ornamental and the elemental, the language of culture and the language of sweat, the democratic ideal and the mulishness of fallen human nature—the Great American Joke. To quote the business partner of Thomas Wolfe's Bascom Pentland in *Of Time and the River,* "the Reverend knows words the average man aint never heard. He knows words that aint even in the dictionary. Yes, sir!—an' uses them too— all the time!"

WALTER BLAIR
HAMLIN HILL

5 No End of Jokes

No truly comprehensive history of American humor
has been written, and such a project would require
several volumes. The title of Walter Blair and Hamlin
Hill's book *America's Humor: From Poor Richard to
Doonesbury* is somewhat misleading, because most of
this study focuses on the nineteenth century, the
period of most interest to both authors. But in their first
chapter, "No End of Jokes," Blair and Hill seek the origins of the rollicking, boastful, exaggerated humor of
the frontier that for them typifies American humor, and
find in the centuries of exploration and colonization
some keys to not only the nineteenth-century humor
they prefer, but also, by implication, twentieth-century
political satire, stand-up comedy, and the television
comedy show. The habit of exaggeration that leads to
caricature or the tall tale, they point out, was ingrained
early on by settlers who deliberately boasted of
America's wonders to attract others to the continent,
or magnified its dangers to excuse their failure to
overcome them. In the disparity between either
extreme and reality lay great comic potential. Like
Blair, Hill was particularly interested in Mark Twain,
editing *Mark Twain's Letters to His Publisher, 1867–1894*
in 1967. In 1993, shortly after Blair's death, Hill edited
a collection of his essays entitled *Essays on American
Humor: Blair Through the Ages.*

*They tell sweet lies of Paradise
And lies—and lies—and lies!*
    —Anita Owen, "Dreamy Eyes," *ca.* 1894.

Europeans who wrote or talked about the New World
during the sixteenth and seventeenth centuries

From Walter Blair and Hamlin Hill, *America's Humor: From Poor Richard to
Doonesbury* (New York: Oxford University Press, 1978), 3–15. © 1978 by Walter
Blair and Hamlin Hill. Reprinted by permission of Oxford University Press.

implied that visitors with a few minutes to spare could easily dig up or liberate from royal treasuries silver, gold and precious jewels. And they could do this anywhere in the area between the Arctic Ocean and the Caribbean Sea. The returned travelers had good news about other attractions. During endless summers, their story went, wine, plants that cured all ailments, fruit, fish, fowl, and every sort of game were so plentiful that nobody had to stir to get them; stretch out a hand and, like love, they came a-tricklin' down. Indians were noble savages built like Renaissance nudes, easygoing about wealth, and with no sticky notions about personal property. If they were heathens, all the better; this meant they were ripe for conversion into Christians, laborers, mechanics, or perhaps slaves.

Late in the sixteenth century, John Donne showed what he had heard about lands overseas in, of all places, a rhapsody about his mistress preparing for bed:

> O my America! my new-found-land,
> My kingdom, safeliest when with one man manned,
> My mine of precious stones, my empery,
> How blest am I in this discovering thee!

But settlers soon found that precious stones and metals always were out beyond the edges of their settlements. The living was not quite as easy as promotional tracts advertised. Master George Percy told how it was in Jamestown in 1607:

> There were never Englishmen left in a foreign country in such misery. . . . We watched every three nights, lying on the bare cold ground, what weather soever came; [and] warded all the next day: which brought our men to be most feeble wretches. Our food was but a small can of barley sodden in water, to five men a day. Our drink, cold water taken out of the river . . . very salt [or] full of slime and filth; which was the destruction of many . . . three or four in a night; in the morning, their bodies being trailed out of their cabins like dogs, to be buried.

The grim statistics: of one hundred and four men and boys in the colony, within six months fifty-one died of starvation and disease.

The experience was all too typical. A few years later at Plymouth, "in two or three months half their company died," often "two or three a day," victims of the New England winter, malnutrition, and sickness.

Early periods were the worst, but for decades, settling in the New World was riskier than Russian roulette. Understandably, even as things became better, rumors proliferated about natural and supernatural forces hell-bent on crushing newcomers. However bad the weather—fierce winds, tornadoes, waves, currents, hail stones the size of bowling balls, tropical heat, and arctic cold—reports predicted worse. Earthquakes, one of which gulped down a river without a hiccup, were said to be rampant. Lists of fauna included not only fierce beasts that actually were ready to prey but also nonexistent tigers, lions, crocodiles, and sea serpents. After King Philip's War wiped out a tenth of the males in Massachusetts Bay Colony and brought rapes, scalpings, and mutilations, red men were pictured as devils incarnate—torturers, murderers, cannibals. Stories had it that—even worse—hordes of fiends temporarily in human form fanned out over the countryside to horrify and harass. On one occasion, four men—all there were left of a party of six hundred colonists and soldiers—"heard much tumult and great clamor of voices, the sound of timbrels, flutes and tambourines as well as other instruments," and almost at once saw their boat teetering on a tree top—surely the work of sorcerers. A visitor to both Southern and Northern colonies in the seventeenth century wrote that the land was cursed with "witches too many, bottle-bellied witches amongst the Quakers, and others that produce many strange apparitions if you will believe report."

Howard Mumford Jones summarizes scores of travel books and settlers' accounts:

> If the modern reader has . . . a feeling of a vague, rich jungle of repellent or terrifying things, animals, plants, and men, it is the impression he would have received, I suggest, had he been a literate European . . . interested in reading about the new found land. . . . The unpredictable, the abnormal, the inhuman, the cruel, the savage, and the strange in terms of European experience were from the beginning part of the image. . . . The New World was filled with monsters animal and monsters human; it was a region of terrifying natural forces, of gigantic catastrophes . . . where the laws of nature tidily governing Europe were transmogrified into something new and strange.

The gulf between the El Dorado, Cockaigne, Arcadia, and Utopia of promotion tracts and the hell on earth of all-too-palpable fact and all-too-inventive rumor provided ample incongruity for the genesis of rib-tickling comedy.

Of course, for the actual production of comedy, conditions had to be right. Colonists who believed that if only they could get out to it, El Dorado was waiting, could not be funny about their impossible dream. A touch of skepticism was needed. As far back as the twelfth century, an Irish author had shown the way when he became dubious about the glorious Otherworld which reverent old narratives had often celebrated—just such a paradise of milk and honey as credulous writers about the New World had pictured. Full of doubts about a host of religious beliefs, the author of *The Vision of MacConglinne* parodied the lot of them. When MacConglinne rows across milk lakes, through seas of soup, and by islands of cheese, as Vivian Mercier puts it, "most of the Otherworld literature . . . is summed up and annihilated in a single devastating work." The lasting appeal of this satire was shown when it was twice adapted in recent times for public performance on the stage in 1936 and on radio in 1953.

Colonists who were being buffeted by nature, stalked and pounced on by wild critters, besieged by Indians, and hexed by witches were hardly in the mood—even if they could find the leisure—to turn out much foolery. As well as skepticism, distance in space or time was helpful.

English playwrights George Chapman, John Marston, and Ben Jonson, an ocean away, could be less involved and more frivolous. Mocking promoters and their wild press releases, this trio in *Eastward Ho!*—performed in London in 1604–05 and revived in 1751 and 1775—had a rascally ship's captain, Seagull, ladle out lies to some potential backers. The Indians, said he, so loved the New World offspring of Britons and squaws that "all the treasure they have they lay at their feet":

I tell thee, gold is more plentiful there than copper is with us. . . . Why, man, all their dripping-pans and their chamber-pots are pure gold; . . . and for rubies and diamonds, they go forth on holidays and gather 'hem by the sea-shore, to hang on their children's coats. . . . As [pleasant a country as] ever the sun shined on; temperate and full of all sorts of excellent viands. . . . And then you shall live freely there, without sargeants, or courtiers, or lawyers, or intelligencers. . . . You may be an alderman there, and never be a scavenger: you may be a nobleman, and never be a slave. You may come to preferment enough, and never be a pander; to riches and fortune enough, and have never the more villainy nor the less wit.

Once they had acquired the distancing they needed, Americans too would be able to burlesque wild claims of promoters, realtors,

Californians, Texans, Alaskans, Chambers of Commerce, and purveyors of publicity everywhere.

Black humor surfaced briefly when time provided distance, and the Rev. W. Simmonds looked back at the winter of 1609 that he underwent in Jamestown. When the silly colonists sent John Smith home "to answer some misdemeanors," they rid that settlement of the only leader who could run it. Within half a year, of about five hundred "not past sixty men, women and children" survived. These miserable wretches fought starvation by eating "roots, herbs, acorns, walnuts, berries, now and then a little fish . . . even the very skins of our horses." One man murdered his wife, "powdered" [i.e., salted] her and, says Simmonds, "had eaten part of her before it was known; for which he was executed, as he well deserved. Now whether she was better roasted, boiled, or carbonado'd [broiled] I know not; but such a dish as powdered wife I never heard of." Since, as a rule, hardships of one sort or another—or maybe both—were always in good supply here for centuries, wags who were frivolous enough would produce black humor about them or exaggerate them and heap them atop one another until they became laughable.

Writing "from Bristow the 13 of November, 1578," Anthony Parkhurst could set down for Richard Hakluyt "merry tales" about the Newfoundland of some years earlier—the sort, as he said, he told "when I please to be merry with my old companions" or when talking to "those that are desirous of strange news." One was about squid, "which I may sweep with brooms on a heap, and never wet my foot." Another was about "trees that bare oysters." His friends, he says, figure these are "notorious lies, but they laugh . . . when they hear the means how each tale is true." Squid, he explained, are chased by cod into shallows, from which they are washed ashore "by the surge of the sea on the pebbles and sands"; and boughs of trees on the shore "hung in the water, on which both oysters and mussels did stick fast, as their property is, to . . . timber." Since peculiar things were always happening in America and uninformed newcomers always lusted for strange news, over the years merry fellows could unwind incredible yarns about flora, fauna, natives, and geography and then give true or untrue but more or less plausible explanations.

Once they had come to be funny on purpose, the lies that old-timers told to explorers, tourists, immigrants, and tenderfeet who were credulous, or to other old-timers who were in on the joke, might serve several purposes. In practically every instance, the humorous liars—peeved or amused by false claims about the splendors or horrors of the new country—parodied them. Some, disgusted by hardships or frightened by rumored menaces, lied about them to exorcise the damned things. Some trotted out lies to befool and show up strangers, or perhaps to initiate them into a new community. And some, the creative ones, revised or invented and embroidered whoppers for their own pleasure and that of appreciative listeners or readers. "A traveller," said one of the most famous of all liars, Baron Münchausen, "has the right to embellish his adventures . . . , and it is very unpolite to refuse that deference and applause they deserve."

As early as 1521, a native of the Cape Fear region, carried home by a Spanish explorer, astonished his hosts with longbows such as the one about neighbors of his who reared themselves up a gigantic king by softening and stretching his serene majesty's bones when he was an infant. Colonists instructed a Swedish scientist about the way a bear usually killed a cow—"bites a hole in the hide, blows with all his power into it, till the animal swells excessively and dies." Inspired no doubt by their own rainy season, natives of Southern California told a Spanish explorer about a tribe that slept under water. A British scientist of sorts heard from helpful New England hosts about a Cape Cod sea serpent, a Casco Bay merman, and a bird called the pilhannow big enough to prey on fawns and jackals. George Washington, famous for being honest though a public figure, passed on lore to a British traveler that did nothing for his reputation: "He was never so annoyed by mosquitoes as in the Skenesborough, for they used to bite through the thickest boot." Hundreds of other stretchers dot sixteenth- , seventeenth- , and eighteenth-century travel books.

Nineteenth-century Americans, still going strong, often had fun feeding fascinating data to tourists who, they believed, would rush home to deliberately libel them. James Kirke Paulding, a popular New York writer, was not completely candid when he told about the reaction of his countrymen to Captain Basil Hall's *Travels in North America in 1827–28*, published in three volumes after he "went grumbling his way, from one end of Jonathan's farm to another, collecting everything." "Jonathan's tenants, who are in the main a cute set of fellows, often bantered him with all sorts of tough stories, which he would write down in his log-book; but little they thought that he was going to put them out as gospel when he got home." The fact was that Americans did their best to deceive strangers and then eagerly watched for printed repetitions of their windies.

A favorite target was Mrs. Frances Trollope, whose *Domestic Manners of the Americans* (1832) irked them because it held that they had no manners, domestic or of any other sort. Mark Twain cited one story that she picked up aboard a river boat as a good example of "stupid and silly lies" natives told tourists so that they could "laugh at them for believing and printing them." It told in gory detail how a Mississippi River crocodile and her young one morning breakfasted on large helpings of a squatter's wife and five children. The story seemed doubtful, since no crocodiles ever have been found in that river—only alligators, which do not relish human flesh. Mrs. Trollope herself seems to have smoked out another yarn she was told at the same time, for though she included it in her manuscript, she left it out of her book in spite of claims that it was "perfectly true." A bear, she was told, evicted an Indian from his canoe, took his place, emptied an abandoned whiskey flask down its throat, and then sailed into New Orleans. The townspeople, she said, had profound discussions—clearly storytellers' exuberant elaborations:

> Some declared it was a savage of a nation hitherto unknown, others that it was an Indian conjuror, in one of their quaint disguises; others again (these were the travelled men) were strongly of opinion that it was an Englishman of fashion, dressed in a driving coat. Some few ventured to differ from the rest, and said they thought it looked very like a bear. A quiet Yankee . . . suggested that, be what it might, they should have a better chance with it on land than on water, and proposed that a hook, attached to a cord of prudent length, should be cast in such a manner as to enable them to draw the canoe to shore. The proposal was acted upon. The prow again touched the land, and the stranger, uttering one loud growl that speedily cleared him a passage, gave another spring that placed him high and dry on land . . . ran through the wondering throng . . . and soon found shelter in the woods.

The Indian, on repossessing his canoe and finding the whiskey gone, philosophized: "Did he too learn to love it? . . . Poor beast! If he tasted it, how could he help it?"

During the 1830s, Mrs. Trollope, renamed Mrs. Wollope, Mrs. Truelip, and the like, as one historian says, "was such a familiar and ridiculous figure to American audiences that comedies seemingly could hardly be without her"; and an obligatory joke was about her credulity. Paulding had at her in a play, a satire on travel books, and a novel. In the next decade, an actor boasted that he had victimized the lady by telling her that Mammoth Cave contained "a natural fountain of pure brandy." Half a century after *Domestic Manners* appeared, Mark Twain—though he liked the book—still got laughs by giving samples of its author's gullibility.

Like other jokes, lies that natives fobbed off on strangers were recycled in different times and places and refurbished to play up local phenomena. In 1714, a stuffy visitor to North Carolina announced that he had "been informed" about a huge tulip tree "wherein a lusty man had got his bed and household furniture, and lived in till his labour got him a more fashionable mansion." In 1837 Westerners substituted a pumpkin for the tree; and in 1951 Vance Randolph included in a book an Arkansas version about a phenomenal potato. He called his book *We Always Lie to Strangers*.

Once America was partially colonized and settled, in addition to reporting on the strange weather, the awful geography, the peculiar flora, and the disquieting fauna, travel writers had much to say about the fascinating men and women. Almost exclusively at first, as superior subjects for humor, they discussed the men.

They tended to play up two flaws—crudity and ferocity. They found the first of these everywhere—in the Northeast, the South, and the West. Visitors reported widespread ignorance, insolence, inquisitiveness, and gaucherie. Just about everybody, they kept saying, was impudent and bad-mannered. Anyone who got half a chance pried into strangers' affairs which were none of his business, asking question after unwelcome question. Everybody spoke the most outlandish patois and assassinated grammar. Every male, seemingly, chawed tobacco. Standard outcries against spitting gave the impression that the settled parts of the continent—and much of the frontier—were shiny, brown, and slippery.

The mayhem, writers believed, was more localized than the disgusting manners—very bad in the South, even worse on the frontier. In both areas, men were hot-tempered, and the heavy drinking of mint juleps, brandy, or kill-devil whiskey fired their ferocity. In no-holds-barred rumpuses, many a poor devil, the books said, had his cheeks clawed, his nose or ear gnawed off, or his eye gouged out. Englishman Isaac Weld in the 1790's put into his book typical if extreme tales about eye-gougings in Maryland and Virginia and "worst of all" a habit fighters had of trying "to tear out each other's testicles." He saw, so he said, "four or five instances . . . of men being confined in their beds from injuries received of this nature in a fight."

Touchy natives and settlers hurried to point out that often reporters of widespread ruffianism on frontiers were not exactly objective. Several foreign writers said frankly in Introductions to books that they hoped their horror stories would keep governments at home from shifting toward radical democratic ways rampant in the New World in general and on its frontiers in particular. Others, less frank, gave away the fact that they were biased by sternly scolding their hosts. Domestic rivalries also brought distortions. Some New England writers, for instance, wrote with the hope that they might slow down their neighbors' stampedes to the West. Only a moron would expect frontiersmen to be pictured as cooing doves in a book titled *Western Migration Journal of Jeremiah Simpleton's Tour of Ohio Containing an Account of Numerous Difficulties . . . which the Doctor and His Family Experienced . . . in that Highly Extolled Country.* Some adverse reports were oral. A Yankee tin-trader, Paulding wrote, who had been caught cheating and who had been walloped, when he got home "of course told terrible stories of gouging and the like; so that in time [his attackers] came to be thought little better than bullies . . . though people who were best acquainted with them knew better."

Humor made use of such calumnies when frontiersmen or playful writers parodied or exaggerated them. Some pranksters put on shows for travelers; others cooked up elaborate lies. In Louisville a gang of young bucks staged a fake free-for-all with horrendous casualties for a genteel visiting man of letters, then enjoyed reading about the carnage in his book. A frontiersman solemnly told a visitor that the best way to gauge the safety of a tavern was to size up its patrons and count missing ears and eyes. A landlord cheerily listed as a morning's task collecting in a bucket eyes, ears, and noses left lying around the night before.

By 1809 Washington Irving, without leaving his native Manhattan, could put together a playful picture of Marylanders drawn from travel reports, burlesques of them, or both:

> a gigantic gunpowder race of men, who lived on hoe-cakes and bacon, drank mint juleps and brandy toddy, and were exceedingly expert at boxing, biting, gouging, tar and feathering, and a variety of other athletic accomplishments, which they had borrowed from their cousins german and prototypes the Virginians, to whom they had ever borne a considerable resemblance.

Eastern stay-at-homes were better equipped to picture such hell-raisers than one might guess. For they had read about English roisterers with somewhat similar ways; they personally knew American kindred spirits; and they themselves just might be part-time libertines. For years British authors made fun of country squires who were boors, fanatical huntsmen, and toss-pots. Fielding's Squire Western in *Tom Jones* (1749) was a famous example, and in Goldsmith's *She Stoops To Conquer* (1773), shabby fellows in a country ale house praised the late Squire Lumpkin because "for winding the straight horn, or beating a thicket for a hare, or a wench, he never had his fellow," and because "he kept the best horses, dogs, and girls in the whole country." When his son Tony sang a song damning bookish schoolmasters and Methodist preachers, and glorifying the fun of getting a skinful, the carousers cheered him and let him buy them drinks. British sporting journals and sketch writers pictured and catered to a drinking, hunting, cock-fighting, and wenching set—"Corinthians," "Nonesuches." A very popular fictional pair of the 1820's, Tom and Jerry, had a hot rum concoction named after them which Americans still drink.

Encouraged, perhaps, by this crowd's example, bucks in the Old South or in Eastern American cities carried on in much the same way. In New York, Washington Irving was a member of a jolly group called the Kilkenny Cats. His pal, collaborator, and fellow member, Paulding, must have been aware of a resemblance between his crowd and Southerners when in 1812 he said the latter were men who "amuse themselves pretty considerably with horse-racing, cock-fighting, barbecues and the like . . . wonderful boys for what they call antifogmatics, being certain mint juleps . . . supposed to make a man somewhat belligerent."

The bully-boy title, held for years by "Southerners," galloped westward ahead of the edges of civilization. "Backwoodsmen" and "Kentuckians" took over for a time. In 1830, a New Englander at home after Western wanderings nominated or reported on a new group of title-holders:

> The character of the citizens of Kentucky . . . is on the whole estimable. . . . I am well aware that it by no means corresponds with the prejudices of the generality of the citizens of the other states. . . . One circumstance which tends to perpetuate the prejudice is the conduct of the Kentucky boatmen on the Ohio and the Mississippi, some of whom appear to pride themselves on the roughness and rudeness of their manners.

A book published in 1847 by an English explorer who had met or heard about some of the mountain men trapping in the Rockies told the world that this group, "callous to any feeling of danger," was closer "to the primitive savage . . . than perhaps any other class of civilized men"; their good qualities were "those of the animal"; they were "White Indians." In the 1850's Texas newspapers broadcast a poem that celebrated a ferocious rumpus between Texans:

> They fit and fit,
> And gouged and bit,
> And struggled in the mud
> Until the ground
> For miles around
> Was kivered with their blood,
> And a pile of noses, ears, and eyes,
> Large and massive reached the skies.

Nevada, Montana, and Alaska were waiting.

These are only a few ways that our country's history inspired and localized laugh-provoking, imaginative works. The history was unique, but the works contained old materials that had been refurbished. Because this process will be repeated in our history again and again, at this stage an initial look at it is useful.

Portraits of bully boys, some of them comic, that we have traced in their essentials changed very little. But—as other portraits would— they changed. As the frontier moved westward, the men's habitats, habits, talk, manners, and occupations were affected. And historic developments during both the nineteenth and twentieth centuries, some of them traumatic, brought additional changes in lifestyles and comic picturings.

Jokesters, we have seen, played with amusing contrasts, between America as a reality, on the one hand, and mythical lands—Arcadia, Utopia, El Dorado, and Cockaigne—on the other hand. Arcadia, dreamed up by the ancient Greeks and Romans, was written about during the Renaissance. Utopia—at least under that name—had been invented in England in 1516, and El Dorado in Spain a few years later. These were visions of satisfied longings—for pastoral innocence, perfect order, and boundless riches. Such wishful fantasies invited mocking parodies. Versions of Cockaigne which appeared long before Columbus sailed the ocean blue provided such take-offs—the Gaelic *Vision of MacConglinne* in the twelfth century; a French fabliau, *Cocagne,* and an English poem, *The Land of Cockagne,* during the thirteenth. These three imaginative burlesques use a similar setting. In a typical version it is a never-never realm soused by wine-filled streams, where roast fowl and suckling pigs with handy knives in their ribs waddle between crepe-roofed cake houses and free delicatessens along pastry-paved streets. Each Cockaigne, though, is pictured in such a way as to enable its creator to satirize his own place and time. The Irishman kids over-pious "visions" of saints, the Frenchman, Avalon—his day's "Island of the Blessed"—the Briton, life in monasteries.

Over the centuries other artists, each in his own way, imagined and portrayed a dream, a nightmare, or a ridiculous world, each using details that hinted at foibles and aberrations of the world in which he himself lived. Aristophanes gave Greek audiences a Cloud-Cuckoo Land inhabited by activist birds; Rabelais and Breughel, their own lusty imaginings of Cockaigne and Schlaraffenland; Jonathan Swift, Lilliput, Brobdingnag, Laputa, and Houyhnhomland. Breughel's painting of Schlaraffenland satirizes Spain's exploitation of the Netherlands; Swift's fabulous countries have England's quirks.

In America, William Byrd located his Lubberland on the North Carolina frontier; Washington Irving (helped by Rabelais) had Diedrich Knickerbocker's New Amsterdam and Sleepy Hollow flow with milk and honey; T. B. Thorpe placed his "creation state . . . without a fault" on Shirt-Tail Bend in Arkansas; Mark Twain loosed a wry Connecticut Yankee on a Twainized Camelot; hoboes hymned "The Big Rock Candy Mountain"; Al Capp drew Dogpatch and Slobbovia; Walt Kelly, Okefenokee Swamp; Ken Kesey, the Cuckoo's Nest.

WILLIAM KEOUGH

6 The Violence of American Humor

It has long been acknowledged that there is a certain strain of violence in American humor. Early studies of American humor tended to concentrate on the nineteenth-century frontier, with its element of law-lessness, and subsequent ones have pointed to verbal battles between men and women and members of different racial and ethnic groups. William Keough takes this understanding a step further by declaring that violence is the key element of American humor, that our "native humor reflects the more menacing aspects of American society." Believing that a culture's humor mirrors its real values and preoccupations, Keough argues that the physical and verbal violence that marks American humor should come as no surprise in a society that not only allows but also celebrates violent behavior.

National humor does much to explain, or betray, a culture. German humor—or lack of it—is itself a joke. Goethe insisted that one cannot have a sense of humor unless one is without conscience or responsibility (perhaps providing additional substance to the gibe that it takes a Prussian three days to understand a joke at which he will laugh for three days). One can make generalizations: Soviet-bloc humor tends to be bleak and nihilistic, e.g., consider the dour political reality of *Krokodil;* French humor, full of double entendre and repartee; Italian humor, gargantuan and full of farce, and so on. But English humor deserves special mention since, as no less a "white savage" than Mark Twain once observed: "Americans are not Englishmen, and American humor is not English humor; but the

From William Keough, *Punchlines: The Violence of American Humor* (New York: Paragon House, 1990), 2–14. © 1990 by William Keough.

American and his humor had their origin in England, and have merely undergone changes brought by changed conditions and environment."

In search, then, of origins, we might note that England has long maintained a distinguished tradition of "genteel" humor—one appreciative of wit and forgiving of foibles, which, in the skillful hands of an Austen or Thackeray, amuses but does not wound, and posits a stable society wherein redemption is not only possible but necessary. Within this tradition, "[c]ontempt," as George Meredith insisted, "is a sentiment that cannot be entertained by the comic intelligence." The English, too, have often expressed a wariness of the comic demon. "Frequent laughter," Lord Chesterfield warned his son, "is the characteristic of ill manner in which the mob express their silly joy in silly things." Not all Englishmen, however, fall into this neat pattern. Swift and Pope created a jugular rather than jocular humor; and the humor of Monty Python, to cite one contemporary example, is certainly far from tame. Malcolm Muggeridge spoke up for this satirical tradition when he observed: "All great humor is in bad taste, anarchistic, and implies criticism of existing institutions [and] beliefs." But (*pace* Swift et al.) we must agree that the English sense of humor, on the whole, has been, as Harold Nicolson describes it, "kind, sentimental, reasonable and fanciful." We might also note that this genteel strain crossed the Atlantic with the early colonists and may be traced through such writers as Washington Irving, Oliver Wendell Holmes, and James Russell Lowell to the *New Yorker* school of E. B. White, Robert Benchley, and the like. Even here, cavils crop up. In one sense, Irving's *Legend of Sleepy Hollow* is the ultimate torture story, anti-intellectual at base, as beefy Brom Bones torments the itinerant schoolteacher Ichabod Crane; and Benchley's vision, like Thurber's, is often dark and misogynistic. But these writers are still in the genteel tradition.

Whatever may be said about the parentage of American humor, something happened—and it happened in the nineteenth century. The child became unrecognizable to many English observers, became nasty, and was disowned. After their American sojourns, English novelists like Mrs. Trollope and Charles Dickens returned to England shaking their heads. The Americans went, *well,* simply too far. "There has always been something sui generis in the American comic spirit," speculated Christopher Morley, "a touch of brutality perhaps? Anger rather than humor? Sardonic, extravagant, macabre." And this "brutality"—often disguised by an edgy deadpan—has put off English critics. W. H. Auden, for instance, noted how remarkably stoical Huck Finn is (how unlike

Oliver Twist!) in the face of the horrors he encounters, and confessed to finding Twain's novel "emotionally very sad." V. S. Pritchett professed similar astonishment, and some manner of disgust, at the frightening assortment of child-beaters, cowards, con men, and cutthroats who people Huck's world. What is interesting is not that Pritchett and Auden point out the violence (American critics have done that as well), but that they should be so shocked as to question the values of the society that can laugh at (and thereby appear to encourage) such antics. And many contemporary English writers have echoed this sense of a special American ferocity. Playwright Jonathan Miller remarked that his own *Beyond the Fringe* was a "pinprick" compared to "the blood-bath" of Lenny Bruce's act; and novelist Martin Amis judged the cynical wisecracking of the reporters covering Ronald Reagan's 1980 campaign all savage and sad, since "like so much American laughter, [it] did not express high spirits or amusement but a willed raucousness."

The debate continues. At the Oxford Student Union recently, American comedians Alan King and Steve Allen took on some students and British comedians to resolve the question of whether American humor is "funnier" than British humor. The approaches were strikingly different. The English humor was cerebral—one Oxfordian, for instance, mocking the Milwaukee cabdriver who thought Botticelli a new pizza topping. King, on the other hand, attacked—declaring war on England and the students with his let-it-all-hang-out Gonzo humor, spewing obscenities and insults along the way—and was rewarded with the biggest laughs. "Gorillas," concluded Allen, "prefer American humor." Gorillas maybe, but not gentlemen.

But it has not been only English observers who have expressed shock at the rawness, cruelty, and lack of restraint of American humor. As Madame Bentzon, a nineteenth-century French traveler, tutted, "there is something in the American spirit, an inclination to gross mirth, to pranks, which reveals that in certain respects this great people is still a childish people." Jean Charpentier referred to Twain as "a Homais dressed in the feathers of the redskin and dancing the scalp dance around the body of Pallas Athene." And high-toned American observers, like Columbia professor H. H. Boyesen and *Atlantic* essayist S. S. Cox, worried aloud as well. Boyesen complained about the "plague of jocularity" that infected us so that "instead of that interchange of thought which other civilized nations hold to be one of the highest social pleasures, we exchange jokes," while Cox insisted our "slashing humor" sacrificed "feeling, interest, sociability, philosophy, romance, art and morality for its joke." Even Josh Billings (himself a low-brow "phunny phellow") noted, "Americans prefer turpentine tew colone-water [and] must have [their] humor on the half-shell with cayenne."

There is no doubt that many of the professors and foreign observers were missing out on the "funning" part. Many of our early native humorists enjoyed "having on" the "dam furriners." If they expected crude, then, by gum, they would show them crude. "Some pranksters," Walter Blair and Hamlin Hill tell us, "put on shows for travellers; others cooked up elaborate lies. In Louisville, a gang of young bucks staged a fake free-for-all with horrendous casualties for a genteel visiting man of letters, then enjoyed reading about the carnage in his book." Washington Irving concocted a Maryland (which he never visited) peopled by a gunpowder race of men who lived on hoecakes, drank gallons of mint juleps and brandy toddies, and spent their days boxing, biting, gouging, and tar-and-feathering. And the humor itself was not only crude but "gigantic," that is, it went beyond the possible. Davy Crockett claimed to be able to "swallow a nigger whole if you but butter his head." John Henry Jarvis's "Wildfire" prated that he was "half-horse, half-alligator, a touch of earthquake, with a sprinkling of the steamboat." Kentucky soil, Jarvis proclaimed, was "so rich that if you but plant a crowbar over night perhaps it will sprout tenpenny nails afore mornin'." Just planting in "Arkansaw" could be plumb dangerous: "I had a good-sized sow killed in that same bottom-land. The old thief stole an ear of corn, and took it down where she slept at night to eat. Well, she left a grain or two on the ground, and lay down on them: before morning the corn shot up, and the percussion killed her dead."

But the violent exaggeration of much nineteenth-century American humor was often the whole point. The Great American Joke, as Louis Rubin defines it, "arises out of the gap between the cultural ideal and the everyday fact, with the ideal shown to be somewhat hollow and hypocritical, and the fact crude and disgusting." This humor, Stephen Leacock notes, also played off "sudden and startling contrasts as between things as they are supposed to be—revered institutions, accepted traditions, established conventions—and things as they are." In a sense, then, our humorists could be said to be poking fun at the American Dream by sticking folks' noses in American reality. "Like many other things this humor," as Leacock suggests, "came out of the west, beyond the plains. You had to get clear away from civilization to start it." Beside the campfires and out on lonely ranges of the Old Southwest, the tall tale, the humorous ghost story, and the raucous practical joke provided welcome relief from the terrible and dangerous conditions of the frontier. Maurice Breton described the humor of the Far West thus: "If men must laugh together in order to forget their hardships, the laughter is loud, nervous, and rough, with overtones of disillusionment and bitterness."

But this "frontier theory" still does not explain the continuance of that tradition long after the disappearance of the actual frontier. The myth persists and even some of our politicians live it. Back in 1964, Ronald Reagan, then governor of California, said of Vietnam, "We could pave the whole country and put parking strips on it, and still be home by Christmas." *Wha-hoo!* Texans still wear cowboy boots and Stetsons (albeit from Neiman-Marcus), and Boston as well as Houston has its urban cowboys; Clint Eastwood continues to "hang 'em high" on the streets of twentieth-century Los Angeles as well as on the crusty plains of the pseudo-West; and many Americans view Bernard Goetz as a vigilante hero for his shooting of subway thugs. American violence is certainly more than a Western phenomenon. Back in the 1930s, Nathanael West, that deft observer of folly, noted: "In America violence is idiomatic. Read our newspapers. To make the front page a murderer has to use his imagination, he has also to use a particularly hideous instrument. Take this morning's paper: FATHER CUTS SON'S THROAT IN BASEBALL ARGUMENT. It appears on an inside page. To make the first page he should have killed three sons and with a baseball bat instead of a knife. Only liberality and symmetry could have made this daily occurrence interesting." In the 1960s, Black Power revolutionary H. Rap Brown said simply, "Violence is as American as cherry pie."

The problem has, if anything, worsened. What are we now to make of such box office heroes as the Popeye-muscled Sylvester Stallone and the steely-eyed Arnold Schwarzenegger, red-white-and-blue heroes who simply blow away the bad guys to stand-up applause? Our cities are under siege from drug dealers and the underclass. Homicide is the greater killer of black males under twenty-five. We are all too accustomed to newspaper front pages such as the one displaying a shadowy photo of a seventeen-year-old who has admitted to keeping a gun under his sweatpants because he liked the feel of it against his skin. "I don't know if I'll ever be 30 years old," says "George," "a lot of people I know don't make it to 30 years old." And there are many "Georges" (certainly not all black) prowling the streets with Magnums, Uzis, and sawed-off shotguns. But aren't these the typical scare tactics of the Fourth Estate, some might argue—overkill—and playing up the exception rather than the rule? *Is* America all that violent? What are the facts?

Well, there are some startling statistics. Between 1882 and 1927, 4,950 lynchings were recorded, lynchings, mind you, and rough estimates double that figure. Further, a simple body count suggests that American society has promoted a gun culture without parallel among all other nations. American domestic firearms fatalities during the twentieth century total more than 265,000 homicides, 333,000 suicides, and 139,000 gun-related accidents—a figure twice the number of Americans killed in all this century's wars. Our homicide rate consistently runs eight times that of Japan and four times that of any European country. In 1988, there were 900,000 Americans incarcerated in prisons (the majority for violent crime) and 3.2 million (one out of every 55 adult Americans) under some sort of correctional supervision; and experts are expecting this figure to double in the next ten years. Sexist violence—date-rape, bedroom rape, just plain rape—abounds. Nationwide there are hundreds of centers servicing the estimated 500,000 women battered every year, as well as thousands of homes for abused children—figures which suggest that the American home itself is too often a battleground.

It is not, however, the figures themselves—horrifying as they are— that shock many observers. It is the widespread proclamation of innocence in the face of such facts that they find most remarkable and most ironic. David Brion Davis sums up the case neatly:

> If we could formulate a generalized image of America in the eyes of foreign peoples from the eighteenth century to the present, it would surely include a phantasmagoria of violence, from the original Revolution and Indian wars to the sordid history of lynching; from the casual killings of the cowboy and bandit to the machine-gun murders of racketeers. [T]his sparkling, smiling domestic land of easygoing friendliness, where it is estimated that a new murder occurs every forty-five minutes, has also glorified personal whim and impulse and has ranked hardened killers with the greatest folk heroes. Founded and preserved by acts of aggression and characterized by a continuing tradition of self-righteous violence against suspected subversion and by a vigorous sense of personal freedom, usually involving the widespread possession of firearms, the United States has evidenced a unique tolerance of homicide.

Richard Hofstadter speculates that this "unique tolerance" is the result of "historical amnesia" which has granted us a history but not an awareness of domestic violence. It is our capacity for self-deception on the subject he finds most telling: "What is most exceptional about Americans is not the voluminous record of their violence, but their extraordinary ability, in the face of that record, to persuade themselves that they are among the best-behaved and best-regulated of peoples." In other words, we *think* we are nice, peaceful folks because we *say* we are.

Such self-deception has certainly not escaped the notice of our humorists, who often direct their barbs at just this hypocrisy in order to expose the violence and cruelty lurking under the mask of assumed goodness. In *Huckleberry Finn,* for instance, Twain ridicules the democratic pretensions of Pap Finn, Huck's reptilian Daddy-O. In "Haircut," Ring Lardner exposes Jim Kendall, the self-styled prankster, as morally debased—even as both Pap and Kendall insist on their own good natures and purest of motives. But there is obvious danger in satirizing such "varmints" if the humorist is also ridiculing the shared delusions of his audience; so we should not be surprised to see our humorists often skirting the issue of violence rather than facing it head on, and frequently masking their assault with some such device as the "poker face."

But often, in this other, distinctly "un-English" strain of American humor, which arose out on the frontiers and edges of civilization, we see no such sophisticated hanky-panky. Here the humor is at once more raucous in tone and concerned with unredeemable "low" types; the jokes come as swift and deadly as bullets, and the laughter is poised a hair's breadth from cosmic grief. This native humor reflects the more menacing aspects of American society, and lampoons certain of our most cherished assumptions, such as the natural goodness of man and the inevitability of progress. We see it in the work of such early humorists as A. B. Longstreet, J. J. Hooper, and George Washington Harris. They created shrewd backwoods rogues who speak "Amurrikan" and demonstrate a practically invincible instinct for survival. With these "crackers," there is no gallantry, no generosity of spirit, no "California dreamin'." In one of Longstreet's "Georgia Scenes," a young "cracker" just about kills himself in a one-man fight—with himself. Proclaiming "It's good to be shifty in a new country," Hooper's Simon Suggs sets out the manual for the con men and flimflammers we meet again in the Duke and Dauphin and in W. C. Fields.

But it is Harris's Sut Lovingood who is the best-conceived, most fascinating, and most frightening specimen of all these early versions of "white trash." *The Tales of Sut Lovingood,* as penned by Harris, a rabid Tennessean Democrat, are extraordinarily violent by any standard; and Sut himself manages, barely, to entertain as he appalls. Sut refuses to accept any insult or injury lying down—"By golly, no body can't tramp on me, wifout gittin thar foot bit." Revenge weighs heavily on Sut's scale of justice, as he sets a horse loose at a quilting bee or "re-decorates" a corpse at a funeral. Sut's victims include snotty old "widders" and sassy "gals" who look down on him and his family; "surkit riders" and other self-styled evangelists who threaten to cut in on any of his "fun"; any helpless blacks or Irishmen who just happen to get in his way.

The typical Sut Lovingood story begins with Sut sipping whiskey with his old friend "George" (played by Harris himself, the bemused observer) before breaking into a *by-the-way* tale of one of his prime escapades, all told in a racy, back-home dialect rich in metaphor and invective. Sut's philosophy is simple: If someone injures you in any way, get him or her and get him or her *good.* Sut's defenses, too, are simple; he makes use of his "durned foolishness" (which is "nat'ral born" and derives from his father "Hoss," who has come by his name honestly for having played horse so well pulling a plow he almost killed himself) and his long, spindly "laigs," which whisk him out of the path of a rampaging bull or an irate "widder." Sut's weapons are simple as well: *one,* his imagination, which thinks up the violent practical jokes; and *two,* his ruthless determination in carrying them out.

In one typical tale, "Parson John Bullen's Lizards," George comes upon a poster setting a reward for Sut:

AIT ($8) DOLLARS REWARD
'TENSHUN BELEVERS AND KONSTABLES! KETCH 'IM!
THIS kash will be pade in korn, ur uther projuce, tu be kolected at ur about nex camp-meetin, ur thararter, by eny wun what ketches him, fur the karkus ove a sartin wun SUT LOVINGOOD, dead or alive, ur ailin, an' safely giv over to the purtectin care ove parson John Bullen, ur lef' well tied, at Square Mackjunkins fur the raisin ove the devil pussonely, an permiskusly discumfurtin wimen very powerfull, an skerin ove folks generly a heap, an' bustin up a promisin, big warm meetin, an' a makin the wickid larf, an' wus, an' wus, insultin ove the passun orful.
TEST, JEHU WETHERO
Sined by me,
JOHN BULLEN, the passun

When George asks what the commotion is all about, Sut explains. It seems that when Bullen came upon Sut and a neighbor girl spooning in the bushes he told her mother, and the girl received an "overhandid stroppin." So Sut sets about sneaking into the next camp meeting of the good parson (or that "durnd infunel, hiperkritikal, pot-bellied, scaley-hided, whiskey wastin, stinkin old groun'-hog," as Sut calls him) and looses lizards up Bullen's pants as he is preaching on "Hell-sarpints," whereupon Bullen is forced to slip out of his pants and run out of the camp meeting, losing a bit of respect along the way, as Sut observes proudly, especially among the womenfolk. So Barbelly Bullen, as he is now known, has declared war on Sut, whom he views as "living proof ove the hell-desarvin nater ove man." But Sut is unafraid and promises that if he is not left alone he'll "lizzard him again." Sut recognizes he has concocted a kind of devious Old Testament justice. "Say George," he concludes, "didn't that ar Hell-sarpint sermon ove his'n, hev sumthin like a Hell-sarpint aplicashun? Hit looks sorter so tu me."

This pattern of insult and revenge runs through all the Sut Lovingood tales—along with an incredible assortment of mayhem involving bulls, horses, bee swarms, snakes, and other animals, including man. While fellow Southern writers such as William Faulkner and Flannery O'Connor have paid tribute to Harris's art and Sut's vigor, not all readers have been equally charmed. After reading Harris's collection of Sut's tales, Edmund Wilson said, "It takes a pretty strong stomach to get through . . . it is by far the most repellent book of any real literary merit in American literature." Wilson is right as usual, but there is more to be said. If Sut's "univarsal onregenerit human nater" is repellent, his sense of life is pagan, based on the here and now. "Men were made a purpos jis' to eat, drink, an' fur stayin awake in the early part of the nites," says Sut, "an' women were made to cook vittles, mix the spirits, an' help the men do the stayin' awake. That's all an' nothin more." Sut has no sense of the transcendental, of life after death ("fur hits onpossibil fur me to hev a soul"); or if there be, Sut knows he is damned, as the Calvinists would have it.

Sut accepts that he is a "nat'ral born durned fool" with white trash poverty and craziness all around him. But what he refuses to accept is the hypocrisy of "sirkut riders" with their promises of heaven and their hands out, or that of "wimen-folk" who claim they want love when they are really looking for a farm; and he rails at them in story after story. Give old Sut a jug of moonshine and a sensible twenty-five-year-old "widder" with a nicely turned ankle who knows just how to move in the saddle, and he's happy. Of course, Sut would like to go to heaven—anything to get him out of his dreadful hand-to-mouth existence—but he's never yet met a fit representative of the hereafter. Sut reminds us of what Lenny Bruce said often: "There was never the what-should-be, there is only what is."

In this sense Sut is in the grand tradition of American humorous characters who attack hypocrisy by deflating pretension. Sut has looked behind doorways, under skirts, and beneath frock coats, so he knows what is going on and uses that knowledge to expose hypocrites. As he says, "Folks in public don't look much like folks in private nohow, dus they, George?" Often Sut's revenge is ugly, his practical jokes cruel, his motives thin and spiteful; and the very idea of a world of Sut Lovingoods is enough to make one shudder. But a Sut-less world would be lacking as well; Sut not only understands and speaks for his own underclass, he understands the losses of other underdogs as well. In the midst of one vituperative diatribe on the Puritans, Sut cries out that, when the *Mayflower* arrived, the Indians "should have carcum-sized the head ove the las'durn'd one, burnt thar close, pack'd thar carkuses heads-and-tails, herrin fashun, in thar old ship, sot the sails, an' pinted her snout the way Ward's ducks went." From the Indian point of view, Sut's tirade makes sense, and Thomas Morton would have approved. "Durn them leather injuns," laments Sut, "they let the bes' chance slip ever injuns had to give everlastin comfort to a continent and to set hell back at leas' five hundred years."

But what does this all mean—what's its "puppus," as Sut would say? Well, Harris has Sut offer his own wish (and slight defense) in the preface to their "collaboration":

> Ef any poor misfortunit devil hu's heart is onder a millstone, hu's ragged children am hungry, an' no bread in the dresser, hu is down in the mud, and the lucky ones a-trippin him every time he strug-gils to his all fours, hu hes fed the famishin an' now is hungry hissef, hu misfortins foller fas an' foller faster, hu is so foot-sore an' weak that he wishes he wer at the ferry—ef sich a one kin fine a laugh, jis' one, sich a laugh as is remembered wif his keerless boyhood atwixt these yere kivers—then I'll thank God that I hes made a book, an' feel that I hev got my pay in full.
>
> Make me a Notey Beney, George. I wants to put sunwhar atween the eyebrows ove our book, in big winnin-lookin letters,

the sarchin, meanin words, what sum pusson writ onto a 'oman's garter onst, long ago—

"Evil be to him that evil thinks."

Them's em, by jingo. Hed em clost apas' yu, didn't yu? I want em fur a gineral skeer—speshully fur the wimen.

Now, George, grease it good, an' let hit slide down the hill hits own way.

Like so much American humor, Sut's *Tales* slid down "hits own way," and there were some who thought evil and saw evil and others who got "sich a laugh." There has always been a battle between those who say, "How dare you?" and others who say, "Thank God." Despite the sometimes impenetrable dialect and heavy doses of violence, Harris accomplished a great deal in defining (and refining) the terms of that important American comic formula by which a rough-hewn rogue with nothing to hide roams free and tells the truth; and he offered one example for Mark Twain to follow. But, as Kenneth Lynn has pointed out, through the narrative device of the "self-controlled gentleman," Harris managed to distance himself from the violence and immorality of his comic creation and thus allowed us to peer safely at Sut as but a peculiar version of a backwoods troll. It would take Twain's substitution of victim's humor for spectatorial humor (and that in midcareer) to humanize the comic treatment of the American frontier. If Sut was not Pap Finn (whom he much resembles), he was kin of a sort, just over-the-"holler," a crude uncle from whom Huck could learn much— but whom he would later repudiate.

JAN HAROLD BRUNVAND

7 Urban Legends

Just as the study of American folklore led Constance Rourke to the study of American humor in the 1930s, so it led Jan Harold Brunvand to the study of what are called urban legends in the 1980s. Brunvand is among those scholars who recognize that folklore does not belong to the past but is created even in modern industrial cultures, and he has taken a close look at stories—sometimes grotesque but often comic—that are transmitted orally as true accounts of human experience, but which usually have little basis in fact. Between 1981 and 1993, Brunvand, a professor at the University of Utah, published five books about urban legends; the essay that follows is composed of parts of his prefaces to two of these: *The Vanishing Hitchhiker: American Urban Legends and Their Meanings* (1981) and *Curses! Broiled Again! The Hottest Urban Legends Going* (1989). Brunvand is also the editor of *American Folklore: An Encyclopedia* (1996).

Urban legends are realistic stories concerning recent events (or alleged events) with an ironic or supernatural twist. They are an integral part of White Anglo-American culture and are told and believed by some of the most sophisticated "folk" of modern society—young people, urbanites, and the well educated. The storytellers assume that the true facts of each case lie just one or two informants back down the line with a reliable witness, or in a news media report. The mass media themselves participate in the dissemination and apparent validation of urban legends, just as they sometimes do with rumor and gossip, adding to their plausibility. But urban legends are folklore, not history.

From Jan Harold Brunvand, *The Vanishing Hitchhiker: American Urban Legends and Their Meanings* (New York: W. W. Norton, 1981), xi–xiii, © 1981 by Jan Harold Brunvand; and *Curses! Broiled Again! The Hottest Urban Legends Going* (New York: W. W. Norton, 1989), 11–24, © 1989 by Jan Harold Brunvand. Reprinted by permission of W. W. Norton.

In common with age-old folk legends about lost mines, buried treasure, omens, ghosts, and Robin Hood-like outlaw heroes, urban legends are told seriously, circulate largely by word of mouth, are generally anonymous, and vary constantly in particular details from one telling to another, while always preserving a central core of traditional elements or "motifs." To some degree—again like much other folklore—urban legends must be considered *false,* at least in the sense that the same rather bizarre events could not actually have happened in so many localities to so many aunts, cousins, neighbors, in-laws and classmates of the hundreds and thousands of individual tellers of the tales. Both the narrative structure of these legends and their characteristic traditional folk motifs and oral variations disqualify them as literal accounts of actual events. The Hook Man's lane is a real locale in numerous communities, and a solid cement Cadillac has been reported "reliably" more than once—even photographed—but the myriad re-tellings and re-localizations (sometimes internationally) of these stories reveal beyond a doubt that they are simply additional instances of our living folklore. Still, like traditional folklore, the stories do tell one kind of truth. They are a unique, unself-conscious reflection of major concerns of individuals in the societies in which the legends circulate.

It is not the purpose of folklore study to debunk oral traditions, although it may seem so to those who may have asked a folklorist about "The Death Car" or "Red Velvet Cake" only to learn that another favorite story has supposedly happened many times before to scores of other people. For a folklorist, collecting a story's variations and tracing its dissemination and change through time and space are only the beginning of an analysis. We may or may not discover an original mouse tail in a pop bottle or a spider in a hairdo, but the wide distribution and acceptance of these and other similar traditions teach us something about how Americans react to situations involving corporate or individual negligence of health and cleanliness standards. Why these stories are told is our major concern. The lessons in the mouse tail or spider legend could just as well have been promoted by means of a factory inspector's directive, but the interesting fact is that the attitudes are much more graphically and memorably conveyed among the folk by these strange, believable, false-true tales. . . .

———

Once upon a time, folklorists were interested only in what one would think of as "folksy" subjects, like ancient ballads or fairy tales. Nowadays, however, we examine things like college customs, drug lore, and office traditions. Even those photocopied fake memos you see posted on the company bulletin board qualify as folklore . . . .

For years I have collected, classified, compared, and even computer-catalogued urban legends, trying to figure out where they come from, what changes they undergo, and why people continue to tell them to each other, despite the power of the mass media, which so much shape our views of the world. In 1986, having published my third book of urban legends—*The Mexican Pet*—and having appeared on countless radio talk shows, been four times on "Late Night with David Letterman," and several times on other local and national television programs, I came to realize how many more stories I was collecting by mail via letters and clippings than by just talking to the people with whom I have personal contact. Readers of my books* and the audiences for my media appearances had become wonderful sources of urban legends, and I joked that I should start a syndicated newspaper column and reach even more people with my collecting and writing.

That summer, to my surprise, David Hendin, editorial director of United Media Enterprises and United Feature Syndicate invited me to write a twice-weekly column for national circulation. Here was my chance to join my heroes like Jack Anderson and Miss Manners, reaching a gigantic audience of daily newspaper readers with my own scoops divulging the real sources and meanings of urban legends and my own replies to readers' questions about which stories to trust and which to bust.

A Swedish folklorist I know, who also writes about urban legends in the popular media, has the wonderful name Bengt af Klintberg. Bengt tells me that newspapers in Sweden now label urban legends "Klintbergers." That has a nice ring to it that I'm afraid "Brunvanders" lacks, though I liked the idea.

My column did not match the circulation of Jack Anderson's, but it was a thrill to see my picture in the United Media catalogue right across the page from J. A.'s portrait and next to Miss Manners's. Her hair was pictured there in perfect control, and her "humor and common sense" were listed as her "weapons against savagery." My hair in the catalogue picture seemed fetchingly rumpled, and my mission was stated as to "uncover the truth behind the legends." Thus began my career as a columnist . . . .

---

*The first two were *The Vanishing Hitchhiker* (1981) and *The Choking Doberman* (1984).

Column No. 1 carried the ambitious headline "Modern Folklorist Tracks Our Subconscious." I began by quoting another folklore scholar who had said: "Being a folklorist means you have to explain yourself a lot." I agreed with her, because, despite public belief to the contrary, folklorists seldom tell stories professionally but instead collect and study them. We are researchers, not raconteurs.

The purpose of the column is to reveal my findings about weird but credible stories—urban legends—that everyone tells as if they are true, though mostly they are fiction. From the start, I urged readers to submit rumors and stories circulating in their own communities.

Things worked out fine in that department. I receive scores of legends from readers every week, probably learning as much from their comments as they do from my essays. Often I see new trends emerging, such as legends about AIDS or about the dangers of tanning salons. I can also track the re-emergence of older legends, which means that a "hot" new legend may actually be a reheated leftover story to a folklorist—still interesting, though not as fresh as the public may think.

Rarely, my queries about stories unearth the apparent origin of a plot. Thus, with readers' help, I tracked through *Reader's Digest* and other publications, and then back to its Midwestern source, a hilarious anecdote about a woman's high heel caught in a grate. Later, a student of mine spotted the same incident dramatized in an old Doris Day film. . . .

Sometimes actual events like this generate urban legends, but legends about real incidents get so localized and stylized that they soon exist independently as oral stories, detached from their origins. For example, a few cars really have been filled with concrete, and perhaps one such case started the legend. But the events described did not occur in all the times and places where "The Solid Concrete Cadillac" is told.

Most urban legends are pure fantasies from someone's imagination. These fictional stories change as they spread but are always told as true—which is really the definition of "legend."

Sometimes readers challenge me that stories I have labeled apocryphal really happened. These people usually either remember an event that slightly resembled a legend, or they repeat a story that they assume (incorrectly) was told by a firsthand witness. Neither "proof" is airtight.

For example, a reader assured me that "The Runaway Grandmother" is "not a myth," because in 1976 she saw a car in Tennessee with what looked like a wrapped corpse tied on top. Having heard the stolen grandmother legend, she figured the body she thought she saw might have gotten lost in a similar manner.

She had observed, as she wrote, "a small older-model car with a strange object on the roof." The package she described was long, well padded, and rounded on one end.

Without even speaking to the couple driving, she decided that their child had died on a trip and that they were transporting the body home for burial on their own because of lack of funds.

The letter concluded, "It is easy to imagine that some prankster stole the bundle at some stop along the route and disposed of it."

You may imagine what you wish, dear reader, but remember that Americans have been telling this "Runaway Grandmother" legend about a supposed vacation mishap in Mexico since the early 1960s. The basic plot goes back to a European legend of the post-World War II days.

Another reader sent this "proof" of "The Nude Housewife" legend: "I happen to know a woman who was doing the laundry in the basement and she took off all of her clothes and put them in the machine. The meter man came, and she covered her head and ran up the stairs! I'm beginning to wonder how thorough you are?"

Gee, I am sorry I wasn't on the scene to interview that woman!

The legend this reader remembered was one in which a woman is caught in the nude except for a football helmet. The scene prompts the gas man to remark, "I don't know what game you're playing, lady, but I hope your team wins."

I have dozens of versions of "The Nude Housewife," many told as true, coming from oral tradition and print over a twenty-five-year period. But I have never spoken to a first-person participant in the supposed event though I've met plenty of secondhand true believers.

Eugene W. Dillenburg of Chicago raised a pertinent point in a letter. He suggested that the average Joe hears several versions of an urban legend from different sources and thinks, "Hey, they can't all be wrong, so there must be some truth to it."

For a folklorist, however, multiple versions from different places betray a story's oral circulation and variation. Even if we find the source of a legend, as I stated before, the story may have a life of its own.

"The Attempted Abduction" was the latest urban legend a reader wrote me about, saying that "somewhere along the way these stories did happen. But in the retelling the location was changed because someone couldn't remember exactly where it happened."

She mentioned the case of a child abducted from a theater restroom a few years ago in her city, the presumed origin of this urban legend. But "The Attempted Abduction" legend has a detailed plot involving cutting and coloring the child's hair, sedating her, changing her clothes except for shoes, the mother's recognition because of the shoes, and suppression by authorities of the crime report.

Numerous shopping malls and stores have had this story told about them, but none ever had exactly that crime committed. Police and journalists have debunked "The Attempted Abduction," and folklorists have found centuries-old antecedents for it.

So the similar crimes in real life must be simply part of the climate in which the old legend still flourishes.

———

With my story files steadily growing as the column continues, so is my level of journalistic accuracy, since readers quickly catch my errors. A recent solid example is a letter from California commenting on my discussion of "The Solid Cement Car." (A man suspects his wife has taken on a lover and fills the competitor's car with cement.) It turns out, as the man wrote, that *cement* is only "the grey powder stuff that you buy in bags"; when mixed with sand, aggregate, and water, he explained, it becomes *concrete, mortar,* or *grout,* depending on the mix.

I should have known that, my father being a retired highway engineer who uses words like "aggregate" when talking of his work. I retitled the story, "The Concrete Car," risking a letter pointing out that the car is merely *filled with* concrete, not made of it.

People wonder why I don't plant invented legends to see how they grow. I do not believe it's my business to make up folklore; nor do I think contrived stories would catch on. But a family in Colorado wrote once saying they had just invented a nifty new legend and were setting it in motion toward me via oral tradition. So far—many months later— no further word of it has arrived, but maybe it got stuck on the grapevine around Grand Junction.

When a reader, in Yellowknife, Northwest Territories, wrote offering to be my listening post for urban legends up there, I thought, "Sure, ha ha; urban and suburban folklore can't possibly get that far into the wilds." A week later, he sent me notes on a couple of good ones he had just heard in Yellowknife. When I got a similar call from White Horse up in the Yukon, I listened. . . .

———

Please keep those cards and letters coming, I asked my readers, and they certainly did keep writing. In one column, I demonstrated what piles of interesting mail I was getting by summarizing only one day's intake—

a dozen letters—from readers of just one newspaper, the *San Jose* (California) *Mercury-News*. In that single stack of correspondence, I found queries about individual urban legends, several new texts, some corrections and additions to my earlier columns, and one complaint from a reader who found my debunking of a sexy legend to be offensive. (She ought to see the ones I have to leave out!) There was even a note from *Mercury-News* feature writer Caroline Grannon, who was forwarding the mail; she couldn't resist adding a question of her own regarding an apocryphal story about Walt Disney.

The sentence "Altered substances are being passed around" headlined another column in which I tried to show by analogy how stories—like other things—may change as they are circulated.

The process of creating variations is like that old parlor game called "Telephone" or "Gossip." The players stand in a circle, and one person whispers a phrase to the person to his or her left, who whispers it to the next person, and so on. When the last player recites the phrase that he or she heard, it's sometimes barely recognizable as a variation of the original.

Perhaps reflecting this process, there are a couple of common legends about objects that are passed around until they return in a new form. The two items passed on in these stories are either a joint of marijuana or a lottery ticket. It's the pot or the lot, so to speak.

I've collected the legend about the joint from people who remember hearing it as long ago as 1968. These particular people heard it in Alaska, California, North Carolina, and Pennsylvania, so I assume that it's known nationwide.

A police officer is giving a lecture about the dangers of drugs to students in a high school. At one point, he puts a real joint of marijuana on a dish and passes it around for the students to see and smell. "When that dish gets back to me, the Cannabis exhibit had better be on it," he warns them. "And if it isn't, there will be an inspection, because I borrowed it from the evidence room at headquarters."

When the exhibit comes back to him, not only is the joint still on the dish, there are three others as well.

In some versions, the policeman's threat has been ignored, and the joint has been exchanged for an ordinary cigarette.

I first came across the lottery-ticket variation of this legend in Michigan. The state began to operate a lottery in 1972, and by the end of the year this story was going around.

A man is in a bar where the lottery numbers are being shown on TV, and he sees that he is a big winner. Thrilled by his good luck, he passes his winning ticket around the bar for everyone to see. When it comes back to him, though, it's not the same ticket.

A reader from New Orleans tells me that he heard virtually the same story in 1969. The only difference is that a winning horse-racing ticket, not a lottery ticket, is passed around.

That such things do sometimes occur in real life is illustrated by a reader's personal experience described in another letter. I'm suppressing the place and name here to avoid embarrassing anyone.

The reader wrote to tell me about the time she had attended the broadcast of a national TV interview program. Among the guests was a celebrity author. Afterward, at a large city bookstore, this reader was able to buy an autographed copy of that author's latest book.

She later told her co-workers about her visit to the show, and several of them asked to borrow the book. She consented, and the book made its way around the office. When it was finally returned to her, after several co-workers had read it, it bore the price sticker of a local bookstore. And the space where the autograph had been was blank.

The lesson of these stories, I suppose, is that you can't trust people when they are in groups. Whether they are passing around contraband or tickets or books—or *folklore*—someone is bound to pull a switcheroo.

Reading a profile in *The New Yorker* ("Boy Wonder" by Lawrence Weschler, November 17 and 24, 1986) about musical lexicographer Nicolas Slonimsky, I discovered that both of us are bedeviled by falsehoods in our fields that seem impossible to eradicate from the popular mind. Slonimsky repeatedly has to debunk fallacies about music history, while I have to deal with fantasies about things like exploding toilets, stolen cat corpses, and the Procter & Gamble company trademark.

As Lawrence Weschler wrote in his essay on Slonimsky: "The horror of horrors [he said] was the inadvertent factual errors that, once born into print, refused to die, and, indeed spread exponentially from one sourcebook to another, eternally. They haunted his sleep like vengeful wraiths."

I know the feeling, Nick! I'm also reminded of a line in Joe Adamson's book *Groucho, Harpo, Chico and Sometimes Zeppo* (New York: Simon & Schuster, 1973) that a column reader pointed out to me: "We have a fascination," Adamson wrote, "for utter transcendent unlikelihoods that we are not likely to shake, so long as we are human." Sounds just like urban legends to me.

With everyday life offering so many chances to be misunderstood, it's not surprising that lots of urban legends—and some true anecdotes— illustrate the difference between what people say and what they mean.

The most common legend of this sort is one I call "The Elevator Incident." At a hotel in New York City, a large man, leading a fierce-looking dog by a leash, boards an elevator occupied by three women tourists. When the man, who happens to be black, commands "Sit, Lady!" the women, apparently believing he is a mugger, sit down on the elevator floor. But it turns out that "Lady" is merely the dog's name, and the man is a celebrity—Reggie Jackson, say, or Lionel Richie. He apologizes profusely and tries to make up for their embarrassment by paying their dinner or hotel bill.

To my knowledge, no such incident has ever occurred to Jackson, Richie, or any other celebrity.

After reading my account of this legend in one of my earlier columns, Dr. K. H. of Syracuse, New York, recalled a similar misunderstanding involving the "teams" of interns and residents in a hospital where he once worked.

At one time, the teams were called red, white, and blue. But one day a female patient who was black asked an intern whether her husband had visited.

Without thinking, the intern replied, "I don't know him. I'm on the white team."

K. H. changed the team names not long afterward.

S. H., also of Syracuse, recalls one from his days as a fighter pilot in the air force. This story sounds awfully legendary, although S. H. says that it really happened.

While training to be a gunner, he was practicing firing at a target pulled by another plane. "SAVE YOUR BRASS," the instructor, sitting behind him in the cockpit, yelled above the noise of the engine—meaning "Save the shell casings." But S. H. thought the instructor said something else: "Save your ass." He pressed the release on his ejection seat and parachuted out of the plane, landing in a Florida swamp.

Not every misunderstanding story is so dramatic. Take the anecdote told among librarians, for instance. A library patron searching for cross references in the card catalogue comes to a card printed with the instruction "Go to Main Entry." So the patron goes to the front door and looks for references there.

That one's drier than a musty old book.

There's the classic story about a new member of Weight Watchers who is trying trying to follow the diet exactly. But one instruction is just too demanding. "I followed the diet as faithfully as possible," the dieter explains at the second week's meeting. "But for the life of me I just could not eat forty-six eggs."

The instructions, of course, were to eat "four to six" eggs per week.

And then there's the story about an amateur cook who was carefully following a recipe for homemade cookies. "Spoon dough on cookie sheet," the recipe instructed. "Leave room to rise."

The cook spooned out the dough and then went into the next room, peeking into the kitchen now and then to see if the cookies were rising.

And every elementary-school teacher has probably heard the story about the teacher who, while on a bus, thinks she recognizes the man sitting a few seats in front of her.

"Hello there, Mr. Johnson," she says, but the man doesn't respond.

She keeps calling out until—with everyone on the bus now looking at her—he finally turns around. And then she sees that she doesn't know him after all. "Sorry," she says, "I thought you were the father of one of my children."

Here's one more story, only faintly related to the theme of misunderstood words, but I happen to like it. It was told to me twice recently with assurances that it had actually happened at an international conference that my source had attended. But only to a friend of a friend (FOAF) of my source, and alleged to have happened on two different continents.

Supposedly, there is a translator provided at the conference who is rendering a talk being given by a German delegate for an English-speaking member of the audience. The speaker proceeds *auf Deutsch,* and the translator whispers each equivalent sentence in English.

It's all going along quite smoothly until at one point in the presentation the speaker has been going on for several minutes without the translator saying anything.

Finally the English speaker whispers, "What's going on?" and the translator hisses, "Shhh! I'm waiting for the verb."

If it didn't happen, it should have.

ROY BLOUNT, JR.

8 | Southern Humor

Periodically, American humorists have undertaken
the editing of collections of American humor. The earliest of these volumes was *Mark Twain's Library of
Humor* (1888), which included the work of many of
Twain's contemporaries. In 1941, *New Yorker* writer
E. B. White edited *A Subtreasury of American Humor,*
which featured the sophisticated wit that characterized much early twentieth-century humor. Following
in this tradition is *Roy Blount's Book of Southern
Humor* (1994), which focuses on a region of America
in part to claim that Southern humor has distinctive
characteristics. Roy Blount is the author of several
humorous works, including *One Fell Soup, or, I'm Just
a Bug on the Windshield of Life* (1982) and *What Men
Don't Tell Women.* In his introduction to *Roy Blount's
Book of Southern Humor,* Blount attempts to define the
humor of this region by citing numerous examples
and by allowing his own style of storytelling to give
readers a sense of what makes it different.

Southerners are too *sportive* with words—frolic-
some and competitive—to use them as neutral ana-
lytical terms. I hate it when I am out on what is known as an author
tour, and some hard-nosed interviewer tries to outflank my shameless
book-mongering by asking questions designed to get to the bottom of
humor: what *is* funny, after all; why *do* we laugh; and how did I, personally, get to be supposedly hilarious?

Sometimes I try hard to be responsive to these questions; sometimes
I try hard to make it clear why I believe that my being responsive to
these questions would be a bad idea; in either case the interviewer eventually looks at me as though he or she wishes I would quit.

So I do. If I am in luck, the next question is "Do Southerners laugh at different things than Northerners do?"

"Yes," I say. "Northerners."

But that is just a joke. At the bottom of Southern humor lies this fundamental truth: that nothing is less humorous, or less Southern, than making a genuine, good-faith effort to define and explain humor, particularly Southern humor.

Why particularly Southern humor? There you go, you're trying to draw me into something that we will both regret. If I had the sense that God gave a goose (and God knows God didn't give a goose much sense), I would introduce this anthology [*Roy Blount's Book of Southern Humor*] by declaring, with simple dignity, "I'm Southern, I'm a humorist, in my book this is Southern humor."

If I had that kind of sense, however, I would not be here before you today. I would be a humor *consultant*—that's where the money is, getting paid by the hour for advice on improving corporate risibility. When you're a consultant you speak with authority, because you and your clients are wearing the same suit. (Maybe your tie is different, has little understated monkeys instead of spots.) "Give your company a funny name," I would be saying, only at greater length in order to stretch out the billable time.

"Well, we're not sure we want to do *that*. Owenco, Inc., is a pretty established name in virtual fundware, and old man Owen is still very much—"

"Oink Oink? Your name is Oink Oink and you come to *me?* Never mind. Give your employees funnier names, then."

"Well, we tried that, but a lot of them didn't like it. And we don't believe in running too roughshod over our people's feelings just for the sake of building their morale through humor. Do you?"

"Believe in it?" I would riposte. "Hell, I've . . . "

That's what the old boy said, you know, when somebody asked him if he believed in infant baptism:

"Believe in it? Hell, I've seen it done!"

For the sake of argument, let's call that statement the quintessential Southern Zen koan. I first heard it some years ago in Yazoo City, Mississippi. What I was doing in Yazoo City is a pretty good story, involving the then President of the United States and an unaccommodating commode, and if I were a less self-effacing person I would have included the written version of that story in this book, but like I say I am *not* less self-effacing, and anyway I had to make some room for Mark Twain. Actually I believe I will quote, from that story, an ancillary story I was told by a Yazoo City native I knew in college, Spencer Gilbert:

"The first time I flew over town in an airplane, coming back from college, I looked down on the top of a water tank, and a sign on it said YAZOO CITY. That was the first time it ever occurred to me that those letters look funny."

The point of Spencer's story, I believe, for our purposes here, is that you have to get back a certain distance from things to see them as comical. And if you live in a part of the country where folks are traditionally liable to hit or shoot you if you get brash with them, and vice versa, then it's a good idea to maintain a certain distance from everybody all the time (which is not to say that you aren't eternally devoted to these people, or sick and tired of them, or both). Let's hold on to that thought—although actually the story is easier to hold on to than the thought. Let's hold on to *that* thought.

If you were to ask me why there have been so many humorists in the South, I might cite this Appalachian folk story recorded by Loyal Jones:

A man came home after working late one night and found his wife in bed and his best friend hiding in the closet.

"Why, John, what are you doing in there?" he asked.

"Well, Bert," his friend answered. "Everybody has to be somewhere."

To that story I would append three stipulations:

First: I was born in Indianapolis. I say this because I don't want somebody popping up waving a certified copy of my birth certificate in an effort to cast this entire collection in doubt. I was born in Indianapolis because the Libby canned goods company transferred my Florida Panhandle father and my Mississippi mother to the Midwest for two years just to complicate my future résumé. My forebears on both sides are Southern as far back as there are unburned courthouses, and I grew up in Georgia from the age of eighteen months. I have been to the Delta, the French Quarter, the Okefenokee, civil rights demonstrations, Klan rallies, juke joints, a rattlesnake roundup, backstage at the old Opry, Willie Nelson's hotel room, Son Thomas's porch, Chet Atkins's golf tournament, Mean Joe Greene's rec room, Bear Bryant's office, George Jones's car, and everywhere else in the South except your mama's wedding, 'cause there weren't no men there, 'cause we all knew better than to get caught like that. Now I live in New York and Massachusetts, but that is because when I'm in the South I wander around wondering where I can get the *New York Times,* and when I'm in the North I wander around wondering where I can get some okra, and I would rather think about some okra than the *New York Times.*

Second: Of the 114 writers in this collection, fewer than 20 of them would be described as humorists. Being humorous in the South is like being motorized in Los Angeles or argumentative in New York—humorous is not generally a whole calling in and of itself, it's just something that you're in trouble if you aren't.

Third: I do not think of Southern as some kind of outlandish separate category of human life. Hey, I had a Southern *mother.* I had a Southern first-grade teacher. I went through measles and puberty in the South. Maybe it's because I'm Southern that I get a certain thrill out of these lines from a postbellum poem called "I'm a Good Old Rebel":

> I hates the Yankee nation
> And everything they do,
> I hates the Declaration
> Of Independence too.

On the other hand, maybe I get that thrill because I learned to appreciate early in life—in the South—both the Pledge of Allegiance and the American tradition of nothing sacred. (Believe in free speech? Hell, I've heard it *denounced.*) Granted, Southern tradition is full of *dumb* sacred things. But Southerners love America—except for its government—all the more because many of our great-great-granddaddies damn near licked it. Incidentally, a Southerner wrote the Declaration of Independence. (These truths be self-evident? Hell, I've held 'em myself!) So don't talk to me, about whatever it was we were talking about.

If you want to, you can say that Southern humor deals with "typical" concerns of the region: dirt, chickens, defeat, family, religion, prejudice, collard greens, politics, and diddie wa diddie. But are not these concerns, boiled down, pretty much like everybody else's? Of course, Southerners boil them down (speaking figuratively, except with regard to collard greens and diddie wa diddie) with hamhock in the pot; although not so much anymore, because believe it or not we too have heard about low-density lipids. But we still know that eating right is more than a matter of molecular chemistry. As the eponymous hero of Charles

Portis's novel *Norwood* says to some boys he comes upon on a sidewalk of New York, as they are toasting marshmallows over a smoldering mattress: "They ain't going to taste like anything cooked over hair."

Demographically, we still fry a lot. Is frying a defining characteristic of the South? A boiled New England dinner eases its way into your system the same way a New England sentence does: without calling much attention to itself. Whereas a dinner of fried panfish (fins and all) and hushpuppies and fried yellow squash says *hot damn, here I am. I got the grit and I got the grease, come on. . . .* And while eating fried things Southerners will often talk about them, even talk *with* them—and I don't mean just that some of us will talk with food in our mouths, excuse me. I mean we will *have conversations with our food.*

That's right. We will pick up a crispy-fried bluegill and say, "My, you're nice. I believe I remember hooking you in particular. Hope you enjoyed that cricket as much as I'm about to enjoy you." And then somebody else will put on the voice of the (just-caught) fish and say, "You can take me home and clean me and eat me, Br'er Fox, but whatever you do, donnnn't throw me back up under them lily pads." Maybe we will usually do that to nonplus Yankees who may be at the table; but here is what we *will* do: we will chew on our choice of *words,* engage in dialogue with our words, roll them around in our mouth, enjoy them for the peculiar artifacts or organisms that they are. And toss a bunch of them scooters protogrammatically together in one sentence like frogs, rabbits, turkeys, cats, snakes, Chihuahuas, katydids, wasps and several other kinds of bugs and dogs in a confined area just to see what they will do. Believe in split infinitives? Hell, I have known infinitives to actually just, truth of the matter, near about evermore before God in broad daylight purely . . . Let's just say I have known infinitives to. To the point where the infinitive was scattered to the winds like an opened-up sack of feed, *and the person speaking didn't even necessarily know what an infinitive was.*

I know I overdid that last paragraph. On purpose, to make a point: Southern humor is usually better when it is trying to do justice to the nature of things than when it is trying to be comical. We see this in Hank Williams: "Did you ever see a robin weep?" is funnier, though it fits right in with the genuine pain of "I'm So Lonesome I Could Cry" than anything in "Kaw-li-ga," the ditty about the romantically frustrated wooden Indian.

Before I got off into extending infinitives into infinity and all, the point I was making was that words in the South have lives of their own.

Here's another of Loyal Jones's Appalachian stories:

> A girl from the country went into town and got a job with a lawyer's family who were pretty high-faluting. The girl cooked, cleaned the house, and did the wash and that sort of thing. The daughter in the family got engaged to a young man up the street.
>
> One day the lady of the house called to the hired girl, "Have you seen my daughter's fiancé?"
>
> "No, she ain't put it in the wash yet."

Let's get back to that infant baptism story. What is essentially Southern humorous about it? One thing is, it's a deep-structural pun, which vivifies and confounds an abstraction by getting physical with it. (Compare the country song title "If I Said You Had a Beautiful Body, Would You Hold It Against Me?") Another thing is, it involves religion. I am not a Southern Methodist anymore, though I was strenuously brought up to be; but I still find myself, as you may have noted above, invoking the Lord. That is because you can't invoke nothing.

Compare the infant baptism story to that well-known *Eastern*-religious koan "What is the sound of one hand clapping?" Southerners don't have to sit mulling that one over. Given the meaning of the word "clapping," there isn't any such thing as one hand doing it. And never has been, except that time when John was sitting out in the yard meditating and his wife said, "John, when are you going to come in here and work on our relationship?" and John said, "What is the sound of one hand clapping?" and she said *Wap* upside his head with the flat of her palm.

Possibly one hand *trying* to clap in thin air is a low, barely detectable whushy sound, maybe something that only a cat could hear. Have you ever noticed how a cat's ears will do—moving around, cocking at various angles, those little hairs sticking out all different ways—when people in the same room can't hear a thing? Personally I think the cat is just trying to get attention, but who knows. I don't think a person could hear one hand clapping against a high whistling wind, even. It's not something I've ever heard. Once I talked to a man who claimed that his wife was driving him crazy because she couldn't tell the difference between the phone ringing on television and the phone ringing there in their house in real life. An unusual dysfunction, but maybe it was part of the Lord's plan. Maybe one afternoon the phone rang on a rerun of *All in the Family* and she picked up her phone—thinking it was ringing—just before it *would have actually* rung if she hadn't picked it up, but since she did pick it up, her line was busy when somebody was trying to call her to tell her something filthy that she had lived too Christian a life to have to hear. We don't know. We just don't know.

If you're not clapping against anything, you're not clapping for anything either, because you're not clapping, you're just waving; of course, if somebody sees you doing it, she might think you're waving at her. Might be worth a try. It's the same with invocation—and if it's the Lord you're invoking instead of, say, Heidegger, then you are empowered to move along a lot quicker from story to story. I've seen it done.

Here's *another* Loyal Jones story:

A woman moved from Kentucky to Dayton, Ohio. One day a fire started in her house, and she called the fire department.

"Hello, I've got a fire out here in my house."

"Okay, where is it?"

"It's in the kitchen."

"I mean how do we get to it?"

"Well, you come in off the back porch or through the living room, either one."

"No, I mean, how do we get from here where we are to you out where you are?"

"Ain't you got one of them big red trucks?"

If you are willing to live with the fact that everything is phenomenal—and you are able to bear in mind, meanwhile, that nobody with any sense ever expected the phenomenological to be logical (because how the hell can it be, when words, the very things the phenomenologist is trying to comprehend phenomena *with*, are phenomena themselves, and wait a minute, isn't the phenomenologist one too, *him*self?)—then there you have Southern humor in a nutshell, except surely you have more sense than to want anything as strong as Southern humor to be packed down that tight. And how about the phenomenologist's mama? She was a sight in this world. I can just hear her now—"Son, don't you come into this house talking about *ab ovo*, that ain't the way you were raised and you know it."

We can't hold ourselves out at arm's length, brethren—and when you consider that I don't have any more rigorous idea of what I am talking about than a man I knew in Georgia did when he realized, while going eighty miles an hour downhill, that the fire ants had got all up inside his motorcycle leathers, you will see why I say: far be it from me to sit here calmly summing Southern humor up.

Others might sum it up, unthinkingly, as crackerishness. But that fiancé won't wash. One thing we need to get straight about Southern humor—Southern culture generally—is that it is Africo-Celtic, or Celtico-African.

According to the scholarly work *Cracker Culture: Celtic Ways in the Old South,* by Grady McWhiney (which I believe in absolutely because it makes me feel less pale), the South was originally settled not predominantly by Anglo-Saxons (as was the North) but by wild, oral, whiskey-loving, unfastidious, tribal, horse-racing, government-hating, Wasp-scorned Irish and Welsh and pre-Presbyterian Scots.

Who then brought in Africans. The ferment that produced Southern culture has *not* been a matter of Wasp civilization guiltily but angrily at odds with (while depending upon) enforced black labor. It has been a profoundly confused struggle to determine who is less like New England—Sut Lovingood or Mudbone, Jerry Lee Lewis or Little Richard. Crackers never did admit that they were oppressors. They could always put that off on Washington. (The fact that Washington, outside the embassies, is in most respects a Southern town, organized around government instead of, say, sawmills, is something that I suppose Northerners might call an irony.) What it came down to was that blacks, after all the exploitation and co-optation they had submitted to, proved in the crunch to be *more Southern.* Years after the news showed white mobs chanting in defiance of desegregation, the following jump-rope rhyme was recorded among black children in East Texas:

Two, four, six, eight,
We ain't gonna integrate.
Eight, six, four, two,
Bet you sons-of-bitches do.

When Rob Slater's class of high school students in Winston-Salem, North Carolina, rebelled against a Northern-devised intelligence test by making up their own "In Your Face Test of No Certain Skills" and sent it up to the testers, who scored C's and D's on it, I counted it as not just a racial but also a regional victory. One question was "Who is buried in Grant's Tomb?" The correct answer was "Your mama."

The civil rights movement, I grant you, was an all-American constitutional triumph (as far as it went) that could not have been achieved without the help of Northern media and activists. But in the local courthouses and on the TV news, where it counted, it was a struggle to prove who were the truest fundamentalists, black ones or white ones—

resulting in an explosive Africo-Celtic fusion (King versus Connor) like the Uncle Remus stories (slave instructing Harris), like *Gone with the Wind* (Hattie McDaniel and Butterfly McQueen supporting the O'Haras), like country music (the Delta Blues seeping into mountain ballads), like Elvis (soul giving body to white gospel keening), like Mark Twain (Jim on the raft with Finn).

(Incidentally, if you wonder whether Southern humor is important enough to devote a whole book to, you might bear in mind that Ernest Hemingway said all of modern American literature grew out of *Huckleberry Finn*.)

What have black Southerners and white Southerners always had in common, aside from the soil and the sweet potatoes and the heat and the possums and just about everything else but rhythm and money and rights? They have had orality. The have had a sense that English—as American infants of whatever ethnicity (and baptized or not) realize when they smile in their first recognition of words—is a comically physical thing for earthy people who bypassed the Enlightenment to wrap their mouths around.

"Nigger, your breed ain't metaphysical," wrote Robert Penn Warren in a 1945 poem—to which Sterling A. Brown riposted, "Cracker, your breed ain't exegetical." Don't white folks ever get the last word? I guess the rule of thumb is, if the first word is "nigger," no. (Warren and Brown were both fine and enlightened writers, but Brown was funnier.)

Let me interject here a story from my experience. I don't mean it to prove anything absolutely positive about Southern race relations, Lord knows: I was attacking Southern race relations, in print, in the South (for all the good it did anybody but me), before I was a legal adult. Southern racism is full of double binds ("We ain't heard *our* Negroes say nothing about freedom") that have been as damnably confining as the infant baptism koan is (sort of) liberating.

But here's what happened. Twenty years ago, I was lying flat on my back in the woods in the middle of the night in Arkansas with a po-white man whose conversation I had been enjoying for a couple of hours. While we waited for his dogs to start going *ba-oooo* in the distance to signify that they were on the trail of a raccoon, we talked about various things. Suddenly, out of the blue (or actually the darkness), he said, "I hate niggers."

My heart sank. "You *do?*" I said.

"Well," he said, sounding surprised that I was surprised, and then he started talking about black people he had known all his life, had swum with as a boy and walked the woods with as a man. Nothing he said was progressive or even sufficiently respectful, but none of it sounded hateful, more like fascinated. And finally he said, "This colored feller Tooley, I'll bring him a possum, 'cause I don't eat 'em. And he'll carry on, 'Lawd, Mr. Bobby, that thing got teeth on him, that thing is ugg-leeeee, Lawd, I always has been mos' bewary of a possum, *hoooo.*' And then be John Brown if I don't come back the next day and Tooley has already cooked that thing and eat it all down to the bones and sucked whatever po' marrer there may *be in* possum bones out of them." What seemed to stick in this man's craw about black people was that they could get more out of a wild animal than he could, on an even smaller budget.

I wish I could pull leprechauns and Yoruba tricksters, Brother Dave Gardner and Little Richard, George Wallace and Stokely Carmichael together into one unified theory of Crackro-African or Africo-Cracker mischief and indirection, but I'm not exegetical enough.

I will say this: I read *The Signifying Monkey,* Henry Louis Gates, Jr.'s book about African-American vernacular irony—which Gates with linguistic nicety calls "Signifyin(g)"—and its traditional uses in fostering tough intimacy among blacks and protecting slaves' pride against white violence. And I kept thinking that this was a lot like Southern white irony and its traditional uses in fostering tough intimacy among whites and protecting them against each other and the overbearing North. (To the extent that Southern white irony is a defense against blacks, on the other hand, it is Br'er Bear trying to position himself against Br'er Rabbit.) "Cracking" is a Scots and Irish term for pointed boastful joshing and also an African-American synonym for "Signifyin(g)." One thing I hope this anthology bears out is the kinship, grossly abused but persistent, between humor of the crackers and humor of the brothers.Without gainsaying that "lynch" comes from a Virginia Irishman's name.

Maybe in some parts of the world, or even of this country, words are taken as givens or as things that grow naturally in the dictionary. But to Southerners (as to Africans and Irishmen I have sat at table with), language is the sound of the tongue and the mind clapping, with an understandable tendency to lose the beat, especially in print. We wrestle with our words the way we do with our children, so as to get syncopated with them.

Here's a story Zora Neale Hurston heard in Florida. A man sent his daughter off to school for seven years, and when she came back he sat her down and began to dictate a letter:

" 'Dear Brother, our chile is done come home from school and all finished up and we is very proud of her.' "

Then he ast de girl "Is you got dat?"

She tole 'im "yeah."

"Now tell him . . . 'Our mule is dead but Ah got another mule and when Ah say (clucking sound of tongue and teeth) he moved from de word.'

"Is you got dat?" he ast de girl.

"Naw, suh," she tole 'im.

He waited a while and he ast her again, "You got dat down yet?"

"Naw, suh, Ah ain't got it yet."

"How come you ain't got it?"

"Cause Ah can't spell (clucking sound)."

"You mean to tell me you been off to school seben yours and can't spell (clucking sound)? Why Ah could spell that myself and Ah ain't been to school a day in mah life. Well jes' say (clucking sound), he'll know what you mean and go on wid de letter."

Writing isn't all language, tooby sho. People who pronounce upon Southern culture cite "sense of place" and "sense of character." Well, Southern humorists have been more likely to ramble than to settle into small-town society, but they have rambled through a physical world, of not just routes but roads, not just areas but woods and neighborhoods, and they have gotten themselves thoroughly embroiled along the way with the horses or the vehicles that they rode through on. When they have put down roots, it has been in settlements where people have known each other for quite likely a lot longer than they ever wanted to, so that they have had ample time, material, and audience for fashioning themselves and each other into characters.

But that doesn't mean that the cream of Southern humor nestles warmly in the South. Traditionally, the Southern writer has had this great advantage: he or she might be not only the only writer in town but also the only free-range reader. Hard-core book larnin' is your town's name written on top of the water tower, up there for strangers to see. So a writer in the South is less likely to be tripping over other writers, less likely to be reduced to writing about what's already paginated. The air is full of unwritten stories ripe for translation to the page. And before the neighbors discover that they have been immortalized, they or the writer may well be safely dead.

Hardly anybody in this book has been sustained in his or her vocation by Southern audiences and media. Of course, artists naturally aspire to national exposure and compensation, but most of these writers, white and black, have had to get a foothold outside the South before they could speak the rough truths that were self-evident to them as Southerners. "Southern Comfort," muses Blanche Du Bois on seeing that brand name on a bottle. "How can that be, I wonder?"

You won't hear a humorous Southern writer proclaiming, like James Joyce in exile from Ireland, that he or she means to "forge in the smithy of my soul the uncreated conscience of my race." Here's what Joseph Mitchell, tobacco country legend of *The New Yorker,* recently told National Public Radio:

> One of the greatest things. . . . One time the state of North Carolina gave me a gold medal. My youngest daughter jokes with me a good deal, and she read in the paper that I had been awarded a gold medal, by the state of North Carolina? And she got on the phone, said, "Daddy, I see that you're still foolin' 'em." Well I can't tell you how that made me feel. . . . The idea that I'm half a swindler delights me more than the literary stuff—though I'm very glad to see these things, God knows, and all that. But at the same time, the feeling that I'm foolin' the population pleases me too. You see when you write these stories, you're not writin' 'em for, God forgive me, posterity, you're writin' 'em for a weekly magazine hopin' some people will laugh at it, see? If I had sat down and said, "I'm going to try and write some literature," do you know what a mess that would've been? Can you imagine? But it's accidental, the fact that somebody will *re-read* these things? That makes me feel, I tell you—that people will go into a store and . . . The damn book costs a lot of money!

That was Mitchell telling the plain truth, but also Signifyin(g). When it comes down to anthology time, the test of humor is whether it will keep.

What makes most Southern humor rot? Not meanness—Sut Lovingood is rough as a cob, Mark Twain damned the human race, Faulkner said a good book was worth any number of old ladies, didn't anybody mess with Memphis Minnie, and Katherine Anne Porter once praised Eudora Welty for "her blistering humor and her just cruelty" in "Petrified Man." Nothing is less enduringly savory than narrow-mindedness that tries to pass for geniality. Whereas a tang of meanness may be a preservative—vinegar for pickling real fellow feeling and love of the world. Mean as in biting, mean as in common, mean as in signify.

Nothing's funny unless it smacks of delight. But what surely leads to spoilage in Southern or any other humor is condescension—or, as Porter put it (describing what Welty eschewed), "that slack tolerance or sentimental tenderness . . . that amounts to criminal collusion between author and character." The Southern humorists who put me off are those who rest their crabby/maudlin appeal upon the assumption that certain of their characters (for instance, themselves) are just about the most precious *thangs*. . . .

Too much Africo-Celtic blood has been shed for Southern humor to be good *and* cozy. The precious thang in any kind of writing is slippery exactitude, such as we see in that infant baptism story. Here's a master-slave exchange that Mel Watkins cites in his book on African-American humor.

> "You scoundrel, you ate my turkey."
> "Yes, suh, Massa, you got less turkey but you sho nuff got mo'
> Nigger."

The word "Nigger," there, digests too many shifting layers to ever settle. When writing keeps, it's not because it finds a niche but because it keeps on moving. Zora Neale Hurston observed that "the colored preacher, in his cooler passages, strives for grammatical correctness, but goes natural when he warms up. . . . The congregation wants to hear the preacher breathing." Believe in it? Heard it done. Now from the white side of the aisle hear Knoxville, Tennessee, newspaper columnist Jimmie Dykes:

> Once, somewhere in Georgia, somebody was watching the rednecks dance. It seemed like they were all bouncing around differently. He asked a good ol' boy nearby what was the trouble. "Hell," he said, "they ain't dancin' to the music. They're dancin' to the words."

If there's anything to which abstract correctness does not apply, it's humor. Almost everything is funny to somebody, and nothing makes everybody laugh. *The New Yorker,* in the days when it was the standard-bearer of American humor, never appreciated Flannery O'Connor, for God's sake. I once heard O'Connor say she had no patience for Dickens. I daresay there are funny writers whom I don't get. For a white boy I do get the blues (Lord, Lord)—here's a verse from "You Got to Love Her With a Feeling," by Tampa Red:

You know the cop took her in, she didn't
Need no bail—
She shook it for the judge, he put
The cop in jail. . . .

P.S. As far as historical sweep goes, the most influential Southern institutions today, I guess, are Wal-Mart, CNN, the Atlanta Olympics, mostly soulless country music, and a feel-your-pain policy-wonk President [Bill Clinton]. Country music can still be good, though. Jimmy Dale Gilmore sings, "I would've killed myself, but it made no sense/Committin' suicide in self-defense." And Bill Clinton is slick, he's up to things, and he comes from a humorous mama. When somebody asked her how it felt when one of her husbands shot at her, she said, "About like when *anybody* shoots at you." There have been all kinds of connections between the South and humor, over the years, that people aren't widely aware of. Oliver Hardy was a Georgian born and raised. He left Milledgeville to seek his fortune in the movies shortly before Flannery O'Connor was born there. Charlotte Moorman, who made a name for herself in New York by playing the cello topless back when that was considered outrageous, was from the South. Did you know that Margaret Dumont, who was so funny in Marx Brothers movies because she was so humorless, was born in Atlanta? George Herriman, creator of Krazy Kat, was born in New Orleans. Jim Henson, creator of the Muppets, grew up in the Delta. And here's something my friend Slick Lawson down in Nashville told me, that a man told him, just the other day, about another man who was bald: "I've seen more hair on a bar of soap down at the Holiday Inn." Holiday Inns started in the South too—and now, finally, there's something funny about them. In any self-respecting library, by the way, you can find William Byrd's fart poem, on page 245 of *Another Secret Diary of William Byrd of Westover,* edited by Maude H. Woodfin. According to that poem, Maids at Court in the days of Queen Anne and Sir Isaac Newton did something with farts, for amusement (I don't know, but it sounds like Byrd may have seen it done), that you may have assumed nobody but awful old Southern boys ever did. Lit them. The Maids' were blue too.

Oh, but that's too low a note to end on. If you want to read something *inspiring* about Southern humor, read Ralph Ellison's essay "An Extravagance of Laughter," in his book *Going to the Territory.* After a Southern boyhood and three years of studying music at Tuskegee Institute, in 1936 Ellison moved to New York, where he loved the freedom but found himself astounded by bad manners on the subway and by the fact that he missed some things about the South. One evening his hero and new-found Harlem friend Langston Hughes invited him to take in a play. Until he arrived at the theater, Ellison didn't know that the play—his first exposure to Broadway—was *Tobacco Road*, Jack Kirkland's long-running adaptation of the Erskine Caldwell novel. "Had I been more alert," he says in the essay, "it might have occurred to me that somehow a group of white Alabama farm folk had learned of my presence in New York, thrown together a theatrical troupe, and flown north to haunt me. But being dazzled by the lights," and so on, Ellison settled back to watch white trash dramatized on the Great White Way. When he saw Ellie May and Lov "uttering sounds of animal passion" and "floundering and skittering back-to-back across the stage," he fell into a laughing fit that embarrassed Hughes and disrupted the proceedings. When other patrons in the balcony saw that this person reduced to helpless laughter was black, they began to "howl and cheer," but theatergoers down below, who couldn't see him, reacted huffily. As for the actors, they "were now shading their eyes and peering open-mouthed toward the balcony." Ellison felt "as though I had been stripped naked, kicked out of a low-flying plane onto an Alabama road, and ordered to laugh for my life." Though part of him was mortified, the rest of him doubled over and straightened back up and doubled over again and wheezed and choked in laughter— all the more convulsively because he was recalling an apropos in-joke that Tuskegee students would elaborate among themselves.

The story was that since African Americans in small Southern towns "were regarded as having absolutely *nothing* in their daily experience which could possibly inspire *rational* laughter," and since a given black person did, however, sometimes find something hilarious even while crossing the town square, he would at such a moment leap headfirst into a "laughing barrel," where he was "apt to double up with a second gale of laughter—and that triggered, apparently, by his own mental image of himself laughing at himself upside down." To their dismay, respectable white citizens would find themselves joining in this laughter—which would cause the embarreled laugher to laugh all the harder, which would cause the whites to suspect that "in some mysterious fashion the Negro involved was not only laughing at *himself* laughing, but was also laughing at *them* laughing at his laughing against their own most determined wills. And if such was the truth, it suggested that somehow a Negro (and this meant *any* Negro) could become with a single hoot-and-cackle both the source and master of an outrageous and untenable situation."

Finally, reduced to tears, Ellison calmed down. He sat there in the balcony awash in "embarrassment, self-anger, ethnic scorn, and at last a feeling of comic relief. And all because Erskine Caldwell compelled me to laugh at his symbolic, and therefore nonthreatening, Southern whites, and thus he shocked me into recognizing certain absurd aspects of our common humanity."

NANCY A. WALKER

ZITA DRESNER

9 | Women's Humor in America

By the 1980s a number of scholars had realized that decades of identifying American humor with the rustic Yankee, with frontier violence, and with politics had served to omit from the tradition the humor created over the years by American women writers. Nancy Walker and Zita Dresner's anthology *Redressing the Balance* (1988) represents one major attempt to reclaim from relative obscurity dozens of examples of women's humor from the colonial period to the 1980s, making them available to others interested in a more "balanced" concept of what American humor has been. Walker is the author of *"A Very Serious Thing": Women's Humor and American Culture* (1988), and Dresner wrote her doctoral dissertation on women humorists of the twentieth century. In their introduction, the editors outline several ways in which women' s humor differs from that of men in theme, tone, and form, and provide a brief history of the way women' s humor developed as a response to their subordination in American culture.

Despite the relative recency of American humor studies, a considerable body of literature has accumulated over the past century concerning the nature and functions of humor. Within the past two decades in particular, psychologists, sociologists, and cultural anthropologists have conducted research into humor motivations and responses and, emphasizing the social uses of humor, have analyzed the roles of the humorist and the humor preferences of different groups within cultures. Looking at women's humor

From Nancy A. Walker and Zita Dresner, eds., *Redressing the Balance: American Women's Literary Humor from Colonial Times to the 1980s* (Jackson: University Press of Mississippi, 1988), xix–xxxiv. Reprinted by permission of the University Press of Mississippi.

in light of humor research and theory, as well as in relation to the critical studies of literary humor and feminist analyses of women's literature that have appeared in recent decades, we can draw some preliminary conclusions about the themes, techniques, and purposes that distinguish American women's literary humor.

First, while America's female humorists have often written in the same modes as their male counterparts, used many of the same devices, and followed similar trends in humor, their work has been neither imitative nor derivative. As a popular art that must appeal to large numbers of readers, humorous writing by both genders is as subject to changes in fashion as are clothing styles and television programming. Public taste and current fads are in part responsible for the subject matter and style of the newspaper column, the book of light verse, and the humorous sketch or novel. But while responding to the pressure to conform to the expectations of the marketplace, American female writers have created a distinctive body of humor with common subjects and themes that set it apart from the male tradition of American humor. Reflecting, by necessity, their roles and positions as women in the culture, female writers have focused largely on the domestic sphere of wife and mother and on the social sphere that, differently in different eras, has been defined as women's work and activities. In short, they have written about "things which women in general find interesting," as Stillman and Beatts note in explaining why their collection, *Titters,* does not contain jokes about "jock straps, beer, trains, mothers-in-law, dumb blondes, cars, boxing, the Navy, chemistry, physics, stamp catalogues, spelunking, pud-pulling or poker."[1]

Second, as Mahadev Apte argues convincingly, because of "the behavioral, expressive, and other sociocultural constraints imposed on women . . . many common attributes of men's humor seem to be much less evident or even absent in women's humor."[2] In particular, Apte notes, cross-cultural research has shown that "women's humor generally lacks the aggressive and hostile quality of men's humor. The use of humor to compete with or to belittle others, thereby enhancing a person's own status, or to humiliate others either psychologically or physically, seems generally absent among women. Thus the most commonly institutionalized ways of engaging in such humor, namely, verbal duels, ritual insults, and practical jokes and pranks, are rarely reported for women."[3] Consequently, the degree to which aggression and hostility are overt in a particular woman's humorous expression depends on the degree of gender equality permitted in her society, as well as on her audience and on those who control the dissemination of her humor. For example, as Apte's research confirms, women are generally more free to ridicule men and make sexual jokes when the audience is exclusively female than they are when it is mixed.

Because of the constraints on women's expression, which in most cultures have included taboos against women's appropriation of sexual subject matter and language, women's humor has been described as more gentle and genteel than men's, more concerned with wit than derision, more interested in sympathy than ridicule, more focused on private than on public issues. These attributes, along with women's greater reliance on verbal devices of understatement, irony, and self-deprecation, have enabled women to mask or defuse the aggressive component of humor making, thereby minimizing the risks involved in challenging the status quo.

Third, because of women's unequal social, political, and economic status in most cultures, and the fact that they are regarded by men as "other" (factors compounded for women belonging to racial or ethnic minorities), women's and men's humor have been directed to different ends and/or realized in different ways. For example, most humor theorists consider the venting of aggression to be a major function of humor. Freud was the first to suggest that humor is a socially acceptable way of releasing repressed antisocial or hostile impulses, and recent proponents of the aggression theory maintain that humorous pleasure drives from the derision, ridicule, deprecation, deflation, degradation, humiliation, and general mockery of individuals, groups, institutions, values, or ideas that threaten one's sense of security or well-being. As has already been suggested, however, most cultures harbor prohibitions against women's expression of aggression and hostility, especially in public and in mixed audiences. Moreover, women have been traditionally conditioned to assume passive, subordinate roles, and as Naomi Weisstein asserts in "Why We Aren't Laughing . . . Anymore," the role of "a funny, nasty clown doesn't go along with the definition of WOMAN that gets us our provider."[4] These factors have not eliminated aggression as a motivation of women's humor, but they have compelled women to exercise it in more covert and indirect ways than men do.

In addition to the release of aggression or hostility, the exposure of incongruity is generally accepted by theorists as a major, universal function of humor. Proponents of the incongruity theory believe that humor operates primarily through surprise, shock, dislocation, or sudden reversal of expectations. However, because the perception of incongruity is based on shared values, beliefs, customs, habits, and experiences, the degree to which the genders (and races or ethnic groups) are differentiated by their cultures into separate classes of people will determine the degree to which they can share and enjoy each other's perceptions of the incongruities that make up their humorous visions. At the same time, as all groups in a society are aware of the values, beliefs, and behaviors that are promoted by the dominant culture, those belonging to the dominant culture do not generally have the same awareness of the attitudes, habits, and experiences of those excluded from or oppressed by it. Thus, as Martha Bensley Bruère and Mary Ritter Beard contend, "the angle of vision from which women see a lack of balance, wrong proportions, disharmonies, and incongruities in life is a thing of their world as it must be—a world always a little apart."[5]

To the extent that woman's world is differentiated from man's, the incongruities revealed in women's humor reflect a world at odds with, and potentially threatening to, that of men. Because in women's humor, frustration and anger at gender-based inequities have had to be expressed obliquely, incongruity has been a major device for decoding the myths of the patriarchy. By exposing the discrepancies between the realities of women's lives and the images of women promoted by the culture, between the inequities to which women have been subjected and the egalitarian ideals upon which the nation was founded, American women humorists have targeted the patriarchal social system. For women of racial or ethnic minorities, of course, the conditions to be attacked and discrepancies to be exposed have been at least doubled.

Finally, the aggression and incongruity theories of humor have been further refined by social theorists who agree with Henri Bergson's position in *Laughter* that humor, in all of its manifestations, has primary social functions; they have argued that both the expression of hostility and the disclosure of discordance through humor depend upon social factors. Analysts have proposed, for example, that humor works in a number of ways as an agent of group enhancement and social control. If the humor expressed in one group (the ingroup) disparages another group (the outgroup), it boosts the morale of and solidifies the ingroup as well as promoting hostility against the outgroup. If the ingroup is culturally dominant (in America, white middle-class men), the humor not only reinforces its sense of superiority but, at the same time, controls the behavior of the disparaged group (e.g., women, minorities) by creating or fostering conflict in or the demoralization of the disparaged group. In other words, humor is used by those in power, whether consciously or not, to preserve the status quo.

On the other hand, humor initiated in a group lacking status in the culture may bolster the members' self-esteem by disparaging the bases of the dominant group's claim to superiority. However, researchers have found that individuals and groups at the top of a social hierarchy use humor more often than those at the bottom, and generally direct it downward, while those at the lower level (e.g., women, minorities), when they use humor, direct it more frequently at themselves or at those below them than at those above them.

The use of self-deprecating humor by women could be a defensive reaction of those who feel themselves too weak or vulnerable to attack with impunity the forces that oppress them, but the seemingly defensive weapons of humor can also become offensive in the hands of women and other outgroups. For example, as psychologists have observed, laughing at one's shortcomings is not only a way of diminishing their importance and potentially overcoming them but is also a technique for cleansing them of pejorative connotations imposed by the dominant culture and, thereby, turning them into strengths. Similarly, the use of incongruity in humor by women as a means of targeting attributes and behaviors prescribed for them by the dominant culture is an act of rebellion. Finally, the use of humor by women against women, when it is used to advance ideas that might conflict with those of the male establishment about women's roles and prerogatives, represents a step toward empowerment rather than capitulation.

These various ideas about the nature, functions, and concerns of women's humor, which account for the different "angle of vision," the "world always a little apart," of American women's literary humor, can be seen in women's writing from the colonial era to the contemporary period. Two types of early American humor, usually identified with male writers, have been described by literary critics and historians: the formal, or "high," literary style of the British satirical mode and the informal, seemingly unconscious ironic style of such personal literary forms as diaries, journals, and travel books. The poetry of Anne Bradstreet (1612–1672), for example, uses devices of wit associated with male Elizabethan and Metaphysical poets, but Bradstreet uses these devices to express a woman's thoughts on marriage, motherhood, creativity, and religion at a time and in a place, Puritan New England, especially hostile to any public role or voice for women. In a poem such as "The Author to Her Book," therefore, Bradstreet adopts an overtly deferential tone about her work to appease her potential critics, but at the same time, the irony with which she presents her anomalous position as a woman poet serves to undermine both the seriousness of her apology and the logic of the patriarchal attitudes that would deny women minds, voices, and talents in anything other than domestic work. Similar uses of such double-edged irony can be found in the "apologies" of succeeding humorists, from Judith Sargent Murray in the eighteenth century to Jean Kerr in the twentieth, especially in what has been called "domestic" or "housewife" humor. As Neil Schmitz writes in reference to Gertrude Stein's work, "What aggression lurks in the deferential tone of the humorous woman, the ironist knows."[6]

The second strain of early American humor appears in Sarah Kemble Knight's diary, which records her five-month journey in 1704 from Boston to New York City and back. While the journal contains many of the elements of humor found in the travel accounts of such early American male writers as William Byrd II, its satiric treatment of regional manners, customs, and dialects reflects Knight's particular concern, as a Puritan woman, with ideas of proper "housewifery." This emphasis on women's roles, as well as the realistic details that make up her humorous depictions of people and places, continues to inform the humor of regional writers, from Caroline Kirkland in the nineteenth century to Betty MacDonald and Cyra McFadden in the twentieth.

During the Revolutionary era, both Mercy Otis Warren and Judith Sargent Murray, like their male contemporaries, used satire to promote the cause of the American patriots, but unlike the men, Warren and Murray were also concerned with women's rights and status in the new republic. Warren's patriotic play *The Group,* for example, closes with a female Patriot speaking about the connections between the Patriots' fight for freedom, women's desire for equality, and nature's revolt against the corruptions of Britain's tyranny. Similarly, while her political poetry has been compared to that of the "Connecticut Wits," other poems reveal that Warren's irony and wit, like Bradstreet's, served to present views that opposed the prevailing masculine views of religion, rationality, and relationship between the sexes.

While Warren's interest in women's rights tended to be voiced covertly in her poetry and plays, Judith Sargent Murray addressed questions of women's place in the new nation more openly. In essays, articles, comedies, and fiction, she directed her wit against those male assumptions about women's physical, mental, and moral weakness that were used to preclude women's political participation in the Republic. Following Mary Wollstonecraft's position in *A Vindication of the Rights of Women* (1792), Murray protested restrictions on women's training, education, and political activity. In addition, in connecting women's moral behavior with civic virtue and in positing a social order based on marital equity and a balance between domestic and political activity, she not only represented what Nancy Cott calls "the equalitarian feminist view" of the late eighteenth century but also anticipated the position of subsequent women writers who employed the devices of humor to deal with similar issues of women's rights in the nineteenth and twentieth centuries.

By advocating education and training for women that would promote their self-sufficiency and informed civic involvement, Murray sought, at least in part, to counter the prevailing sentimentalism of late eighteenth-century popular literature. As the sentimental novel proliferated in the nineteenth century, later humorists attempted to do the same by painting satirical portraits of women suffering from the disease of sentimentality. The earliest of these, Tabitha Tenney's satirical novel, *Female Quixotism* (1801), recounts the lifelong romantic delusions that leave the heroine, Dorcasina Sheldon, in old age, with a wasted life, for which she blames her addiction to sentimental novels. Similarly, Caroline Kirkland's depiction of the "poet" Miss Eloise Fidler, in *A New Home—Who'll Follow?* (1839), ridicules both the claptrap of sentimental poetry and the pretensions of Miss Fidler herself, whose behavior and dress, modeled on sentimental literature, are particularly absurd in the backwoods Michigan environment that Kirkland describes. Continued satirical treatment of sentimental women in the work of Frances Whitcher and Marietta Holley prefigure the portraits in twentieth-century humor, from Betty MacDonald in the 1940s to Erma Bombeck in the 1970s, of women who accept and promote romanticized fantasies of female attributes and roles.

In Kirkland's work, the portrait of Miss Fidler is just one example of the "strong antiromance sentiment"[7] that, as in the work of later male frontier humorists, served to counterbalance increasingly romanticized accounts of life in the American West. But what differentiates Kirkland's work from that of the male humorists/realists is her emphasis on the problems and hardships faced by women living on the fringes of civilization. In addition, Kirkland's antiromanticism; descriptions of regional characteristics, language, and customs; and emphasis on depicting the realities of women's lives place her work in a line of women's humorous writing that began with Sarah Kemble Knight and extends to the work of journalist Mary Abigail Dodge (pseud. Gail Hamilton) and the local color realists of the latter part of the nineteenth century, as well as to twentieth-century writers who have used irony and satire to challenge prevailing myths about women's roles and about the communities in which they live.

As the cult of domesticity and the notion of separate spheres for men and women gained adherents in the nineteenth century, the contrasts between Kirkland's perspective and that of male humorists expanded to include other differences in men's and women's humorous literature. While men were developing a brand of American humor that began, as Bruère and Beard wrote, "in the robust expression of frontiersmen and [remained] in that gusto and temper while a new world was subdued to the plow, while an agricultural civilization swung toward an industrial one, while the nation was hammered into form by war and peace, prosperity and depression" (v), women were increasingly restricted to roles and admonished to cultivate qualities that were at odds with these changes and developments. Consequently, in the work of nineteenth-century female humorists, from Caroline Kirkland to Marietta Holley, there is a concern with the discrepancies between the opportunities opening up for men and the constraints closing in on women.

This concern appears most obviously in the locale of women's humorous stories: the kitchen or the sewing circle, the parlor or the dress shop, rather than the mining camp, the riverboat, the business or political office, or the saloon. The world perceived to be comically askew is the world of children and neighbors and teakettles, of relationships between men and women in the family and in society, of all that constituted what has traditionally been designated women's "proper sphere." Throughout the nineteenth century, most female humorists took as their subjects the domestic environment that formed a large part of their acquaintance with the world: the home, courtship and marriage, and those community activities assumed to be the special province of women—shopping, volunteer work, church and school groups. Ann Warner's "Susan Clegg" stories, for example, published at the turn of the twentieth century, show the garrulous and unconsciously funny Susan enmeshed in housework and the care of her invalid father, having postponed thoughts of marriage in order to fill the role of housekeeper and nurse. Even Emily Dickinson, who did not participate directly in most community activities, comments ironically on woman's "sphere" and the social perception of her role, and the imagery of domestic life permeates both her comic and serious poetry.

Along with this common subject matter, women who have written humor have pursued several common themes. The most pervasive of these has been a concern with the incongruities between the realities of women's lives and the sentimental or idealized images fostered by the culture; between women's awareness of their abilities and ambitions, and their perception of the laws and conventions that have restricted them to a limited sphere of activity. In pointing out these incongruities, female humorists have encouraged an enlargement of woman's sphere and protested the restrictions that, in barring women from utilizing their talents and abilities in the public arena, have countenanced their dissipating their energies in the pursuit of husbands, social status, fashion, spotless floors, perfect bodies, and super momism. Their techniques have included realistic portrayals of women's lives; contrasts between what the authors believe to be strong, positive images of women and weak, negative stereotypes; and deflation of masculine notions of male superiority.

These themes and techniques were first evident in nineteenth-century works, from Anna Cora Mowatt's popular comedy *Fashion* (1850) to Marietta Holley's "Samantha Allen" series, published between 1873 and 1914. While Mowatt satirizes the genteel pretensions and frivolous behavior of middle-class urban women through the characters of Mrs. Tiffany and her daughter, she also shows, through the contrasting character of Gertrude Truelove, that women become virtuous and self-reliant when they are raised with traditional rural values and taught the skills with which to support themselves. Frances Whitcher's work also ridicules the excesses of gentility by using women as both subjects and objects of her humor. The Widow Bedott, the narrator of her most popular work, is a garrulous, middle-aged widow obsessed with finding a second husband. In lampooning Bedott and her circle for self-righteousness and malicious gossiping, however, Whitcher did not intend, as did her male counterparts, merely to perpetuate negative stereotypes of women. Rather, as her "Aunt Maguire" letters and her novel *Mary Elmer* illustrate, she hoped to motivate change by depicting the ways in which women betray their nature, themselves, and each other by adopting the cold, commercial values of the male world. Marietta Holley, whose books rivaled Mark Twain's in sales at the turn of the twentieth century, followed Whitcher's Aunt Maguire in creating as her spokesperson Samantha Allen, an unsophisticated farm wife who combines commonsense practicality with the simple logic born of experience. Through Samantha's discussions of her domestic responsibilities with Betsey Bobbet—another caricature of a sentimental spinster given to perorations about women as ivy needing man as oak to cling to—Holley exposes the contradictions between the illusions and the realities of married life. In the twentieth century, the tradition of using contrasting characters to explore the conflict between the real and ideal is continued in the juxtaposition of the compulsive Mrs. Hicks to the slovenly Mrs. Kettle in Betty MacDonald's *The Egg and I*, and of black domestic servant and white employer in Alice Childress's *Like One of the Family*.

This conflict between real and ideal serves to point up another theme in women's humor: the need to be taken seriously. Sara Willis Parton, for example, a newspaper columnist who published two volumes of articles titled *Fern Leaves from Fanny's Port-Folio* (1853 and 1854) using the pseudonym Fanny Fern, is in the tradition of those, from Bradstreet to Beatts, who have attacked male attitudes toward women writers, as well as exposed the difficulties of trying to combine a literary career with housework and child rearing. As a social commentator, she used satire to expose, in particular, the ways in which an obsession with power and money corrupts. As an advocate of education and independence for women, she challenged the idea that married women were happy, or at least happier than single women, echoing Judith Sargent Murray in attributing much of the unhappiness in marriage to imbalances of power and calling for greater equality for women. Harriet Beecher Stowe's "The Minister's Housekeeper" similarly urges a revision of women's talent and worth, as represented by the efficiency and common sense of Huldy. And Marietta Holley, in her twenty-one humorous books, used Samantha Allen in part to illustrate that although "women's work" has been presumed to be trivial, it is, in fact, important and should be taken seriously. As Samantha avows in Holley's first book, *My Opinions and Betsey Bobbet's* (1873), "Why jest the idee of paradin' out the table and teakettle 3 times 3 hundred and 65 times every year is enough to make a woman sweat."[8] Women's work was also vehemently defended by Phyllis McGinley for several decades of the twentieth century and, slyly, by Shirley Jackson, who remarks in *Life among the Savages* (1953) after a flurry of housework and child care, "I don't care what *any*one says, that's a morning's work."[9]

Taking women seriously, for Marietta Holley, also meant granting them equal rights, and by focusing on the issues that most concerned women's rights proponents of the late nineteenth century—suffrage, temperance, entry into the professions, equal pay for equal work—Holley introduced a feminist theme that sharply distinguishes women's humor from men's. As Jane Curry notes in her introduction to *Samantha Rastles the Woman Question,* a selection of excerpts from Holley's books, "When one reads the Samantha books, she begins to view the 19th century not as 'then' so much as it was the beginning of 'now.' "[10] Like Jonathan Slick, the "wise fool" figure of Ann Stephens's work, and the popular personae of early nineteenth-century "Down East" humor, Samantha exposes pretentiousness and hypocrisy through her ability to see and call a spade a spade. Throughout the many Samantha books, Holley's implacable logic contrasts with other people's illogicality of sentiment or prejudice. In her first book, for example, Holley reverses the traditional images of the genders, depicting Josiah, Samantha's husband, as physically smaller and weaker than she, less rational, more susceptible to fads and fashions, and more dependent. Consequently, the arguments advanced by Josiah against women's rights—based on popular notions of woman's weakness, fickleness, and irrationality—are reduced to absurdity. Holley's use of ironic role reversal and her concern with social issues, particularly political equality for women, anticipate the suffrage work of Alice Duer Miller and Josephine Daskam in the early twentieth century, as well as the more recent feminist humor of the 1970s and 1980s. Similar techniques have been used by ethnic humorists to undermine the cultural assumptions of inferiority that have been used to deny them equal rights.

By the turn of the century, some of the characteristics that had distinguished women's humor through the nineteenth century began to change as American humor in general began to reflect the shift in population from rural areas to the cities and as new magazines emerged to appeal to the values and tastes of an increasingly urbane, cosmopolitan audience for humor. Providing outlets for cartoons, light verse, and humorous sketches that emphasized sophisticated wordplay rather than dialect humor, these new publications also reflected the new interest of an urban cultural elite in technological advances, in the social sciences and psychology, and in the images of the "new woman" and "little man" that were transforming American life.

The increased freedom that women achieved in the decades just before and after the passage of the suffrage amendment in 1920, at the same time that men were experiencing what Norris Yates describes as a diminution of their status and influence,[11] contributed to the "war between the sexes" that American humorists of both genders waged in their work during the first three decades of the twentieth century. At the same time, the new freedoms for women increased the opportunities for social mingling of men and women, while the growth of the media promoted a popular culture of interests and activities, fads and fashions that cut across gender and even class lines. In Bruère and Beard's selection of humor by women after 1900, these shifts are apparent both in the subject matter and in the publications in which the humor originally appeared. Working as journalists, columnists, and cartoonists for major newspapers in New York and Chicago and for magazines such as *Harper's, The New Yorker, Vanity Fair, The Saturday Evening Post,* and even political organs such as the *New Leader,* these early twentieth-century female humorists had a less restricted audience than did many of their nineteenth-century counterparts. Consequently, their humor reflects greater diversity of subject matter, as well as concern with gender roles and relationships in a rapidly changing society.

One indication of these changes is that the prevalent nineteenth-century notions of separate spheres for men and women and of distinct masculine and feminine natures and functions do not serve as a basic premise for this later humor. For example, in the political satire of Alice Duer Miller and Charlotte Perkins Gilman, it is not women's special, feminine contributions that are emphasized to justify their gaining the vote so much as their simple right as human beings in a democratic society to legal and political equality with men. Similarly, tacit assumptions about woman's moral superiority, nurturing qualities, and instinctive sensitivity to others are challenged by writers such as Josephine Daskam, Helen Rowland, and Florence Guy Seabury, who work both with and against established stereotypes of men and women to give the genders "realistic" advice about, and images of, each other. Moreover, in the work of such writers as Dorothy Parker and Anita Loos, who deal with the "war between the sexes," women characters are portrayed as being just as morally and psychologically confused, self-absorbed, and manipulative as their male counterparts. Finally, the expansion of women's options is reflected in Mary Roberts Rinehart's "Tish" stories, published between 1910 and 1937, which present an embodiment of the "new woman" in the attitudes and behavior of Letitia "Tish" Carberry, an independent spinster who, content with her single status, engages herself and two spinster friends in a variety of activities and adventures, from automobile racing, flying, and camping to catching crooks and even liberating a town from the Germans in World War I.

Despite the proliferation in the early decades of the twentieth century of female humorists exhibiting a wide diversity in style, form, and subject matter, the main thread that continued to run through women's humor of the 1930s and 1940s was the "little woman," the counterpart of the "little man" of male humorists such as Thurber and Benchley. Whether urban, suburban, or rural, the young housewives and new mothers depicted first by Parker and later by Cornelia Otis Skinner and Betty MacDonald are as bewildered by the conflicting demands of other people, as controlled by the technology and bureaucracy of modern life, and as intimidated by their own fear of failure as the "little men."

By the fifties and sixties, the "little woman" had become the housewife heroine of the "domestic" humor that dominated the period. Inspired by the post-World War II campaign to return the American woman to the home, this humor concerns the trials and tribulations of middle-class housewives who, in increasing numbers, inhabited suburban communities featuring commuting husbands, children, and other frantic women. Disseminated primarily in magazines and sections of newspapers addressed to women, this humor spoke to an audience that could be characterized by the title of Phyllis McGinley's poem "Occupation: Housewife." Like their nineteenth-century forebears, these women were cut off from the public world of business and enterprise that their husbands inhabited and restricted to a routine of domestic chores and child rearing. Domestic humor provided a way for both writer and audience to minimize through laughter, and thereby better cope with, the frustrations and demands of their lives.

Betty Friedan's 1963 analysis of the housewife's discontent, *The Feminine Mystique,* not only helped to spark the rebirth of a movement for female equality but also abetted the emergence in the late sixties and early seventies of a feminist humor more overt and aggressive than the political humor of the suffrage era. The women who created this humor were influenced by the iconoclastic style and irreverent tone of a new generation of black and white male comics, beginning with Lenny Bruce, whose political and social satire appealed to increasing numbers of college students and young adults who were in rebellion against the competitive and conformist values of the fifties and inspired by the civil rights and peace movements of the sixties.

Selecting specific agents of oppression as targets, women humorists of the seventies and eighties attacked the greater privilege and freedom of men, derided patriarchal institutions, and ridiculed social, sexual, and racial stereotyping. Influenced by the new wave of male comics, women humorists have appropriated subject matter once considered taboo for women, accepting the totality of female experience—including sexual relationships, menstruation, lesbianism, anxieties about one's attractiveness, and the ineptitude of men—as material for humor. Moreover, humorists such as Erica Jong have addressed these topics with a bawdy tone and in graphic sexual and scatological terms that, because they came from a woman, still shock or offend segments of the population. Although domestic humor has maintained its popularity alongside feminist and new wave humor, women's humor of the seventies and eighties has generally become more confrontational on social and political issues, rather than sly or cute.

NOTES

1. Deanne Stillman and Anne Beatts, eds., *Titters: The First Collection of Humor by Women* (New York: Collier, 1976), 4.
2. Mahadev L. Apte, *Humor and Laughter: An Anthropological Approach* (Ithaca, N.Y.: Cornell University Press, 1985), 69.
3. Ibid., 70.
4. Naomi Weisstein, "Why We Aren't Laughing . . . Anymore," *Ms.* (November 1973): 89.
5. Martha Bensley Bruère and Mary Ritter Beard, eds., *Laughing Their Way: Women's Humor in America* (New York: Macmillan, 1934), viii.
6. Neil Schmitz, *Of Huck and Alice: Humorous Writing in American Literature* (Minneapolis: University of Minnesota Press, 1983), 210.
7. Josephine Donovan, *New England Local Color Literature* (New York: Frederick Ungar, 1982), 26.
8. Marietta Holley, *My Opinions and Betsey Bobbet's* (Hartford: American Publishing, 1873), 59.
9. Shirley Jackson, *Life among the Savages* (New York: Farrar, Straus and Young, 1953), 2.
10. Jane Curry, Introduction to *Samantha Rastles the Women Question* (Urbana: University of Illinois Press, 1983), 1.
11. Norris Yates, *The American Humorist: Conscience of the Twentieth Century* (Ames: Iowa State University Press, 1964), 38.

M. THOMAS INGE

10 Comics as Culture

M. Thomas Inge has written extensively on both American popular culture and Southern literature. Among his many books are *Faulkner, Sut, and Other Southerners: Essays on Literary History* (1992) and *Perspectives on American Culture: Essays on Humor, Literature, and the Popular Arts* (1994). For several decades, Inge has been the leading expert on one of the most widespread and familiar forms of American humor: comic art in the form of the comic strip and the comic book. The comic strip, which began in the 1890s, is one of America's truly original art forms, and it has become a feature of daily life for most Americans as well as achieving popularity in other countries. Inge's central point in *Comics as Culture* is that the comic strip and the comic book are not isolated phenomena but have been closely tied to other aspects of American culture. They reinforce some of America's most cherished values, they have influenced and been influenced by American literature, and they have contributed words to the vocabulary and visual images of the American experience.

The comic strip may be defined as an open-ended dramatic narrative about a recurring set of characters, told in a series of drawings, often including dialogue in balloons and a narrative text, and published serially in newspapers. The daily and Sunday comic strips are part of the reading habits of more than one hundred million people of all educational and social levels. During the first half of this century, surveys have indicated that sixty percent of newspaper readers consider the comic page the priority feature in

From M. Thomas Inge, *Comics as Culture* (Jackson: University Press of Mississippi, 1990), xi–xii, xiv–xv, xvii–xxi. Reprinted by permission of the University Press of Mississippi.

their reading. Along with jazz, the comic strip as we know it perhaps represents America's major indigenous contribution to world culture.

Comic books, on the other hand, originally an offshoot of the comic strip, are regarded with considerable suspicion by parents, educators, psychiatrists, and moral reformers. More than one critic has called them crude, vulgar, and ultimately corrupting. They have been investigated by governmental committees and subjected to severe censorship. Yet even in today's uncertain market, more than two hundred million copies are sold a year, and the comic book collecting business has become an important area of investment with its own price guide and publications to facilitate exchange and trade.

Any phenomenon which plays so heavily on the sensibility of the American populace deserves study purely for sociological reasons if for no other. The comics serve as revealing reflectors of popular attitudes, tastes, and mores. Because comic strips appear in daily newspapers, a publication designed for family consumption, the syndicates, editors, and publishers submit strips to the severest kind of scrutiny and control to be sure that no parent, political bloc, or advertiser whose support they court will take offense. In the thirties conservative Harold Gray once had to redraw a *Little Orphan Annie* sequence because of its attack on one of Franklin Delano Roosevelt's New Deal programs, and the liberal slanted *Pogo* strip by Walt Kelly was often banned in the fifties in southern newspapers because of its satiric thrusts at school segregationists.

Examine the comics in any daily newspaper and each will be found to support some commonly accepted notion or standard of society. *Blondie, Archie, Mary Worth, Li'l Abner,* and *Gasoline Alley* in different ways support the idea that the family is the basic social unit. *Judge Parker, Rex Morgan, Mark Trail,* and *Gil Thorpe* support the concepts of decency and fair play among the professions. While *The Wizard of Id, B.C., Peanuts, Funky Winkerbean, Doonesbury, Bloom County,* and *Shoe* are overtly satirical, they also provide a rational standard against which the aberrations they portray can be measured and found laughable. Why is Andy Capp, who drinks heavily, gambles, and commits adultery, permitted to violate these social taboos on the pages of the funny papers? Possibly because he is British and Americans are willing to forgive such behavior on the part of Europeans. It is little wonder that Andy has such a large following—he is a stubbornly unpredictable and incorrigible individualist among many repetitious and mindless Caspar Milquetoasts. In the 1980s, I should note, a few strips have daringly dealt with such hitherto forbidden topics as homosexuality, pre-marital sex, unmarried teenage mothers, and mental retardation, but with trepidation and frequent local censorship.

Comic books are submitted for approval prior to publication to the Comics Code Authority, which exercises the most severe censorship applied to any mass media. Guidelines prohibit displays of sex, adultery, divorce, drugs, corrupt authority, or unpunished crimes. Submission to the authority requires a medium mainly irrelevant to reality; thus characters escape into a world of fantasy, dominated by superheroes, a world in which both might and right are on the side of morality. When needed to support his country in time of war, however, no superhero has ever dared to refuse. The recent development of adult comic books and graphic novels, it should be noted, as well as alternative methods of publication and distribution have greatly eroded the influence of the Authority.

The underground press comic strips and books of the 1960s and 1970s, which came into being partly to defy the restrictions of the Comics Code Authority, ironically failed to escape the basically political nature of American comic art. The defiance of American materialism by Robert Crumb, however, approaches anarchy, the rejection of society's sexual taboos by S. Clay Wilson is absolute, and the doomsday vision of Spain Rodriguez predicts the total destruction of civilization. These are radical stances beyond the pale of political ideology, but the underground cartoonists had the incredible luxury of unrestricted artistic freedom. This freedom has yielded brilliant results in the work of Art Spiegelman and Harvey Pekar, both of whom emerged from the underground comic book movement. Spiegelman's impressive retelling of the Holocaust in animal fable form *Maus*, haunting and moving in its intelligence and sincerity, brought a nomination for a National Book Critics Circle Award in 1987, the first comic book to be so honored, and Harvey Pekar's philosophic disquisitions on the nature of mundane life in Cleveland collected in *American Splendor* and *More American Splendor* in 1986 and 1987, have made him an influential force on the national cultural scene. These are obviously comic books with a serious purpose and something important to say about modern human life and history.

The comics also derive from popular patterns, themes, and symbols of Western culture. Chester Gould credited Sherlock Holmes as the inspiration for Dick Tracy (compare the shape of their noses), and Superman was partly based on Philip Wylie's 1930 novel *Gladiator*.

Bringing Up Father, better known as "Maggie and Jiggs," by George McManus was inspired by a popular play, *The Rising Generation,* and Philip Nowlan based *Buck Rogers* on his own short story "Armageddon 2419." Dick Tracy's gallery of grotesque villains draws on the gothic tradition and follows the medieval concept that the outward appearance reflects the inner character. Flash Gordon, Prince Valiant, Captain Marvel, and the Fantastic Four draw on the heroic tradition to which Hercules, Samson, King Arthur, Beowulf, Davy Crockett, and Paul Bunyan belong.

If the comics have absorbed much of Western tradition, they have also had their influence on popular language and culture. Word coinages deriving from comic strips, and still found in general currency, include *jeep, baloney, yardbird, horsefeathers, google-eyed,* and *twenty-three skidoo.* There are Rube Goldberg contraptions and Mickey Mouse college courses. Certain foods are inextricably associated with certain characters: Popeye's spinach, Wimpy's hamburgers, Jiggs's corned beef and cabbage, and Dagwood's incredible sandwiches. Buster Brown clothes and shoes can still be bought, and the Prince Valiant haircut has been popular at times. While Charlie Brown did not invent the expletive "Good Grief!" it will be a long time before anyone can use the phrase without automatically associating it with Charles Schulz's diminutive loser in the game of life.

Perhaps a major reason for recognizing and studying the comics is the fact that they are one of the few native American art forms. Literature, drama, music, film, and the other forms of popular culture were largely established in Europe and most American practitioners (with perhaps the exception of film) have followed the patterns and standards established by foreign masters—Joyce in the novel, Ibsen in the drama, or the Beatles in popular music. In the comic strip and comic book, however, Americans have defined the forms, expanded their aesthetic possibilities, and become the first masters of their unique visual and narrative potential. Winsor McCay, George Herriman, Alex Raymond, Hal Foster, Roy Crane, Milton Caniff, Will Eisner, and Harvey Kurtzman are just a few of the internationally recognized geniuses of the comic strip, and all are Americans.

In a great variety of ways, the comics have influenced the general culture of the United States and the world. Pablo Picasso was supplied with American funny papers in France by his friend Gertrude Stein, and he drew inspiration from them for much of his work, such as *The Dream and the Lie of Franco* (1937). When samples of George Herriman's brilliant *Krazy Kat* pages circulated in France, they were recognized as early examples of Dada art, and a few great modern masters, such as George B. Luks and Lyonel Feininger, produced comic pages early in their careers. The pop art movement of the 1960s witnessed the wholesale appropriation of the forms, symbols, and style of comic art for the individual aesthetic intentions of a number of contemporary artists such as Andy Warhol, Roy Lichtenstein, Mel Ramos, Claes Oldenburg, and Ray Yoshida, among others. They saw the iconography of comic art as an appropriate idiom for communicating their contemporary visions. Comic imagery is liable to crop up in the most unlikely places. In Crystal City, Texas, the "Spinach Capital of the World," there stands a statue of Popeye, erected by a grateful community. The command module of the crew of Apollo 10 answered to "Charlie Brown," while the LEM was named "Snoopy." Blondie has helped sell margarine in Norway, and in France Mandrake the Magician once promoted Renault automobiles. The Phantom is the subject of a series of highly popular novels published in ten languages throughout all of Europe.

In addition to their sociological value and their cultural significance, the comics are also of importance unto themselves, as a form of creative expression apart from their relationship to other forms of art. This is the most difficult area to write about because we lack the critical vocabulary and have only begun to define the structural and stylistic principles behind successful comic art. Instead we tend to rely on terms borrowed from other areas of creative expression.

For example, we can talk about the comics as a form of communication and how they can be used as propaganda, in advertising, for the dissemination of information, or as instructional aids. Reading teachers have only recently begun to realize the effectiveness of comic books in teaching reluctant or unresponsive children to read—fascinated by the pictures and the story being portrayed, they are led to study the words to figure out what is happening. Contrary to the notion that comic book reading serves as a cop-out and escape from reading "real" books, young readers are often led to novels and plays after reading the comic book adaptations, in the same way adults want to read a book after viewing the movie version of it (a trend so popular that now a book is often not written until after the film version has been released).

We can talk about the comics as graphic art, and clearly the visual attraction is the first thing that captures our attention. The comic artist must confront and solve the same problems of spatial relationships, balance, and form that every artist must face, and nearly all modern artistic movements and styles have either been anticipated by or reflected in the comics. In the case of pop art, they inspired a whole school of painting.

Narration or storytelling is also a main function of the comics. They are meant to be read, as opposed to traditional narrative art meant to be viewed and interpreted. While they have never competed with the classics, they have seriously altered popular reading habits by attracting readers away from pulp magazines, dime novels, and cheap tabloids (only detective and science fiction have withstood the competition and survived). The total work of some cartoonists constitutes something like a novel on the pattern of Balzac's human comedy or Faulkner's Yoknapatawpha County cycle. *Little Orphan Annie* follows the picaresque pattern of *Adventures of Huckleberry Finn,* and *Gasoline Alley* anatomizes an entire midwestern community much in the tradition of Sherwood Anderson's *Winesburg, Ohio* or Sinclair Lewis's *Main Street* (especially with the recent emphasis by Dick Moores and his successor Jim Scancarelli on the provincial grotesque).

It has been suggested that the comics are closest to drama in that both rely on the dramatic conventions of character, dialogue, scene, gesture, compressed time, and stage devices, but probably the motion picture is closer. Will Eisner, distinguished for his visual innovations in comic art, has stated that "comics are movies on paper." Eisner's work in *The Spirit* has always demonstrated a brilliant use of angle shots, framing, lighting, mood, and detail characteristic of the film medium. When William Friedkin, producer of *The French Connection, The Exorcist,* and other films, announced his intention to do a film version of *The Spirit* for television, he paid tribute to Eisner's influence on his own work: "Look at the dramatic use of montage, of light and sound. See the dynamic framing that Eisner employs, and the deep vibrant colors. Many film directors have been influenced by *The Spirit,* myself included." Displaying an Eisner cover with a man being chased by an elevated train, Friedkin noted, "This is where I got ideas for the chase in *The French Connection.*" Federico Fellini, Orson Welles, Alain Resnais, and George Lucas are other film makers who have acknowledged their indebtedness to the comics for cinematic concepts and techniques. In fact, many standard techniques were first employed in the comics—montage (before Eisenstein), angle shots, panning, closeups, cutting, framing, etc.

Yet none of these relationships and functions discussed so far elucidate comic art for the distinctive and separate medium it happens to be. Text, artwork, and meaning cannot be judged independently of the whole work. Word and picture interact in the best examples without one dominating the other, and quite literally the medium is the message. There has been nothing else quite like comic art on the cultural scene since the invention of the novel for potential in creative challenge and imaginative opportunity.

Historical studies, biographies, critical appreciations, anthologies, encyclopedias, and periodicals on the subjects of comic art and artists have begun to proliferate in recent years. Partly this has resulted from publishers wishing to tap the lucrative nostalgia market, but in many cases because individuals have begun to recognize the importance of documenting this part of our national heritage. The study of comics has become a part of high school, college, and university curricula throughout the country and abroad, and numerous museums have hosted major exhibitions of original comic art. At least five research centers now exist in the United States and are available to scholars: the San Francisco Academy of Comic Art; the Museum of Cartoon Art in Rye/Port Chester, New York; the Library for Communication and Graphic Arts at Ohio State University in Columbus; the Russel B. Nye Collection of Popular Culture at Michigan State University in East Lansing; and the Cartoon Art Museum in San Francisco.

Those who hesitate to accept comic art as a significant form of expression might remember that Shakespeare was once merely a contributor to Elizabethan popular culture who spoke to the pit as well as the gallery (and ultimately the ages), and it took decades for the elite to grant his work the respectability it deserved. Perhaps the day will come when some of our major comic artists will be granted the place they deserve in the pantheon of American culture. . . .

The comics are a form of legitimate culture quite capable of confronting the major questions of mankind, but they do it with a gentler spirit that leads to laughter at the moment of recognition. The comics are well and deservedly loved, but they should also be respected for what they have contributed to the visual and narrative arts of the world.

LAWRENCE E. MINTZ

11 | Stand-up Comedy as Social and Cultural Mediation

In the 1970s and 1980s many who studied and wrote about American humor were turning their attention to media other than the printed page. Lawrence E. Mintz, who has also written about racial and ethnic humor and who edited *Humor in America: A Research Guide to Genres and Topics* (1988), is a scholar particularly interested in comic performance, both live and on the screen. What we today call "stand-up comedy," in which a single comedian performs a comic monologue for an audience in a nightclub or a comedy club, actually has a long history; Mintz, in fact, maintains that it is the oldest form of humorous expression other than the joke. In "Stand-up Comedy as Social and Cultural Mediation," Mintz defines this humorous genre broadly, and concentrates on how such a comic performance works within society to create a sense of shared values and assumptions.

Stand-up comedy is arguably the oldest, most universal, basic, and deeply significant form of humorous expression (excluding perhaps truly spontaneous, informal social joking and teasing). It is the purest public comic communication, performing essentially the same social and cultural roles in practically every known society, past and present. Studies dealing with humor often begin

From Lawrence E. Mintz, "Stand-up Comedy as Social and Cultural Mediation," *American Quarterly* 37, no. 1 (1985): 71–80. © 1985 by The Johns Hopkins University Press. Reprinted by permission of The Johns Hopkins University Press.

with defensive, half-hearted apologies for taking so light a subject seriously or for failing to reproduce the spirit and tone of the entertainment examined; this one will argue that humor is a vitally important social and cultural phenomenon, that the student of a culture and society cannot find a more revealing index to its values, attitudes, dispositions, and concerns, and that the relatively undervalued genre of stand-up comedy (compared with film comedy or humorous literature, for example) is the most interesting of all the manifestations of humor in the popular culture. In this essay, at least, Rodney Dangerfield and his colleagues will finally get some respect.

A strict, limiting definition of stand-up comedy would describe an encounter between a single, standing performer behaving comically and/or saying funny things directly to an audience, unsupported by very much in the way of costume, prop, setting, or dramatic vehicle. Yet stand-up comedy's roots are, as I shall discuss below, entwined with rites, rituals, and dramatic experiences that are richer, more complex than this simple definition can embrace. We must therefore broaden our scope at least to include seated storytellers, comic characterizations that employ costume and prop, team acts (particularly the staple two-person comedy teams), manifestations of stand-up comedy routines and motifs within dramatic vehicles such as skits, improvisational situations, and films (for example, Bob Hope in his "Road" pictures, the Marx Brothers movies), and television sitcoms (Jack Benny's television show, Robin Williams in *Mork and Mindy*). To avoid also having to include all theatrical comedy and its media spinoffs, however, our definition should stress relative directness of artist/audience communication and the proportional importance of comic behavior and comic dialogue versus the development of plot and situation. Such a definition is hardly pure, but it is workable.

Stand-up comedy has been an important feature of American popular culture since its earliest days.[1] Popular theater incorporated variety comedy as complement to the main plot. Circus clowns provided verbal stand-up comedy in the early years of these productions, as well as physical and prop comedy, in the tradition of fools, jesters, clowns, and comics, which can be traced back at least as far as the Middle Ages. The enormously popular minstrel theater featured the comic interaction of the two end-men, Tambo and Bones, and the Interlocutor, a straight-man, as well as various comedy routines within the show itself. The lecture circuit in the nineteenth century supported dozens of successful humorists, the most famous of whom were Mark Twain and Artemus

Ward. Medicine shows, tent shows, and other traveling variety entertainments all boasted stand-up comedy as a central element.

In the twentieth century, stand-up comedy has been the back-
bone of vaudeville and burlesque and the variety theater (for example,
Earl Carroll's *Vanities,* the *Ziegfeld Follies*), as well as nightclub and
resort entertainment. More recently, stand-up comedy has spawned a
popular entertainment movement of its own, the comedy clubs, where
a rather lengthy bill of comics have exclusive possession of the stage
and audience for a long evening of laughter. Stand-up comedy has also
contributed to all of the mass media in America, from the silent films
through radio, to the record industry and, of course, to television. Clearly
it is a popular art that is central to American entertainment, but in the
universal tradition of public joking rituals it is more than that as well;
it is an important part of the nation's cultural life.

The motives and functions of stand-up comedy are complex,
ambiguous, and to some extent paradoxical. Anthropologists and sociologists have paid some attention to teasing relationships and the
roles of social joking. Students of theater and humor have recognized
comedy's more profound aspects, but there is no developed study of
the social and cultural functions of stand-up comedy as such. In his
book, *Heroes, Villains, and Fools,* Orrin Klapp does, however, briefly
mention a few of the functions of stand-up comedy in his discussion
of fools. He observes that

> Every kind of society seems to find fool types useful in: sublimation
> of aggression, relief from routine and discipline, control by
> ridicule (less severe and disruptive than vilification), affirming
> standards of propriety (paradoxically by flouting followed by
> comic punishment), and unification through what Henri Bergson
> and Kenneth Burke have called the communion of laughter.[2]

In her vitally important work on public joking, the anthropologist
Mary Douglas emphasizes properly that the contexts and processes of
joke telling are at least as important as the texts of the jokes themselves
to any understanding of the meaning of humor. This is obviously the
case with stand-up comedy performance as well. As Douglas observes,
"the joke form rarely lies in the utterance alone, but . . . can be identified in the total social situation." Douglas further concerns herself with
the joking activity as *rite* and *anti-rite,* or as public affirmation of
shared cultural beliefs and as a reexamination of these beliefs. She notes
that the structure of jokes tends to be subversive; in other words,

jokes tear down, distort, misrepresent, and reorder usual patterns of expression and perception. Yet she also agrees with Victor Turner that the *experience* of public joking, shared laughter, and celebration of agreement on what deserves ridicule and affirmation fosters community and furthers a sense of mutual support for common belief and behavior (hence *rite*).[3]

Turner's work is also helpful when thinking about stand-up comedy. His concept of "plural reflexivity," or "the ways in which a group or community seeks to portray, understand, and then act on itself" has important implications for our understanding of art, popular culture, and humor. In addition, his discussion of *liminal* or *liminoid* activity in the rituals of performance and of artistic expression is potentially adaptable to a theory of public comedy. Turner sees rituals as an opportunity for society to explore, affirm, deny, and ultimately to change its structure and its values:

> Public liminality can never be tranquilly regarded as a safety valve, mere catharsis, "letting off steam," rather it is communitas weighing structure, sometimes finding it wanting, and proposing in however extravagant a form, new paradigms and models which invert or subvert the old.[4]

Other writers whose work contributes to this view of the social functions of comedy include Hugh Dalziel Duncan in his book *Communication and the Social Order* (1970), and William Martineau in his article outlining the various social motives of humor.[5]

The key to understanding the role of stand-up comedy in the process of cultural affirmation and subversion is a recognition of the comedian's traditional *license* for deviate behavior and expression. Probably originating in the cruel but natural practice of ridiculing physical and mental defectives, this license presents a paradox crucial to the development of the stand-up comedy tradition. Traditionally, the comedian is defective in some way, but his natural weaknesses generate pity, and more important, exemption from the expectation of normal behavior. He is thus presented to his audience as marginal. Because he is physically and mentally incapable of proper action, we forgive and even bless his "mistakes." This marginality, however, also allows for a fascinating ambiguity and ambivalence. In his role as a *negative exemplar,* we laugh *at* him. He represents conduct to be ridiculed and rejected, and our laughter reflects our superiority, our relief that his weaknesses are greater than our own and that he survives them with only the mild punishment of verbal scorn. Yet to the extent that we may identify with his expression or behavior, secretly recognize it as reflecting natural tendencies in human activity if not socially approved ones, or publicly affirm it under the guise of "mere comedy," or "just kidding," he can become our *comic spokesman*.[6] In this sense, as a part of the public ritual of stand-up comedy, he serves as a *shaman*,[7] leading us in a celebration of a community of shared culture, of homogeneous understanding and expectation.

The oldest, most basic role of the comedian is precisely this role of *negative exemplar*. The grotesque, the buffoon, the fool, the simpleton, the scoundrel, the drunkard, the liar, the coward, the effete, the tightwad, the boor, the egoist, the cuckold, the shrew, the weakling, the neurotic, and other such reifications of socially unacceptable traits are enacted by the comedian to be ridiculed, laughed at, repudiated, and, finally, symbolically "punished." Modern American stand-up comedy reflects the universal range of this phenomenon, from Jerry Lewis's grotesques, to the many fools and simpletons of the genre: Jackie Gleason's Poor Soul, Irwin Corey's mindless professor, Dean Martin's drunkard, the legion of "transvestites," and the "little men" or weaklings portrayed by such comics as Woody Allen and Rodney Dangerfield, among others. We laugh at the egotism of Bob Hope and Jack Benny, at the frustration of Alan King, the sex-role inadequacy of Joan Rivers and Phyllis Diller, the promiscuity of Redd Foxx and Richard Pryor, the boorishness of Steve Martin and Martin Mull, and at a host of other follies and frustrations reflected by the army of self-deprecating comedians whose domestic life is a disaster, whose battles with everyday life become overwhelming routs, and whose flaws are immense exaggerations of all we fear and reject in our own self-definitions.

Though the time-honored function of the stand-up comedian has been to provide a butt for our humor, this function is perhaps less interesting, even less important than his role as our comic *spokesperson*, as a mediator, an "articulator" of our culture, and as our contemporary *anthropologist*.[8] To be sure, the separation of the two roles is rarely absolute or even entirely clear. For instance, Joan Rivers's comic persona is established as essentially negative. We laugh at her characterization of herself as a failed or flawed woman, because she is unattractive, lacks the proper female attributes, is unpopular, rejected by parents and friends, and inept in domestic skills such as cooking and housekeeping. Yet over the years her act has begun to emphasize an expression of pride in these very "failings." Rivers in fact often seems aggressively to repudiate these traditional cultural values, and to attack more "perfect" cultural role models, such as Elizabeth Taylor and Cheryl Tiegs. She seems to engage in a conspiracy with women in the audience to reject male demands that women fulfill their romantic and domestic fantasies. Indeed she shares the perspective with Phyllis Diller, another stand-up comedienne, and with Erma Bombeck, the columnist and comic-lecturer. It seems likely, therefore, that these female comics are voicing changing attitudes about gender roles that have begun to take hold in American society as a result of the most recent wave of feminist agitation.

Similarly, Alan King serves as a comic spokesperson for contemporary Americans by outlining his frustrations with the bureaucracy, with doctors, with all of the pitfalls of modern American life. His persona, however, is also clearly negative; he is a bully, a boor, a malcontent, a loudmouth, and a loser.

The ambiguity, then, is an essential feature of an audience's reaction to stand-up comedy.

Redd Foxx's Las Vegas routine, like so many other comic acts, is based on a persona that is sexually libertine. He is a constant violator of both verbal and behavioral taboos. I witnessed one of his sets, for instance, in which virtually all of his jokes dealt with the topic of oral sex. Foxx presented himself as a successful practitioner of these taboo arts and repeatedly claimed that all successful lovers indulge in the techniques whether nor not they admit it. The audience laughed loudly and enthusiastically, but a close look at the physical responses in the room revealed two different types of laughing behavior. The older people in the audience gasped, flinched, physically backed away while laughing at the punchlines, and frequently looked at each other nervously, perhaps for confirmation that the license of comedy was still in effect. They seemed to be saying to themselves and each other, "Can you believe that he is as daring to say these things in public? Isn't this exciting, dangerous stuff?" The younger people in the audience were laughing in a manner that I term "anthemic." They leaned *toward* Foxx, often applauded, raised their hands or fists as though cheering a political speaker with whom they were in agreement, while occasionally yelling, "yeah," or "right on," or "all right," or just yelping with delight. For them Foxx was the counter-culture spokesman with the courage (and the comically protected situation) to state publicly and openly that the sexual taboo against oral sex was, in their view at least, no longer valid or operative. Foxx led them in an expression of their cultural truths.

This role of the comedian as social commentator is surely not a new one. Shakespeare made extensive use of the fool's traditional license to have the innocent but sharp, shrewd observer speak the "truth" which was universally recognized but politically taboo. If nineteenth-century Americans laughed *at* the racist images of Tambo and Bones for their licentiousness, they probably also laughed *with* their Dionysian freedom to enjoy life and their common-sense victories over the stuffy, pompous, dull Interlocutor. No doubt, they identified also with their topical commentaries expressing the democratic, popular, if often cynical, opposition to "official" social attitudes and public positions.[9] Twain, Ward, and the other platform lecturers similarly offered a down-to-earth, comically acceptable, but "opposition line" to the views of polite society. Ethnic and blue-collar comics of vaudeville and the variety theater were vulnerable fools, frequently, but they also won ironic victories and expressed many of the social proclivities of their audiences, as well as a more realistic if not more admirable view of their worlds.

It might be said, then, that the trickster, con-man, and likeable rogue all turn dishonesty, selfishness, disruptive and aggressive behavior, and licentiousness into virtues, or at least into activity that the audience can applaud, laugh with, and celebrate. The pleasure the audience derives from this sanctioned deviance may be related to the ritual violation of taboos, inversion of ritual, and public iconoclasm frequently encountered in cultural traditions. If, as Freud posited, there is a battle going on between our instincts and our socially developed rules of behavior, comedy provides an opportunity for a staged antagonism.[10] Another way of expressing the same process would be as a dialectic in which a thesis—basic human traits and characteristics—is confronted with an antithesis—polite manners and social restraints—with a synthesis perhaps being tolerance or at least a relaxation of hostility and anxiety.[11]

Given this analysis, it is possible to see that our modern American stand-up comedians provide us with some of our most valuable social commentary. While some critics of popular entertainment try to distinguish between a traditional stand-up comedy characterized by an irrelevant quest for laughs, and a so-called new wave comedy which is more socially and politically satiric or insightful, such categorization belies the consistent role of stand-up comedy as social and cultural analysis. Traditional comics like Bob Hope, Johnny Carson, and Alan King are less openly "counter-culture," certainly, but their complaints contain a critique of the gap between what is and what we believe should be. Moreover, the "new wave" comics were not always exclusively, openly political or even satiric. Mort Sahl, Lenny Bruce, Dick Gregory, and others were controversial because many of the issues they addressed were causing social divisions. Yet other "new wave" comedians—Jonathan Winters, Shelley Berman, Mike Nichols and Elaine May, Bill Cosby, and Joan Rivers chose less openly divisive material. Even the informal "new wave" style—casual dress, the use of longer "bits," fewer "punchlines," and more spontaneous improvisation—recalls the nineteenth-century platform lecturers as much as it heralds a break with tradition.[12]

The young comedians currently [mid-1980s] performing on the club circuit[13] reflect the entire range of stand-up comedy performance, from one-liners, verbal games involving puns, malapropisms, double-entendres, and the violation of socially acceptable language taboos to physical and prop comedy, insult comedy, parodies and put-downs of current popular culture, and of course social and political criticism.[14]

Perhaps the best, if not the only, place to witness stand-up comedy as true social and cultural mediation is in live performance, preferably at one of the small comedy clubs or intimate night-club rooms where the interaction between the comedian and the audience is more prominent. The comedian begins by performing two important functions. He or she establishes the nature of the audience by asking questions of a few people close by or by making statements about the audience followed by a call for agreement or acknowledgement (if the audience is too large for the question-and-answer session). This function is often performed by an MC or a warm-up comic, but it is not merely a matter of gathering information. The comedian must establish *for the audience* that the group is homogeneous, a community, if the laughter is to come easily.[15] "Working the room," as comedians term it, loosens the audience and allows for laughter as an expression of shared values rather than as a personal predilection (since people are justifiably nervous about laughing alone and what that might reveal). This interaction with the audience often, but not always, includes ritual insults directed at audience members, and sometimes heckling and the putting down of the heckler (also relaxing the audience, making them feel less vulnerable [it doesn't *really* hurt . . . much . . . even if you are the target]). So-called kamikaze comedians such as Don Rickles make the insult banter a feature of their act, but that is a special brand of stand-up comedy not necessarily connected with the process of establishing a community.

The comedian then establishes his or her comic persona, discussing personal background, lifestyle, and some attitudes and beliefs. This allows the audience to accept the comedian's marginal status and to establish that the mood of comic license is operative. This mood is accentuated by encouraging applause and laughter, thereby establishing a tone of gaiety and fun. Then the comedy routine itself can begin.

The styles of stand-up comedy differ almost as much as the content of jokes and joke routines themselves, but the essence of the art is creative distortion. Such distortion is achieved through exaggeration, stylization, incongruous context, and burlesque. (Treating that which is usually respected disrespectfully and vice versa.) These and other techniques all disrupt expectation and reorder it plausibly but differently from its original state. There are dozens of theories explaining why this is humorous, ranging from formal analyses that stress incongruity reconciled or the simultaneous consideration of opposites to theories that stress socially functional factors such as superiority, hostility, aggression, taboo violation, and so forth.[16] Comedians themselves, like most popular artists, tend to eschew theory in favor of trial-and-error practice ("I don't know why it works and I don't care," "I learn from others and try things out, keeping what works for me," "I express what *I* think is funny and let the audience decide," are the frequently voiced opinions).

The observer has to agree that it does work, most of the time. Audiences laugh and enjoy themselves, but they also express themselves, nodding concurrence, applauding, and offering verbal encouragement. When members of the audience are asked to discuss what they liked about comedy performance and why they liked it, they are usually not much more helpful than the performers. "It was funny," "He was cool, great," "I could really identify with that," "That's just like my life," "He's crazy, really nuts," "He was wild, far out." When pressed they will often assert agreement with the content of the comedy or sympathy with the comedian's persona, but perhaps here they are pushed into such overt self-perception by their knowledge of what the questioner wants to hear.

There is much more work to be done if we are to appreciate properly the role of stand-up comedy in America. An authoritative, comprehensive history of the genre is necessary so that we can appreciate what has changed as well as what has remained constant. Thorough studies of joke texts and comedy routines are needed as well as more careful analyses of forms and techniques. We need ethnographic and demographic research to clarify, to substantiate, and no doubt to correct the theoretical assumptions about the performer-audience relationship and the motives and functions of the ritual. Until stand-up comedy is studied as a social phenomenon, we can only speculate concerning its real meaning. It is safe to say, however, that stand-up comedy in America operates within a universal tradition, both historically and across cultures, that it confronts just about all of the profoundly important aspects of our culture and our society, and that it seems to have an important role allowing for expression of shared beliefs and behavior, changing social roles and expectations.

NOTES

1. There is no comprehensive, definitive history of stand-up comedy in America. Phil Berger calls his book *The Last Laugh* (New York: Morrow, 1975), a history of the genre, but it is impressionistic, more "new journalism" than anything else. Joe Franklin's *Encyclopedia of Comedians* (Secaucus, N.J.: Citadel Press, 1972) is helpful, as are Steve Allen's *Funny Men* (New York: Simon and Schuster, 1956); *Funny People* (New York: Stein and Day, 1981); and *More Funny People* (New York: Stein and Day, 1982).
2. Orrin E. Klapp, *Heroes, Villains, and Fools: The Changing American Character* (Englewood Cliffs, N.J.: Prentice-Hall, 1962), 60.
3. Mary Douglas, "Jokes," in *Implicit Meanings: Essays in Anthropology* (Boston: Routledge & Kegan Paul, 1978), 93.
4. Victor Turner, "Frame Flow, and Reflection: Ritual and Drama as Public Liminality," in Michael Benamou and Charles Caramello, eds., *Performance in Postmodern Culture* (Madison: University of Wisconsin Press, 1977), 33. See also Turner's books, *The Ritual Process: Structure and Anti-Structure* (1966: rpt. Ithaca: Cornell University Press, 1977); and *Dramas, Fields, and Metaphors: Symbolic Action in Human Society* (Ithaca: Cornell University Press, 1974).
5. Hugh Dalziel Duncan, *Communication and Social Order* (New York: Oxford University Press, 1970), 373–424: William H. Martineau, "A Model of the Social Functions of Humor," in Jeffrey Goldstein and Paul McGhee, eds., *The Psychology of Humor* (New York: Academic Press, 1972), 101–24.
6. Recent studies dealing with the personality of stand-up comedians suggest that they tend to accept this role more or less consciously, viewing their art as a protection of society. Most comedians have had troubled pasts, view themselves as outcasts to some extent, and express a need for the approval of the audience. See Susan Witty's review of this research, "The Laugh Makers," *Psychology Today,* (August 1983) for the views of Samuel Janus, Waleed Salameh, and others. Seymour Fisher and Rhonda Fisher, *Pretend the World Is Funny and Forever: A Psychological Analysis of Comedians, Clowns, and Actors* (Hillsdale, N.J.: Erlbaum, 1981) is the essential book-length study. See also collections of interviews with performers, notably Larry Wilde's *The Greatest Comedians* (Secaucus, N.J.: Citadel Press, 1973); and Wilde, *How the Great Comedy Writers Create Laughter* (Chicago:

Nelson-Hall, 1976); and William Fry and Melanie Allen, *Make 'Em Laugh: Life Studies of Comedy Writers* (Palo Alto: Science and Behavior Books, 1975).

7. Albert Goldman uses the term in his discussion of comedians such as Lenny Bruce in *Freakshow* (New York: Atheneum, 1971). See also E. T. Kirby, "The Shamanistic Origins of Popular Entertainments," *Drama Review*, 18 (March 1974), 5–15.

8. See Stephanie Koziski, "The Stand-up Comedian as Anthropologist," *Journal of Popular Culture*, 18 (Fall 1984), 57–76. Her dissertation on stand-up comedy is in process. The term "articulator" is used by Chauncy Ridley in an unpublished ms., "Insight and Regeneration in Richard Pryor's Stand Up Comedy."

9. See Robert Toll, *Blacking Up: The Minstrel Show in Nineteenth Century America* (New York: Oxford University Press, 1977), which emphasizes the racism of the characterizations; and William Stowe and David Grimsted's review which corrects Toll by calling attention to the more positive functions of the portrayal, "Review Essay: White-Black Humor," *Journal of Ethnic History*, 3 (1975).

10. Sigmund Freud, *Jokes and Their Relation to the Unconscious*, ed. James Strachey (New York: Norton, 1960).

11. An important essay by Louis D. Rubin, Jr., "The Great American Joke," reprinted in Enid Veron. ed., *Humor in America* (New York: Harcourt Brace Jovanovich, 1976), 255–65, maintains that the consistent feature of American humor is its examination of our ideals in the light of the reality of our lives. [See Chapter 4, this volume.]

12. The March 1961 issue of *Playboy* magazine features an interesting symposium on the "new wave" stand-up comedy, involving Lenny Bruce, Mort Sahl, Jonathan Winters, and Jules Feiffer among others.

13. Several articles in the popular press and entertainment industry newspapers have chronicled the growth of comedy clubs throughout America in recent years. Nightclubs such as San Francisco's *The Hungry I* and New York's *The Bitter End* promoted the genre in the 1960s and Budd Friedman's *The Improvisation* led to the establishment of several clubs in New York and Los Angeles. Today almost every American city has a small comedy club or two, offering young comedians a chance to learn their craft through frequent appearances. These comedy clubs generally feature one or two "name performers" who travel the circuit and whose reputations are fostered by television exposure (Jay Leno, Byron Allen, and David Brenner, among others), local professionals, and amateur, would-be stand-up comedians. The success of the urban comedy clubs alone would suggest that stand-up comedy in contemporary America is experiencing its finest hour, certainly since the days of vaudeville.

14. James Walcott argues that today's club comics are not worthy successors of the "new wave" tradition. Rather, he sees them as heirs of the traditional professional stand-up comedy with its emphasis on commercial success, mass-media exposure, shorter routines, more concern with laughter and entertainment than message, and slick, polished style. Moreover, Walcott laments that the young professionals today are less interesting, less socially relevant: "most comedians are ignoring the shifts in American Society, mostly ignoring politics . . . ignoring quirks in the quest for status and power in a society that demands success, overlooking even the anomalous state of affairs between men and women, a great subject in these

confusing, post-liberation days." "The Young Comedians: But Seriously Folks," *Village Voice.* 30 (December 1974), 8. While it is easy for comedy aficionados to share Walcott's nostalgia for the more pointed satire of some of the "new wave" comedians, his charges simply do not stand up after even an introductory tour of the clubs today [mid–1980s]. The stand-up comedians of the past decade [the 1970s] compare favorably in style and substance with those of any previous era.

15. See studies by Howard Pollio and various associates: Pollio and John Edgerly, "Comedians and Comic Style," in Antony Chapman and Hugh Foot, eds., *Humour and Laughter: Theory, Research, and Applications* (London: Wiley, 1976); Pollio, John Edgerly, and Robert Gordan, "The Comedians World: Some Tentative Mappings," *Psychological Reports,* 30 (1972), 387–91; and "Predictability and the Appreciation of Comedy," *Bulletin of the Psychonomic Society,* 4 (1974), 229–32.

16. Humor theory is an indispensable if unpleasant part of any study of the social and cultural meaning of comedy. Recent books such as Antony Chapman and Hugh Foot, *It's a Funny Thing, Humour* (London: Wiley, 1977); and the two-volume *Handbook of Humor Research,* ed. Paul McGhee and Jeffrey Goldstein (New York: Springer-Verlag, 1984) survey the entire field of contemporary humor research and introduce the appropriate, more specific studies.

JOSEPH BOSKIN
JOSEPH DORINSON

12 Ethnic Humor
Subversion and Survival

As a nation composed largely of people with origins in other cultures, differences among racial and ethnic groups have been the source of violence and disruption, but they have also created a great deal of American humor—both humor that ridicules those who are "different," and humor developed by members of ethnic groups to defend themselves against such slurs and celebrate their own cultural heritage. In describing ethnic humor as "subversion and survival," Joseph Boskin and Joseph Dorinson trace a process by which ethnic humor takes the very weapons used against members of these groups and uses them to promote pride and self-esteem. Underlying their analysis is the assumption that humor is closely tied to power and to social class structures. Joseph Boskin is the author of *Urban Racial Violence in the Twentieth Century* (1976) and *Sambo: The Rise and Demise of an American Jester* (1986).

People have undoubtedly always laughed at others who seemed "distinct," to reassure themselves and to blunt the threats implicit in differences. Ethnic slurs in joking form have reflected the tensions of social difference in America, and they continue to serve important, though sometimes distasteful, functions in American life. Active and resurgent, intentionally cruel and demeaning, ethnic humor has a lengthy past characterized by resiliency and forward-looking adaptability. Ethnic humor against supposedly "inferior" social groups initially conveyed the thrusts of the well-entrenched

From Joseph Boskin and Joseph Dorinson, "Ethnic Humor: Subversion and Survival," *American Quarterly* 37, no. 1 (1985): 81–97. © 1985 by The Johns Hopkins University Press. Reprinted by permission of The Johns Hopkins University Press.

members of society, the white, mostly Protestant "haves," against the newly arriving immigrants or their imperfectly assimilated offspring, or against black slaves, freedmen, their children, and children's children. It also designated other unfortunates typically of red, yellow, and brown complexions. Ethnic humor in the United States originated as a function of social class feelings of superiority and white racial antagonisms, and expresses the continuing resistance of advantaged groups to unrestrained immigration and to emancipation's black subcitizens barred from opportunities for participation and productivity. In time, ironically, the resulting derisive stereotypes were adopted by their targets in mocking self-description, and then, triumphantly, adapted by the victims of stereotyping themselves as a means of revenge against their more powerful detractors.

Such humor is one of the most effective and vicious weapons in the repertory of the human mind. For this reason, Thomas Hobbes related laughter to power and traced the origins and purposes of laughter to social rivalry. The passion of laughter, he sensed, was nothing more than the proclaiming of "some eminency in ourselves by comparison with the infirmity of others" or with our own one-time lowly position.[1] In the Hobbesian jungle of our contemporary world, ethnic humor's primary form revolves around the stereotype. Highly developed images today, stereotypes may once have originated in the stuff of social reality, but they have long since been embellished and taken on a life of their own. As Gordon W. Allport has aptly noted, "Some stereotypes are totally unsupported by facts; others develop from a sharpening and over-generalization of facts."[2] Yet, once formed, they assume certain features of a circular structure within which all behavior conforms to the internal directives of the stereotypical image.

Although ethnic humor demonstrates aggressive intentions, empirical studies suggest that it possesses a salutary side as well. Lawrence LaFave and Roger Mannel, for example, argue that some jokes of this genre actually compliment the maligned group.[3] The disparaged group absorbs the barbs and, in fact, defuses them by passing them along as of their own manufacture. Thus, the humor of ridicule may serve to support the ladder for upward social mobility. In Buffalo, for instance, Polish Americans were reported to relate the following quips upon the elevation of Polish-born Pope John Paul II to the Holy See:

Why doesn't the Pope let any dogs into the Vatican?
Because they pee on poles.
___

When asked what he thought of the abortion bill, the Pope replied, "Pay it."[4]

Alan Dundes suggests that such Polish jokes are demeaning, but Lydia Fish disagrees. She argues that they actually affirm ethnic pride.[5] Is either position correct? A Yiddish joke, in which a rabbinical sage listened to a dispute, adds perspective. The rabbi found merit in each position. When the *rebbitzen,* his wife, complained that both parties could not be right, the rabbi impartially conceded: "You're right too!" Ethnic jokes have occasionally appeared as light-bulb riddles:

How many WASPs does it take to change a light bulb?
Two. One to call the electrician and one to mix the martinis.
_____

How many Jewish children does it take to change a light bulb?
None. "I'll sit in the dark!" the mother *kvetches* (whines).[6]

Clearly, jokes of this kind reflect, or can be fused with, contemporary circumstance. The Polish joke cycle, as Dundes observed, transfers heat from other ethnic groups including Jews and blacks to the lower socioeconomic classes in general.[7] It could be argued, however, that Polish jokes also manifest revenge by blacks and Jews against whites, Christians or *goyim,* presumably for centuries of indignities.[8]

Concealed by a "smile through one's teeth," aggressive humor or wit serves two salient functions: conflict and control. Conflict, which is implicit in a variety of forms—satire, irony, sarcasm, parody, and burlesque—reinforces the in-group and weakens the out-group. Stereotypes figure prominently in most conflict humor. Obstinately rigid, devilishly tenacious, the stereotypes have colored our thinking processes from early times. Because they are so deeply embedded in our individual memory and so firmly anchored in our collective folklore, stereotypes tend to be extremely difficult to dislodge. Witness, for example, the cartoons of Herblock, Jules Feiffer, and David Levine, the movies of Mel Brooks and Woody Allen, the stand-up comedy of Lenny Bruce, Dick Gregory, and Richard Pryor. Humor based on stereotype, the nastiest cut, can emasculate, enfeeble, and turn victims into scapegoats. *Die Sturmer* caricatures of the Jews spring painfully to mind.[9]

In origin and development, ethnic slurs are best understood in historical context. The Irish, for example, became victims of Irish jokes soon after their arrival in the United States. Thus:

Why is the wheelbarrow the greatest invention ever made?
It taught a few Irishmen to walk on their hind legs.[10]

Reputedly the Irish embodied propensities for brawling, drinking to excess, contradicting themselves unwittingly, and making incongruous statements—brutal or foolish behavior, in other words. Accident victims Pat and Mike have suffered a great fall. "Are you dead, Pat?" "I'm badly bruised, Mike, but quite alive." "I hope you are but you're such a liar, I don't know whether to believe you." Blacks sometimes employed these jokes because they conferred on themselves feelings of superiority over the Irish along with some degree of revenge against all white folk.[11] A visitor in Hell saw all kinds of ethnics—Germans, English, Japanese, and Negroes—burning in torment. "Where are the Irish?" he asked. Escorting him to a room filled with Irish, the Devil said: "We are just drying them here; they are too green to burn now." At another level, an Irish orator covered a litany of ethnic achievements. "Who puts up all the fine buildings?" The audience responded on cue: "The Irish." "And who puts up the court house?" "The Irish." "And who builds the state penitentiaries?" "The Irish." "And who fills them?" "The Irish."[12]

On stage, the Irish carved out a distinctive image for themselves. Vaudeville or burlesque teams including Needham and Kelly, Rooney and Rogers, the Shamrocks, and others, engaged in tongue-twisters, brawling, and blarney. They conjured up a vivid portrait described by "a figure in a derby hat and dudeen pipe, a melodic if not sentimental songster having a belligerent attitude, a love for the bottle, a penchant for politics, . . . a quizzical look." In the newspaper comics, Irish folks inhabited shanties where the chimney, a patched stovepipe, pitched crazily. One needed a ladder to get into the house filled with children and dominated by a hot-headed, washer-woman wife.[13]

This kind of cruel caricature flourished at a time when the nation was confronted by a large number of impoverished immigrants who could not easily be assimilated. Older-stock Americans aimed jokes against these newcomers and their unusual customs as one method of promoting cultural conformity. The Irish responded to such oppressive humor, however, using a counter-assertion of aggressive humor in return. If, indeed, the Irish represented unwanted alien characteristics, they readily employed their own wits to criticize American values and peculiarities, and maintained thereby a measure of self-respect. Eventually Chicago's Irish dialect commentator on public affairs turned the tide in favor of his countrymen. From his saloon on Archey Road, Mr. Dooley satirized fraud, pretense, and materialism in the American grain. He tackled Andrew Carnegie's philanthropies at the time when they were almost universally celebrated. ("Ivry time he gives a libry, he gives himself away in a speech.") He supplied the most cogent appraisal of reform politics:

> Th' noise ye hear is not th' first gun iv a rivolution. It's on'y th' people iv th' United States batin' a carpet. Ye object to th' smell? That's nawthin! We use sthrong disinfectants. A Frenchman or an Englishman cleans house by sprinklin' th' walls with cologne; we chop a hole in th' flure an' pour in a kag iv chloride iv lime. Who is that yallin'? That's our ol' friend High Fi-nance bein' compelled to take his annual bath. . . .[14]

Mr. Dooley marveled at American society with its "invintions—the steam-injine an' th' printin'-press an' th' cottin'-gin an' th' gin sour an th' bicycle an' th' flyin' machine an' . . . crownin' wur-ruk iv our civilization—th' cash raygisther." In retrospect Dooley stands equidistant between immigrant scapegoat Teague O'Regan, Brackinridge's cunning but cowardly rogue figure in the *Modern Chivalry* series (1792–1815), and martyred hero John Fitzgerald Kennedy.[15]

Jesse Bier has suggested that Dooley's unyielding opposition to American business, militarism, politics, and customs was a displacement of his Irish and his Catholic hostilities against the English. Dooley's egalitarian needling deflated the powerful, a tendency rooted in Irish comic tradition. Indeed, Irish bards, as Vivian Mercier has argued, constantly stirred up trouble in Ireland. Dooley questioned the conventional wisdom of his day. He functioned as a critic with a paradoxical bent, in that he was "provincial and broadminded, anti-intellectual but thoughtful, pugnacious but humanitarian."[16] In time Dooley seemed to grow more peaceful. Perhaps he, likewise, had joined the "cash raygisther" crowd along with other successful Irishmen. The Irish left ethnic humor to other ethnics who followed after them, principally Jews and blacks.

Jewish ethnic humor builds on its folk sources, as these examples reveal:

> An elderly orthodox Jewish man was walking his dog. He approached a stranger with an attractive dog. "What breed is he?"
> "A cross between a Jew and a mongrel."
> "Oh!" said the elderly Jew, "then he is undoubtedly related to both of us!"

Priest: "When will you give up those silly dietary laws?"
Rabbi: "At your wedding, excellency."[17]

Such jokes reveal distinctive aspects of Jewish humor, the wit of retaliation and the comedy of revenge.

American Jews found the origins of their comic voice in medieval Europe. Precursors of modern stand-up comedians, *badchonim* and *marshalliks* enjoined each other to "tell it like it is" well before the advent of Jackie Mason. A seasonal event, the *Purimshpiel* (Purim Play) sanctioned irreverent humor and granted license to a number of fools—the *lets, nar,* and *payats*—to act comically. Droll characters—*shnorrers, shlemiels, shlimazels,* and *luftmentshen*—originated in the East European *shtetl* or village.[18] Some, like Motke Chabad and Hershl Ostropolier, were real people. One night while dining, the story goes, Hershl broke into a loud wail. "Is there anything wrong?" asked the concerned proprietor. "Oy!" cried Hershl, "to think that for this little morsel of meat a great big ox had to be slaughtered." Fired from a menial job for excessive jesting, Hershl was hired by a melancholy Hassidic rabbi to serve as his court jester. The rabbi rebuked him on one occasion for spending so little time at prayer. Hershl protested:

> You have so much to be grateful for! Your carriage and your fine horses, your gold and silver, your fancy dishes. But look at me. I have a nagging wife, my six children and a skinny goat. And so my prayers are very simple: 'Wife, children, goat'—and I'm done.

As he lay dying, Hershl was visited by members of the Burial Society. He advised: "Remember, my friends, when you lift me up to lay me in the coffin, be sure not to hold me under the armpits. I've always been ticklish there." He died with a smile on his lips, and laughed all the way to the grave (*keyver*). Like his fellow imps, Froyim Graydinger and Shayke Fayfer, Hershl played the wise fool. He unmasked the rich who pretended to be righteous and the ignorant who pretended to be learned. By reinterpreting his predicament, the fool triumphed in the end.[19]

Other forms of folk humor flowered in the *shtetl*. Stories from the mythical village of Chelm parodied the Jewish preoccupation with learning bereft of common sense. They poked fun at sages fixed on millenial concerns, mindless of mundane reality. Children still love these stories, because adults act foolishly in them and education leads to futility. When two wise men of Chelm went for a walk, it started to rain. "Quick, open your umbrella!" "It won't help. My umbrella is full of holes." "Why then did you bring it?" "I didn't think it would rain." In another example of inspired nonsense, the village elders of Chelm refuse to grant a raise to the underpaid Messiah-watcher because, although the salary is low, the work is steady.[20]

Some scholars contend that Jewish humor is a product of emancipation and did not blossom until the late nineteenth century, while others argue that following the Holocaust and the rise of a Jewish nation-state in Israel, this genre has expired. Jewish jokes attracted and stimulated Sigmund Freud, who, in his analysis of Jewish humor, found that it exemplified the "tendency wit" of skepticism and self-criticism.[21] Freud's supposition finds confirmation in the penchant of contemporary Jewish comedians for assailing established institutions, as in the antics of Groucho Marx, Sid Caesar, Lenny Bruce, Jackie Mason, Don Rickles, and Mel Brooks, to name only a few comic wreckers. Building on his mentor's work, Theodore Reik, like Freud, focused on Jewish wit's intimacy, its dialectical process, and its releasing of unmerry laughter at a moment of subjective truth or profound insight.

In Immanuel Olsvanger's comic treasure-trove, *Royte Pomerantsen,* we discover this gem:

> When you tell a peasant a joke he laughs three times; once
>   when you tell it, once when you explain it, and once when
>   he understands it.
> When you tell a land-owner a joke he laughs twice; once when
>   you tell it and once when you explain it—he'll never
>   understand it.
> When you tell a military officer a joke he laughs only when you
>   tell it. Because he won't let you explain it and of course he
>   does not understand it.
> But when you tell a Jew a joke, he tells you that he's heard it
>   already—and besides, you're telling it all wrong.[22]

Often some other national or ethnic representative appears in this kind of anecdote, but the Jew always get the punch in the tag line and the rabbi frequently functions as a trickster. Does Jewish humor always indicate self-hatred? Most psychiatrists who treat this subject seem to have fixed on "psychic masochism" as their descriptive explanation. However, Elliot Oring delineates a basic dichotomy in humor theory between humanists and social scientists. While humanists prefer incongruity as the primary mode of humor, as they see it, social scientists stress catharsis via "drive reduction."[23]

Unencumbered by such divergent and humorless theories, Yiddish writers Mendel Mocher Sforim and Sholem Aleichem created comic characters who snatched ironic victories from the jaws of defeat. They further improved that delicate balance between piety and complaint, the humor of marginality as epitomized earlier by Heinrich Heine and expressed in a joke cycle concerning cleanliness, sexual permissiveness, identity problems, and war.[24] To explain what happened to this humor as it crossed the Atlantic Ocean to America, Lawrence Mintz has pinpointed four stages in the process: the first featured critical humor that targeted the out-group; the second involved self-deprecatory humor; the third stressed realism; and finally, the fourth stage reversed the first stage as the oppressed minority gained revenge by assaulting the majority culture. In stages one and four, critical hostility gained license. This helped to deflect aggression through ritualistic, as opposed to real, punishment because, as Mintz argues, the joking relationships and resulting ritual banter serve to reduce irritants.[25]

Jews in the United States in the nineteenth century were caricatured in jokes and cartoons published in *Puck, Judge, Life,* and *Leslie's Weekly.* The jokes concerned money, bargains, and fraud (mainly arson). The graphic stereotypes reflected a mixture of "good" and "bad" traits. However maligned, Jews actually received better treatment than a number of other groups, particularly Italians, blacks, Chinese, and, surprisingly, Mormons. John Appel has charted the evolution of the Jew in caricature from the money bags of the fifteenth century to the long beards, grotesque noses, open palms, and pawnbrokers' signs prevalent in eighteenth- and nineteenth-century European cartoons. In contrast to the Irish, for example, the Jews appeared more likable in American caricatures. Harry Hirshfield helped to create a counter-image with his Abe Kabibble comic strip in 1914. With his striped trousers, saucer eyes, small bulb nose, familiar accent, and peculiar syntax, Abe represented middle-class Jewish aspirations. He loved family, country, business, and pinochle.[26] As their co-religionists owned and operated many theatres, Jews flocked into vaudeville, where budding careers opened to their talent and *chutspe.*

Old Jewish jokes found renewed expression on stage:

"Have I got a girl for you!" the *shadchan* (matchmaker) insists. On cue, as rehearsed, the *shadchan*'s apprentice embellishes. *Shadchan:* "A pretty girl." Apprentice: "A beauty. Queen Esther." "Intelligent." "Brilliant. She knows six languages." "She's from a good family." "The highest *yichus* (status). Her grandfather was a famous scholar." "She's rich." "Her uncle is Rothschild." "She has only one fault. She has a little hump." "A hump!" cries the apprentice. "A regular Mount Sinai!"[27]

With a gift for cultural pastiche, Jewish comedians engaged in "ethnic acts." Joe Weber and Lew Fields did Mike and Meyer, a "Double Dutch Act." Mike, a fat little man in a bizarre checkered suit, yelled at Meyer, tall, lean, and unctuous, who twisted Mike's nose. The shorter man flailed helplessly at his taller adversary. They argued over politics. Mike scored with his punch line: "Banners don't vote. Budt dey shure do show vhich vay der vindt is plowing." Mike was shoved off stage as he bellowed: "Dondt poosh me, Meyer!" When they met again, they greet each other:

"I'm delightfulness to meedt you."
"Der disguzt ist all mine."[28]

Smith and Dale's classic routine of 1906 was a thinly veiled Dutch Act. Beneath Dr. Kronkhite's German accent coursed choice bits of Jewish humor.

Patient: What do I owe you?
Doctor: You owe me $10 for my advice.
Patient: $10 for your advice? Well, Doctor, here is $2. Take it, that's my advice.
Doctor: You cheap skate! You *shnorrer*, you low life, you raccoon, you baboon!
Patient: One more word from you, you'll only get $1.
Doctor: You . . .
Patient: That's the word! Here's a dollar.[29]

Jews also put on burnt cork. Blacking their faces to impart their *shmaltz* (literally, chicken fat; figuratively, sentimentality bordering on bathos), Sophie Tucker, Al Jolson, George Jessel, and Eddie Cantor became stars. Their black masks guaranteed freedom from conventional restraints. Perhaps the grimness of industrialization helps to explain the enormous popularity of Al Jolson, whose songs conjured up a mythical magnolia-scented South teeming with togetherness. If so, while Spenglerians were lamenting western decadence, and poets in exile were raining metaphors of sterility on their respective wastelands, Jews were imitating the black libidinous style and developing a coarse, vital humor with music to match.[30]

The Marx Brothers carried on the vaudeville tradition minus the minstrel masks. Fortified with S. J. Perelman scripts, they plunged into gleeful nihilism. Listen to Groucho, the *shnorrer* as explorer. "When I came to this country, I didn't have a nickel in my pocket. Now I have a nickel in my pocket." Resigning from the Friars Club, he explained: "I do not care to belong to a club that accepts people like me as members." Yet there were many more kicks for Groucho's straight-woman, Margaret Dumont. "That remark covers a lot of territory," he observed. "As a matter of fact, you cover a lot of territory. Is there any truth to the fact that they're going to tear you down and put up an office building?"[31] No one remained safe from Marx's demolition derby, least of all, Margaret Dumont, pillar of piety and symbol of WASP respectability.

Jack Benny, however, typified newer trends on radio. Born Benny Kubelski, he married Sadie Marks, who, like her husband, metamorphosed herself with a new nose and a new name into Mary Livingstone. Ethnic humor issued only from the subsidiary characters in Benny's cast, like Eddie "Rochester" Anderson, Dennis Day, and Messrs. Kitsel and Schlepperman, who presented stereotypes reminiscent of those on the vaudeville circuit. Vain, stingy, pompous, violinist *manqué* Benny played the butt and imparted his Jewish flavor almost subliminally. As Harry Popkin contends, the Hitler years constituted a period of relative silence on Jewish topics and actual de-Semitization. After World War II, however, defiant in the wake of the Holocaust and proud at Israel's birth, Jewish comedians as well as Jewish writers emerged from the cultural closet. Among them Sid Caesar, Jack E. Leonard, Milton Berle, Mort Sahl, Lenny Bruce, Woody Allen, Mel Brooks, Saul Bellow, Bernard Malamud, and Philip Roth laughingly carried their low comedy into virtually every avenue of popular culture. They freshened up old stereotypes and injected doses of Jewish comic wisdom into American life. Their message was strong and clear: *mir zeinen doh* (we are here).[32]

Black comedians responded differently to the stresses affecting them than did their Jewish counterparts. True enough, blacks and Jews shared the humor of the oppressed. Inwardly masochistic, indeed tragic, externally aggressive, even acrimonious, their humor generated several distinctive forms of expression such as gallows humor, the ironic curse, double meanings, trickster tales, and retaliatory jokes.

Black humor's outstanding traits include its play quality, which seeks to ward off punishment and thus permits quick retaliation; its deep scrutiny; and a type of control humor which is vital for the maintenance of a highly attuned and carefully sensitized community.[33] Springing from its folk sources, Afro-American humor has proceeded mainly along two tracks destined to provoke laughter. Externally, it represents an accommodation to white society and functions as a mechanism for survival. Slaves used veiled humorous language to vent anger, just as they employed coded sayings to mask true feelings. The John-Master stories illuminate this process. John cussed out his massa whenever he pleased—whenever the massa is up at the big house and John is down in the field. John steals food and lies his way out of trouble by turning a pig into a baby and, when caught, reversing the magic. Slave stories featured outwardly docile subjects paying homage to their master as in this deathbed scene: "Farewell, massa! Pleasant journey! You soon be dere, massa—[it's] all de way down hill!" Some slaves refused to be buried in the same gravesite with their masters for fear that the Devil, "old Sam," might take the wrong body. Blacks chortled as they slipped past white scrutiny:

> I fooled Old Master seven years,
> Fooled the overseer three.
> Hand me down my banjo.
> and I'll tickle your bel-lee.[34]

John, the stereotype, epitomizes the rewards, the limits, and the hazards of the "trickster," wherein even verbal facility and skill in role playing were not enough. In one tale, John's absolute faith in prayer betrays him as the massa's cruel children prey on his gullibility and pelt him with "God's stones." To track the inner feelings of the Afro-American in servitude, one has to turn to the animal trickster. Rabbit is correctly identified with the slave, yet he also mirrors the oppressor's cruelty. Lawrence Levine cautions against simplistic equations. He prefers to view trickster tales as profound parodies of white society. Because the whites held such awesome power, their human chattels preferred to seek revenge disarmingly with guile and indirection. Even if the meek fail to inherit the earth, they might occasionally enjoy a last laugh. Slaves laughed "to keep down trouble and to keep our hearts from being broken." As John Little put it, "I have cut capers in chains."[35]

Folktales, in the useful paradigm of Arnez and Anthony, constitute "an oral tradition in which the group pokes fun at its customs, idioms . . . folkways." Such in-group humor fosters social cohesion. When black humor went public with burnt offerings, a ritual sacrifice occurred. In American popular culture, the black as comic figure crept into our group fantasy as the smiling descendant of Pan. He lusted after chicken, watermelon, pig's feet, and white women. He feared ghosts (particularly in white sheets) and spoke in malapropisms. White performers Thomas Rice and Dan Emmett swooped down South in the wake of Reconstruction to cannibalize black culture. Two blatant stereotypes surfaced, Jim Crow and Jim Dandy: the former, a rural, slow-witted buffoon; the latter, an urbane, effeminate city-slicker. Prodded by the upper-class, white-faced interlocutor, who played it straight, Coon and Dandy created havoc on stage. These types, contends Robert Bone, triggered laughter as audiences perceived the gap between affectation and reality. The travesty sought "to keep the pretender in his place."[36]

Sambo, Crow's cousin, a Darwinian loser and preindustrial primitive, became the nation's demeaned alterego or, in Bone's formulation, its anti-self. To whites he was

> slow-witted, loosely-shuffling, buttock-scratching, benignly-optimistic, superstitiously-frightened, childishly lazy, irresponsible-carefree, rhythmically-gaited, pretentiously-intelligent, sexually-animated. His physical characteristics added to the jester's appearance: toothy-grinned, thick-lipped, nappy-haired, slack-jawed, round-eyed.[37]

Unlike Lear's fool, Ahab's Pip, or Bergen's McCarthy, our Sambo lacked wisdom. He was, in short, a buffoon.

The white performer who put on his blackface minstrel mask was performing a rite of exorcism. He was operating a safety valve for repressed emotions. The black persona he portrayed—indolent, inept, indulgent—embodied the anti-self and objectified the distance between social norms and man's instincts. Imparting a sense of freedom and inviting a return to childhood, minstrelsy answered deep psychic needs for white audiences, "the mammy for security and comfort; . . . the Negro male for ridicule and jest."[38] For blacks themselves, this ridicule forged psychic chains: a bag for Uncle Ben, a box for Aunt Jemima, a cabin in the sky for Uncle Tom, a pancake restaurant chain for Sambo, and a joke for Rastus.

To survive, the black artist had to participate in self-caricature. To succeed, he had to perpetuate vile stereotypes. Billy Kersands juggled a cup and saucer in his mouth. Ernest Hogan, Ma Rainey, and Bert Williams donned the mask to conceal as well as to express true feelings. Williams, in fact, used two sets of jokes: one for white folks, the other for black. As "Jonah Man," Williams, helped and comforted by "Nobody," successfully pulled laughter from pain. Most of his peers, however, coupled their painful indignities with derisive laughter. Kersands and Hogan performed coon songs. Dunbar wrote them.[39]

Blacks' humor of accommodation was the only kind to which whites were ordinarily exposed until recently. To laugh openly at "the Man," "Mr. Charlie," "Miss Ann," "pig," "honkey," "vanilla," was to invite certain punishment. Blacks, therefore, developed a gaming stance stoically laughing on the outside to cope with their pain inside. Black humor served many important functions including group survival, escape into pride and dignity, self-criticism, and the resolution of conflict.[40] Getting past society's censors, internal and external, as Freud maintained, brings pleasure even in the presence of pain, because a joke saves energy normally expended on upholding inhibitions or disguising aggression. Such jokes function, in fact, as miniatures of rebelliousness. In Daryl Dance's rich anthology of materials, which often pits the poor against those with power, one set of selections used the Negro preacher as the target to expose vanity, ignorance, hypocrisy, lechery, alcoholism, gluttony, and materialism through his misadventures and misfortunes. For example:

> The church people were having a party at which they served some punch, but the punch was so weak that, every time they got a chance, some of the men would sneak in a bottle and pour some whiskey into the punch. The Preacher enjoyed it so much, he just kept nipping. Later, when he was called to pray, he said: "God, bless the cow that gave this milk."[41]

When another minister and his son encountered a bear in the woods, the son urged, "Let us pray!" The minister responded: "Let us run. Son, prayers is all right in a prayer meetin' but they ain't no good in a bear meetin'!"[42]

The elephant riddle-jokes, which achieved great popularity in the 1960s, frequently depicted the elephant as sexually superior, a crude disguising, in the suggestion of Abrahams and Dundes, for the stereotypical black male. Thus:

Why does the elephant have four feet?
It's better than six inches.

———

How do elephants make love in the water?
They take their trunks down.

In another cycle, the elephant is symbolically castrated!

> How do you keep an elephant from charging?
> Take away his credit card.

Before long, color riddles appeared, as:

> What's black and has a red cape?
> Super Nigger.

> What is black and white and rolls in the grass?
> Integrated sex.

The prospects of black liberation often spurred anxiety among whites, triggering repressive responses in turn.[43] At times, in the great urban riots of the 1960s, the responses and counterresponses could erupt violently and self-destructively.

Why, then, was it that American audiences responded so favorably to black comedians in this period? Perhaps the answer lies in the role that stand-up comics play as cultural anthropologists. Lawrence Mintz's insight is crucial:

> As a licensed spokesman he is permitted to say things about our society that we want and need to have uttered publicly, but which would be too dangerous and too volatile if done so without the mediation of humor; and as a comic character he can represent, through caricature, those negative traits which we wish to hold up to ridicule, to feel superior to, and to renounce through laughter. Thus, for example, the blackfaced minstrels can be the objects of racist ridicule as a part of a ritualized experience in venting hostility and in defining socially undesirable behavior, yet at the same time they can function as positive, likeable spokesmen for topical satire. . . . Similarly the ethnic comedians could represent "greenhorns" to be laughed at for their ignorance, gullibility, poverty, and vulnerability, but laughed with for their street-wise insistence on survival and their ironic exposure of injustice.[44]

Stephanie Koziski has demonstrated that comedians can jar audiences into awareness of deeply buried cultural underpinnings. Like a Margaret Mead, the stand-up comedian "gets down" into primal roots. Comparable to the ancient storyteller in "primitive" cultures, he or she may also communicate shared values as well as the common knowledge.[45]

Building folk sources and in-group banter, black comedians joined their Jewish and other ethnic counterparts in imparting cultural commentary and anthropological insight. Dick Gregory carried the ball directly into enemy territory in the early 1960s. As a civil rights activist-commentator, he repeatedly scored:

Restaurateur: "We don't serve Nigras!"
"That's cool. I don't eat them."

I sat in so long at lunch-counters. It took me ten years to discover that they didn't have what I wanted.

It's kinda sad, but my little girl doesn't believe in Santa Claus. She sees that white cat with the whiskers and even at two years old she know damn well that no white man coming to our neighborhood at midnight.

Makes you wonder . . . when I left St. Louis I was making $500 a week for saying the same thing loud that I used to say under my breath.

Wouldn't it be a hell of a thing if all this was burnt cork and you people were being tolerant for nothing?[46]

Godfrey Cambridge laughed at his wife's "Back to Africa" kick. "She did the bedroom in brown, the whole thing, drapes, ceiling, carpet, spread, pillow. One day she took a bath, came into the room and it took me three hours to find her." Cambridge roasted whites, too, with his "How to Hail a Taxi" routine and their concern over property values. "Do you realize," he asked, "the amount of havoc a Negro couple can cause just by walking down the street on a Sunday morning with a copy of the *New York Times* real-estate section under the man's arm?"[47]

Redd Foxx brandished his own weapons. He once threatened a less-than-enthusiastic, predominantly white audience with "Why should I be wasting time with you here when I could be knifing you in an alley?" He ruefully observed that the first black to receive an athletic scholarship from "Ole' Miss" was a javelin catcher. He parodied Tarzan of the Apes and derided Long Beach, California, blacks as "the ugliest Negroes I have ever seen." Foxx confessed the ambivalences inherent in mulattodom: "You wake up in the morning with a taste for . . . filet mignon with biscuits." Unmasking Sambo, Foxx confided that "'Boss' spelled backwards is double SOB."[48] He had come a long way from the restraints of minstrelsy.

Jackie "Moms" Mabley and, more recently, Richard Pryor also found rich veins of humor in folk sources. Mabley's appearance, her references to soul food, and her earthy wit established the appropriate image and tightened the bonds of kinship with her black audiences, while in comic reversals, she addressed powerful white men as "boy" and called prestigious white women "girl." Once she offered an account of a major United Nations conference:

> Aw, everybody was there. They had a ball. Yeah. All them men from the Congo, some of 'em was late getting there 'cause they had plane troubles, and they had to be grounded in Arkansas, Little Rock. One of them Congo men walked up to the desk in Little Rock and said, "I'd like to reserve a room, please." The man said, "We don't cater to your kind." He said. "No, you misunderstand me. I don't want it for myself. I want it for my wife. She's your kind."[49]

Such humor, as Dwight MacDonald once observed, is like guerilla warfare. Success depends on traveling light, striking unexpectedly, and getting away fast.[50] Yet ethnic humor, because of its agitational elements, must return to the action repeatedly. Skirting the edge of gallows laughter, it cannot afford to escape into fatalism. Thus, in its quest for control over events and lives, ethnic behavior demonstrates that both oppressors and their adversaries use humor, but for strikingly different ends. The oppressors employ ridicule to maintain conformity to the status quo by adhering to iron-bound stereotypes. Ethnics in retaliation have created a world of internal joking where, in Langston Hughes's observation, "certain aspects of the humor of minority groups are so often inbred that they are not palatable for outside consumption."[51] Moreover, they often reverse roles and turn the tables on their adversaries by striving for a language of self-acceptance. Poet Marianne Moore perceptively noted that "one's sense of humor is a clue to the most serious part of one's nature." Mocking the features ascribed to them by outsiders has become one of the most effective ethnic infusions into national humor, particularly by Afro-Americans and Jews. Minority laughter affords insights into the constant and often undignified struggle of upwardly striving Americans to achieve positive definition and respectable status.

NOTES

1. Thomas Hobbes, "Human Nature, or the Fundamental Elements of Policy," in Sir William Molesworth, ed., *The English Works of Thomas Hobbes*, vol. 4 (London: John Bohn, 1840), 46. For examples of *blaison populaire*,

see Alan Dundes and Carl R. Pagler, eds., *Urban Folklore from the Paperwork Empire* (Austin: Publications of the American Folklore Society, 1975), 174–79; and Sterling Eisiminger, "Ethnic and National Stereotypes and Slurs," *American Humor: An Interdisciplinary Newsletter* 7 (Fall 1980), 9–13.

2. Gordon W. Allport, *The Nature of Prejudice* (Garden City, N.Y.: Doubleday/Anchor, 1958), 186.

3. Lawrence LaFave and Roger Mannel, "Does Ethnic Humor Serve Prejudice?" *Journal of Communication* 26 (1976), 116–17, 122.

4. Lydia Fish, "Is the Pope Polish? Some Notes on the Polack Joke in Translation," *Journal of American Folklore* (hereafter *JAF*), 93 (1980), 450–54.

5. Ibid.

6. The "power" jokes are found in Judith B. Kerman, "The Light Bulb Jokes: Americans Look at Social Action Processes," *JAF*, 93 (1980), 454–55, 457–58. For further illumination, see Alan Dundes, "Many Hands Make Light Work: or Caught in the Act of Screwing in Lightbulbs," *Western Folklore*, 40 (1981), 266; Joseph Boskin, "Obscure Humor: Comments on Contemporary Laughter, Circa. 1980s," paper presented at the Third International Conference on Humor, 9–10 Aug. 1982, The Shoreham Hotel, Washington, D.C.

7. Alan Dundes, "A Study of Ethnic Slurs: The Jew and the Polack in the United States," *JAF*, 84 (1971), 186–89, 202–03.

8. Dundes, "Many Hands," 266; Boskin, "Obscure Humor," 9–10.

9. Joseph Boskin, *Humor and Social Change in Twentieth-Century America* (Boston: Boston Public Library, 1979), 28–31; Richard M. Stephenson, "Conflict and Control Functions of Humor," *American Journal of Sociology*, 56 (1951), 569.

10. Ray Ginger, *Ray Ginger's Jokebook about American History* (New York: Franklin Watts/New Viewpoints, 1974), 31.

11. Isaac Asimov, *Isaac Asimov's Treasury of Humor* (Boston: Houghton Mifflin, 1971), 287; Lawrence W. Levine, *Black Culture and Black Consciousness: Afro-American Folk Thought from Slavery to Freedom* (New York: Oxford University Press, 1981), 302.

12. Ibid., 302–03.

13. Boskin, *Humor and Social Change*, 31; Douglas Gilbert, *American Vaudeville: Its Life and Times* (New York: Dover, 1940), 62.

14. Finley Peter Dunne, *The World of Mr. Dooley*, ed. Louis Filler (New York: Collier, 1962), 151.

15. Jesse Bier, *The Rise and Fall of American Humor* (New York: Holt, Rinehart and Winston, 1968), 179.

16. Ibid., 181; Arthur Power Dudden, ed., *The Assault of Laughter: A Treasury of American Political Humor* (New York: Thomas Yoseloff, 1962), 285–87; Charles Fanning, "The Short Sad Career of Mr. Dooley in Chicago," *Ethnicity*, 8 (1981), 169–73. Irish comic sensibility is canvassed in Vivian Mercier, *The Irish Comic Tradition* (Oxford: Oxford University Press, 1972).

17. Nancy Levy Arnez and Clara B. Anthony, "Contemporary Negro Humor as Social Satire," *Phylon*, 29 (1969), 340; the mongrel-Jew joke is related by Howard J. Ehrlich, "Observations on Ethnic and Intergroup Humor," *Ethnicity*, 6 (1979), 394; while the priest-rabbi repartee—one of several versions—can be found in a fascinating study by Ed Cray, "The Rabbi Trickster," *JAF*, 77 (1964), 342.

18. Nathan Ausubel, *A Treasury of Jewish Folklore* (New York: Crown, 1948), 264–87, 304–19. There is a wonderful evocation of the Purim Plays in Nahma Sandrow, *Vagabond Stars: A World History of Yiddish Theater* (New York: Harper and Row, 1977), ch. 1.
19. Ruth Wisse, *The Schlemiel as Modern Hero* (Chicago: University of Chicago Press, 1971), 11–12; William Novak and Moshe Waldoks, eds., *The Big Book of Jewish Humor* (New York: Harper and Row, 1981), 26–27; Sig Altman, *The Comic Image of the Jew: Explorations of a Pop Culture Phenomenon* (Madison, N.J.: Fairleigh Dickinson University Press, 1971), 131–32.
20. Ausubel, *Treasury,* 338; Israel Knox, "The Wise Men of Helm," *Judaism,* 29 (1980), 187–88; Allen Guttman, "Jewish Humor," in Louis D. Rubin, Jr., ed., *The Comic Imagination in American Literature* (New Brunswick: Rutgers University Press, 1973), 331, contains the Chelm Messiah-watcher anecdote.
21. The "bath" jokes are collected in Salcia Landman, *Der Jüdische Witz* (Olten: Walter-Verlag, 1960), 87, 453. Also see Sigmund Freud, *Jokes and Their Relation to the Unconscious,* trans. and ed. James Strachey (New York: W. W. Norton, 1963), 49–51, 55–56, 61–63, 111–15.
22. Immanuel Olsvanger, *Royte Pomerantsen* (New York: Schocken, 1965), 3; Theodore Reik, *Jewish Wit* (New York: Gamut Press, 1962), 182–240; Dan Ben-Amos, "The 'Myth' of Jewish Humor," *Western Folklore,* 32 (1973), 112–15, 118–21, 129–30.
23. Elliot Oring, *Israeli Humor: The Content and Structure of the Chizbat of the Palmach* (Albany: State University of New York Press, 1981), 39–40.
24. Altman, *Comic,* 141–45, 163–68.
25. Lawrence E. Mintz, "Jewish Humor: A Continuum of Sources, Motives and Functions," *American Humor,* 4 (Spring 1977), 4.
26. John J. Appel, "Jews in American Caricature: 1820–1914," *American Jewish History,* 71 (1981), 103–18. For a similar thesis, namely, that the caricature of Jews was more benign in America than in Europe, see Rudolph Glanz, *The Jew in Early American Wit and Graphic Humor* (New York: Ktav, 1973), 237. The cartoons, however, on 67, 88, 113, 115, 117, appear less than benign.
27. Nahma Sandrow, " 'A Little Letter to Mamma': Traditions in Yiddish Vaudeville," in Myron Matlaw, ed., *American Popular Entertainment* (Westport: Greenwood Press, 1979), 90.
28. Paul Antonie Distler, "Ethnic Comedy in Vaudeville and Burlesque," in ibid., 127–31.
29. Joe Smith, "Dr. Kronkhite Revisited," in ibid., 127–31.
30. Ronald Sanders, "The American Popular Song," in Douglas Villiers, ed., *Next Year in Jerusalem* (New York: Viking Press, 1976), 197–98; Lewis A. Erenberg, *Steppin' Out: New York Night Life and the Transformation of American Culture, 1890–1930* (Westport: Greenwood Press, 1981), 190–95; Stanley White, "The Burnt Cork Illusion of the 1920s in America: A Study in Nostalgia," *Journal of Popular Culture,* 5 (1971), 543.
31. Bier, *Rise,* 270–71; Altman, *Comic Image,* 188–89.
32. Irving Howe, *World of Our Fathers* (New York: Harcourt Brace Jovanovich, 1976), 565–70; Wallace Markfield, "The Yiddishization of American Humor," *Esquire,* 64, Oct. 1965, 114. For a succinct summary of this evaluation, consult Joseph Dorinson, "Jewish Humor: Mechanism for Defense, Weapon for Cultural Affirmation," *Journal of Psychohistory,* 8 (1981), 447–64.

33. Boskin, *Humor and Social Change,* 49–56.
34. Afro-American humor's twin tracks are charted in Joseph Boskin, "Goodby, Mr. Bones," *New York Times Magazine,* 1 May 1966, 31. The roguish John stories are conveyed in a variety of sources: Daryl Cumber Dance, *Shuckin' and Jivin': Folklore from Contemporary Black Americans* (Bloomington: Indiana University Press, 1978), 189–90; Richard Dorson, *American Folklore* (Chicago: University of Chicago Press, 1959), 186–90; Norine Dresser, "The Metamorphosis of the Humor of the Black Man," *New York Folklore Quarterly,* 26 (1970), 216–19; Gil Osofksy, ed., *Puttin' on Ole Massa: The Slave Narratives of Henry Bibb, William Wells Brown, and Solomon Northrup* (New York: Harper and Row, 1969), 21–23; Harry Oster, "Negro Humor: John & Old Marster," in Alan Dundes, ed., *Mother Wit from the Laughing Barrel: Readings in the Interpretation of Afro-American Folklore* (Englewood Cliffs, N.J.: Prentice-Hall, 1973), 550–55. The "getting over" song is cited in Levine, *Black Culture,* 125.
35. Osofsky, *Puttin' on Ole Massa,* 39–40; Levine, *Black Culture,* 118–19.
36. Robert Bone, *Down Home: A History of Afro-American Short Fiction from Its Beginning to the End of the Harlem Renaissance* (New York: G. P. Putnam and Sons, 1975), 59, 60–61; Arnez and Anthony, "Contemporary Negro Humor," 339–40; Nathan I. Huggins, *Harlem Renaissance* (New York: Oxford University Press, 1971), 261–83.
37. Joseph Boskin, "The Life and Death of Sambo: Overview of an Historical Hang-Up," *Journal of Popular Culture,* 4 (1971), 649.
38. White, "Burnt Cork," 543; Albert F. McClean, Jr., *American Vaudeville as Ritual* (Lexington: University of Kentucky Press, 1965), 24–26; Robert Toll, *Blacking Up: The Minstrel Show in Nineteenth Century America* (New York: Oxford University Press, 1974), 29; Huggins, *Harlem Renaissance,* 260–74, offers a brilliant analysis of travesty.
39. Toll, *Blacking Up,* 245–48, 254–59, 262, 274; Robert Toll, *On with the Show: The First Century of Show Business in America* (New York: Oxford University Press, 1976), 123; Morris Goldman, "The Sociology of Negro Humor," Diss. New School for Social Research 1960, iv, refers to the dual set of jokes used by Bert Williams.
40. Boskin, *Humor and Social Change,* 57; Robert Brake, "The Lion Act Is Over: Passive/Aggressive Pattern in American Negro Humor," *Journal of Popular Culture,* 9 (1975), 551–53.
41. Dance, *Shuckin',* 41–76; Levine, *Black Culture,* 321.
42. For the "bear meetin'" joke, see Mary Frances Berry and John Blassingame, *Long Memory: The Black Experience in America* (New York: Oxford University Press, 1982), 102.
43. Roger D. Abrahams and Alan Dundes, "On Elephantasy and Elephanticide," *Psychoanalytic Review,* 56 (1969), 230, 231, 233, 237, 238–39.
44. Lawrence E. Mintz, "The 'New Wave' of Standup Comedians: An Introduction," *American Humor,* 4 (Fall 1977), 1. The comedian who made the biggest waves is still mired in myth. See Joseph Dorinson, "Lenny Bruce, A Jewish Humorist in Babylon," *Jewish Currents,* 35 (Feb. 1981), 14–19, 31–32.
45. Stephanie Koziski, "The Standup Comedian as Anthropologist: Intentional Cultural Critic," paper presented at the Third International Conference on Humor, Aug. 1982, 8, 15. The Shoreham Hotel, Washington, D.C.
46. Dick Gregory with Robert Lipsyte, *Nigger: An Autobiography* (New York: Pocket Books, 1970), 132; Dresser, "Metamorphosis," 226–27; William

Schechter, *The History of Negro Humor* (New York: Fleet Press, 1970), 186–88, 189.

47. Ibid., 105–06, 192–94; Levine, *Black Culture,* 362; Mel Gussow, "Laugh at this Negro but Darkly," *Esquire,* 62, Nov. 1964, 94–95.

48. Redd Foxx-isms are found in Boskin, *Humor and Social Change,* 50–51; Levine, *Black Culture,* 361, 365; Schechter, *History,* 196; Redd Foxx and Norma Miller, *The Redd Foxx Encyclopedia of Black Humor* (Pasadena: Ward Ritchie Press, 1977), 234–56.

49. Arnez and Anthony, "Contemporary Negro Humor," 342; Levine, *Black Culture,* 363–66.

50. Dwight MacDonald, *On Movies* (Englewood Cliffs, N.J.: Prentice-Hall, 1969), 160–61.

51. Langston Hughes, "Jokes Negroes Tell on Themselves," *Negro Digest,* 9 (June 1951), 25.

GERALD MAST

13 Comic Films

Comedy has been associated with motion pictures since the beginning of the American film industry in the early twentieth century. Silent film comedies, with their pantomime, slapstick, and exaggerated facial expressions, still seem to some observers a high point of the film medium's possibilities for comic communication. Yet a number of types of film comedy have developed over the years as technology has allowed different possibilities and as tastes in comedy have changed. Gerald Mast has written extensively about film; his books include the co-edited volume *Film Theory and Criticism: Introductory Readings* (1985) and *A Short History of the Movies* (1992). In his detailed analysis of film comedy, Mast first identifies eight different comic plots in which filmmakers have "organized their human material," pointing out that most of these basic plots are to be found also in stage drama and the novel. In "Comic Thought," Mast analyzes the various ways in which comic films make audiences think about serious issues, and then in "Categories and Definitions," he analyzes how film comedy may either uphold or challenge the dominant values of society. What Mast provides, then, is a framework for thinking about film comedies in terms of their structures, effects, and cultural commentary.

Comic Plots

There are eight comic film plots, eight basic structures by which film comedies have organized their human material. The film shares six of the eight with both the drama and the novel, one of the eight with only the novel, and one seems completely indigenous to the cinema.

From Gerald Mast, *The Comic Mind: Comedy and the Movies*, 2d ed. (Chicago: University of Chicago Press, 1979), 4–27, 343. © 1973 and 1979 by Gerald Mast. Reprinted by permission of the University of Chicago Press.

1. The first is the familiar plot of New Comedy—the young lovers finally wed despite the obstacles (either within themselves or external) to their union. Boy meets girl; boy loses girl; boy gets girl. Many twists and surprises have been injected into this structure—in fact, it was full of twists and surprises in its infancy with Plautus and Terence. Shakespeare used transsexual twists in *Twelfth Night* and *As You Like It*; in *A Midsummer Night's Dream* he twists the romantic platitude that beauty is in the eye of the beholder; in *Much Ado About Nothing* the twist is the irony that the boy and girl do not know they are the boy and girl. Shaw reversed the active and passive sexes of New Comedy in *Man and Superman*. Ionesco burlesqued boy-gets-girl in *Jack, or The Submission*. This plot, with or without unexpected wrinkles, serves as the structural model for such films as *Bringing Up Baby* (the girl is the aggressive kook), *The Marriage Circle, Adam's Rib*, and *The Awful Truth* (boy and girl happen to be husband and wife), *It Happened One Night, Trouble in Paradise, Seven Chances, The Graduate* ("the other woman" is the girl's mother), and many, many more.

Merely concluding the action with a marriage (or an implied union of the romantic couple) is not sufficient for creating a comic plot. Many non-comic films end that way—*The Birth of a Nation, Stagecoach, The 39 Steps, Way Down East, Spellbound*. But in such films the final romantic union is parenthetic to the central action—the overcoming of a series of dangerous, murderous problems. After successfully combating terrible foes, the protagonist earns both life and love as his rewards. This is the typical plot of melodrama (in more dignified terms, "action" or "adventure" films). The adventure plot is a contemporary, totally secularized descendant of the medieval romance, and such films might be truly labeled "romances." In the comic plot, however, the amorous conclusion grows directly and exclusively from amorous complications.

The next three comic plots are all distillations of elements that were combined in Aristophanic Old Comedy.

2. The film's structure can be an intentional parody or burlesque of some other film or genre of films. Aristophanes parodied Euripides; Shakespeare parodied both classical heroism and courtly romance in *Troilus and Cressida*; Fielding began by parodying Richardson in *Joseph Andrews* and heroic tragedy in *The Tragedy of Tragedies* and *The Covent Garden Tragedy*; Ionesco parodies the well-made *boulevard* play in *The Bald Soprano*. In films there were specific parodies of silent hits— *The Iron Nag, The Halfback of Notre Dame*. Mack Sennett parodied

melodrama and Griffith's last-minute rescues in *Barney Oldfield's Race for Life* and *Teddy at the Throttle.*

Parody plots flourished in the days of the one- and two-reelers. Feature-length parodies have been rarer. Keaton's *The Three Ages* is a parody of *Intolerance,* and his *Our Hospitality* parodies both the stories of the Hatfield-McCoy feuds and Griffith's last-minute rescue from the murderous falls in *Way Down East.* Many Abbott and Costello films parodied serious horror films. Woody Allen's *Take the Money and Run* is a series of parodies of film genres and styles; his *Bananas,* a series of parodies of specific films. The parodic plot is deliberately contrived and artificial; it is not an "imitation of a human action" but of an imitation of an imitation. Perhaps, for this reason, it is best suited to the short form.

3. The *reductio ad absurdum* is a third kind of comic plot. A simple human mistake or social question is magnified, reducing the action to chaos and the social question to absurdity. The typical progression of such a plot—rhythmically—is from one to infinity. Perfect for revealing the ridiculousness of social or human attitudes, such a plot frequently serves a didactic function. After all, reduction to the absurd is a form of argument. Aristophanes used it by taking a proposition (if you want peace, if you want a utopian community, if you want to speculate abstractly) and then reducing the proposition to nonsense—thereby implying some more sensible alternative.

But the *reductio ad absurdum* need not serve didactic purposes exclusively. Feydeau typically takes a small human trait—jealousy, extreme moral fastidiousness—and multiplies it to infinity. Ionesco combines the farcical and intellectual potential of the *reductio ad absurdum* in plays such as *The Lesson*—which reduces the process of education to the absurd—and *The New Tenant*—which reduces man's dependence on material objects to the absurd.

In films, too, the *reductio ad absurdum* has served as the basis for both pure farce and bitter intellectual argument. The Laurel and Hardy two-reelers are the perfect example of the *reductio ad absurdum* as pure fun—a single mistake in the opening minutes leads inexorably to final chaos. However, some of the most haunting and bitter film comedies are those which take some intellectual position and reduce it to horrifying nonsense. The reason both *Monsieur Verdoux* and *Doctor Strangelove* are comedies structurally (they are comedies for other reasons, too), despite their emphasis on deaths and horrors, is that they share this common comic shape. Verdoux reduces to the absurd the proposition that murder serves socially useful and emotionally necessary purposes; *Strangelove* deflates the proposition that man needs atomic weapons and military minds to preserve the human race. There is also an implied reduction to the absurd in Renoir's *The Rules of the Game,* although that is not its primary structural principle. Renoir's film is built on the proposition that good form is more important than sincere expressions of feeling. He reduces the proposition to death.

4. The structural principle of this Renoir film is more leisurely, analytical, and discursive than the taut, unidirectional, rhythmically accelerating *reductio ad absurdum.* This structure might be described as an investigation of the workings of a particular society, comparing the responses of one social group or class with those of another, contrasting people's different responses to the stimuli and similar responses to different stimuli. Such plots are usually multileveled, containing two, three, or even more parallel lines of action. The most obvious examples of such plots are Shakespeare's comedies in which love (*A Midsummer Night's Dream*), deceptive appearances (*Much Ado About Nothing*), or the interrelation of human conduct and social environment (*As You Like It*) is examined from several social and human perspectives. Many Restoration comedies (Congreve's *Love for Love,* Wycherley's *The Country Wife*) and their descendants (Sheridan's *The Rivals*) are constructed on similar principles. In films, this multilevel social analysis serves as the basis of many Renoir films (*Boudu sauvé des eaux, The Rules of the Game, The Golden Coach*), of Clair's *À Nous la liberté,* Carné's *Bizarre, Bizarre,* and Chaplin's *The Great Dictator.* In films there is something very French about this structure.

5. The fifth comic-film structure is familiar in narrative fiction but very uncommon on the stage. It is unified by the central figure of the film's action. The film follows him around, examining his responses and reactions to various situations. This is the familiar journey of the picaresque hero—Don Quixote, Huck Finn, Augie March—whose function is to bounce off the people and events around him, often, in the process, revealing the superiority of his comic bouncing to the social and human walls he hits.

This form is probably less suited to the stage simply because its sprawling structure requires a series of imaginative encounters for the *pícaro* that could not be effectively depicted on a stage, given the theater's boundaries of time and space. But the film, completely free from such tyrannies (one of the points at which the film is closer to narrative fiction than to the drama), can give the *pícaro* as interesting and believable a series of opponents as any novelist. The most outstanding film *pícaro* is, of course, Chaplin. Significantly, he begins to use the picaresque structure as he begins to mature with the Essanay films of 1915 (very few of his Keystones use it) and keeps it until *Modern Times* (1936), after which he drops it (for aesthetic reasons that will become clear). The other major film *pícaro* is Jacques Tati. But few of Chaplin's silent rivals ever used the loose, personality-centered structure: Langdon (traces of the picaresque only in *Tramp, Tramp, Tramp* and *The Strong Man*), Keaton (perhaps in a few two-reelers but not in the features), Lloyd (never the *pícaro;* always up to his neck in a very clear, goal-oriented plot). The picaresque structure also shapes such bitter comedies as *Nights of Cabiria* and *A Clock-work Orange.*

6. The next comic-film plot is one that would seem to have no analogue in any other fictional form. The structure might best be described with a musical term—"riffing." But it could as easily be called "goofing," or "miscellaneous bits," or "improvised and anomalous gaggery." This was the structure of most of Chaplin's Keystones, simply because it was one of the two major Sennett structures (parody was the other). The Sennett riffing films take some initial situation—perhaps a place (a beach, a lake, a field), an event (auto races, a dance contest, a circus), an object (Tin Lizzies), an animal (lion), and then run off a series of gags that revolve around this central situation. The only sources of such a film's unity (other than the place, event, thing, or animal) are the performers' tendency to reappear from gag to gag and the film's unceasing rhythmic motion. Pace and motion become unifying principles in themselves. Perhaps the riffing film has no literary analogue because no other form (dance and music would be the closest) is so dependent on pace, motion, and physical energy. The outstanding examples of more recent riffing films are the two Richard Lester-Beatles pictures, *A Hard Day's Night* and *Help,* Louis Malle's *Zazie dans le métro,* and the Woody Allen comedies, which riff with a fairly anomalous collection of parodies and jokes.

Each of these six plots usually produces a comedy, though there are obvious exceptions. *King Lear* uses the multi-plot structure (4) for tragic ends, and many Elizabethan and Jacobean plays (*Doctor Faustus, The Changeling,* Beaumont and Fletcher's) interweave multiple lines of action for non-comic effects. In films, *Children of Paradise, Ship of Fools,* and *The Magnificent Ambersons* might be described as non-comic films with multilevel structures. And the amorous plot of boy-eventually-gets-girl (1) can serve as the basis of weepy melodramas as well as comedies.

The difference between Lubitsch's *The Merry Widow* (1934) and von Stroheim's (1925) is the difference between a comic and non-comic use of the same structural pattern.

Finally, there are two other plots that have been used as frequently for non-comic ends as comic ones.

7. One is the kind that is also typical of melodramatic (or adventure or "romance") films. The central character either chooses to perform or is forced to accept a difficult task, often risking his life in the process. The plot then traces his successful accomplishment of the task, often with his winning the battle, the girl, and the pot of gold at the end of the rainbow. Non-comic versions of this plot include *My Darling Clementine, North by Northwest, Rio Bravo, Tol'able David, The Maltese Falcon, The Thief of Bagdad* (1924), and thousands of other films—many of which contain comic elements and touches. Comic versions of the plot include *The General, The Navigator* (indeed, most of Keaton), *The Kid Brother, The Mollycoddle, The Lavender Hill Mob*, and many others. The difference between a comic and non-comic use of the plot depends entirely on whether the film creates a comic "climate" in the interest of arousing laughter or a non-comic one in the interest of arousing suspense, excitement, and expectation.

8. The same distinction holds true for the final plot form of comic films—the story of the central figure who eventually discovers an error he has been committing in the course of his life. This is, of course, the plot of *Oedipus Rex, Macbeth, Othello*, and any prototypic Aristotelian-Sophoclean tragedy. But it is also the plot of *Tartuffe, The Plain Dealer*, and *Major Barbara*. In films, the plot serves comically in *Mr. Smith Goes to Washington, The Freshman, Sullivan's Travels, Hail the Conquering Hero* (indeed, much of Sturges), *The Apartment* (and much of Wilder), and many others. The comic versions of the plot take place in a comic climate, which is a function of who makes the discovery, what the discovery is, and what the consequences of the discovery are.

Comic Climate

This term condenses the notion that an artist builds signs into a work to let us know that he considers it a comedy and wishes us to take it as such. Once again, it is functional to sidestep theory on the premise that we pretty much know what *a* comedy is even if we do not know what Comedy is. What are the signs by which we recognize that we are in the presence of a comic work?

Here, Elder Olson's concept of "worthlessness" is useful. A worthless action is one that we do not take seriously, that we consider trivial and unimportant rather than a matter of extreme importance, of life and death.* Now, if comedy does indeed depict matters of life and death, then the reason such depiction remains comic is because *it has not been handled as if it were* a matter of life and death. This device will, at some point, lead the audience to reflect that it has been lulled into taking the supremely serious as trivial—a reflection that is precisely the aim of much contemporary comedy. But whether a comedy asks for such reflection or not, the comic craftsman plants a series of signs that lets us know the action is taking place in a comic world, that it will be "fun" (even if at some moments it will not be), that we are to enjoy and not to worry.

1. When the film begins, perhaps even before it, the filmmaker transmits cues to our responses. The first might be the title. It is not worth making too much of titles, and obviously titles such as *The General, Modern Times,* and *The Marriage Circle* do not tell us a lot—although Bergson notes that most comedies bear generic titles (*The Alchemist*) rather than specific names (*Macbeth*). But titles such as *Much Ado About Nothing, Super-Hooper-Dyne Lizzies, Three's a Crowd, Sullivan's Travels,* and *Doctor Strangelove, or How I Learned to Stop Worrying and Love the Bomb* tell us a good deal about what to expect from what follows.

2. The characters of the film rather quickly tell us if the climate is comic. If a familiar comedian plays the central role, we can be *almost* certain that the climate is comic (unless the filmmaker deliberately plays on our assumptions). Keaton's presence makes *The General* take place in a comic world—despite the fact that the film is full of adventure, suspense, war, and death. When Chaplin dropped the picaresque journey for other plot structures, he still used our expectations about Charlie to tell us in what light to view the action. He first appears in *Monsieur Verdoux* trimming flowers, showing great concern for a tiny caterpillar, his familiar mustache turned up in an insane, amputated version of Dali's. Meanwhile the remains of his last wife are going up in smoke (literally) in an incinerator in the rearground of the frame. Chaplin's comically finicky character informs us how to

*Elder Olson, *The Theory of Comedy* (Bloomington: Indiana University Press, 1968), 35–44, defines comedy as "the imitation of a worthless action . . . effecting a *katastasis* of concern through the absurd." The other key term, "*katastasis*," will receive discussion here shortly.

view the grisly activities in his incinerator. His familiar comic *persona* influences every reaction we have to the film, much as the sight of Will Kemp or Robert Armin must have done for audiences in the Theater or the Globe.*

One-dimensional characters who represent comic types, either physically or psychologically, also line up our responses in the intended direction. Because of the pervasiveness of these types, critics have consistently identified comic character with "the base," "the lowly," "the mechanical," or "the ridiculous." But such identifications are not necessarily valid. Such terms fail to fit any of the great comic film *personae.* Many comic films deliberately use inelastic, mechanical types in the minor roles and perfectly supple, non-stereotypic human beings in the major ones—just as Shakespeare did in his comedies.

3. The subject matter of the film's story might also inform us of a comic climate. Subjects such as trying to invent doughnuts without holes or participating in a cross-country walking race are necessarily comic. But if the subject matter is not intrinsically trivial, a comedy reduces important subject matter to trivia. In *Doctor Strangelove* a serious subject, the destruction of the human race, is treated as if it were no more important than inventing hole-free doughnuts. And in *Bananas,* a political assassination (a topic horrifyingly fresh in the American memory) is staged as if it were a televised sporting contest.

4. The dialogue can let us know the climate is comic—because it either is funny or is delivered in a funny, incongruous, mechanical, or some other unnatural way. The opening sequence of Preston Sturges's *Sullivan's Travels* is a breathless series of one-line jokes in which a studio chief and a young, idealistic director debate the validity of making films with a social message. The comic dialogue of this opening scene is essential to the effect of the rest of the film, which gets precariously close to the edge of bathos in its later sequels (indeed it may fall over that edge despite the opening jokes). The suave dialogue between Herbert Marshall and the waiter taking his order for supper in *Trouble in Paradise* informs us that the action and the world to follow are comic, as do the subjects and manner of Cary Grant's breathlessly rapid discussion with his former wife in the opening scene of *His Girl Friday.*

5. Any hint of artistic self-consciousness—that the filmmaker knows he is making a film—can wrench us out of the illusion of the

---

*In *King Lear,* Shakespeare toyed with his audience's expectations as much as Chaplin did in *Verdoux* or *Limelight* by casting the clown, Armin, as a very wise, philosophical fool.

film and let us know that the action is not to be taken seriously. Such self-consciousness can assert itself in moments of burlesque or parody of topical issues or figures, parodies of other films or film styles, in gimmicky cinematic tricks, or in any other device that reminds the audience it is watching something artificial, "worthless." *Singin' in the Rain* self-consciously parodies the story of a star's meteoric rise from obscurity to fame and fortune; *Trouble in Paradise* parodies picture-postcard romance by juxtaposing a garbage collector and a shot of romantic Venice; *Doctor Strangelove* begins with a parody of a love scene as two planes enjoy sexual intercourse to the violinic strains of "Try a Little Tenderness." One trend in recent films is to add self-conscious, intrusive manipulation of cinematic elements to non-comic films as well. Such films, while proclaiming the film event as "not real," attempt to create an intense kinetic metaphor for the feeling of an event rather than comic detachment.

6. The examples above reveal that the motion picture can use distinctly cinematic tools to create its comic or non-comic climate. What the director shoots, how he shoots and edits it, and how he underscores the pictures for the ear establish the way an audience responds. A piece of comic business at the beginning of a film can color our responses for the next two hours—or until the film informs us to alter them.* Chaplin and Lubitsch are two masters at creating hilariously informative business for the beginnings of their films. In *The Gold Rush,* Charlie enters the screen world unknowingly pursued by a bear; in *City Lights* he is grandiosely unveiled as he sleeps on the statue of Civic Virtue and Justice. Whatever else such shots mean in the films—and they mean plenty—they are hilariously funny surprises. Lubitsch's *So This Is Paris* begins as an apparent parody of a Valentino sheik-type movie, only to surprise us by revealing an ordinary domestic couple practicing a dance routine. *The Merry Widow* captures a gaudy military parade as Maurice Chevalier sings "Girls, Girls, Girls." Then two oxen walk ploddingly down the street in the opposite direction, disrupting the order and precision of the singer and the marching band. The apparent "seriousness" of this display of European pageantry has been permanently and effectively ruptured. The manipulation of physical business, so important to an art that depends on the visual and, hence, physical, provides one of the important clues about a film's emotional climate.

*Although the comic climate persists throughout a comic film, I have been concentrating on how we feel that climate at a film's beginning. Establishing the comic climate is, in effect, an element of exposition.

So does the director's handling of camera angle, editing, lighting, and sound. Are the shots close or distant? Does he shoot from below, from above, or at eye level? Is the lighting bright and even, or somberly tonal? Is the editing invisible or obtrusive, rapid or languid with dissolves? Is the soundtrack cheery, tense, contrapuntal, silent? There are no formulas as to what techniques and methods will or won't inevitably produce comic effects, but that the union and combination of lighting, camera angle, decor, editing rhythm, music, etc. do shape the way we respond is undeniable.

In the film medium the handling of physical action, the photographing of images, the styles of camera, editing, and sound are far more important than Aristotle accorded "melody" and "spectacle" in the drama. Whereas Aristotle relegated these two concrete physical assaults of the drama to the two least important aesthetic places, the motion picture, given its greater physical freedom, is far more dependent on them. The handling of image and sound becomes, literally, a part of a film's "diction"—its method of "saying" what it has to "say." The common view that there is a grammar and rhetoric of film underscores the fact that cinematic technique is a kind of language. Whereas imagery in a literary form transmits itself verbally, imagery in the films is explicitly visual. Just as jokes, puns, wit, or comic imagery shape our reaction to a comic novel or play, a film's cinematic "diction" shapes our awareness that the action takes place in a comic or non-comic world.

A comic film, then, is either (a) one with a comic plot and comic climate; or (b) one with a not necessarily comic plot but a pervasive enough comic climate so that the overall effect is comic. For example, the reason von Stroheim's *Merry Widow* is melodrama while Lubitsch's *Merry Widow* is comedy is that Lubitsch has created a comic climate for his film by almost all available means. Von Stroheim's subject matter is gloomy and brutal (duels, deaths, and semi-rapes); his characters are often vicious and perverted; and his manipulation of cinematic devices—camera angle, rhythms of cutting, lighting—is quiet and gloomily tonal. Lubitsch, using the same basic story and characters with the same names, fleshes out the structure with frivolous incidents; and he uses song, farcical minor characters, clever physical business, and self-conscious games with the camera and sound track.

An even more revealing (and more complicated) contrast is that between a comic film such as *The General* and a non-comic one such as *The 39 Steps.* Both use the same plot (the series of dangerous obstacles), the same motivation (both protagonists must overcome obstacles to survive), the same conclusion (both men succeed and win the lady fair). Both films are journeys. Both turn upon accidents and ironies.

But *The 39 Steps* is a heroic action performed by a non-heroic character; *The General* is a heroic action performed by a comic character. *The General* establishes a comic climate early and maintains it throughout the film. Gags define Buster Keaton's character as comic before he ever begins his adventure in search of a locomotive; *The General* introduces slapstick gags even at the most perilous moments. While *The 39 Steps* has wonderful comic moments—the feuding man and woman handcuffed together in a double bed; the man delivering a rousing impromptu political speech although ignorant of the views of the expected speaker—these moments of themselves do not, and are not intended to, create a comic climate.

Comic Thought

The difference between the function of the comedy in *The 39 Steps* and in *The General* is crucial to a definition of the comic film. In the former, comic moments work to make a potentially unbelieving audience *accept as credible* a farfetched heroic tale. Comic touches are used similarly in other Hitchcock films and in such exciting, heroic movies as *Stagecoach* and *The Big Sleep*. In these films we are asked to accept the action as "true," as "fact," to enter into the emotions of the characters and experience their adventures as ours. The heroic "romance" seeks to convince us that the represented action is humanly probable and, consequently, important, of value, "worthwhile."

The function of comedy in *The General* is exactly the opposite: to make the audience accept a potentially exciting, heroic adventure as not strictly credible, as not real, as "worthless." The comic climate subverts our belief in what we see. This reduction of probability is at the heart of film comedy. One kind of film comedy deliberately flaunts its impossibility (*The Gold Rush*, most of Mack Sennett, *À Nous la liberté*, *Boudu sauvé des eaux*, *La Ronde*), exuberantly reducing reality (or elevating it!) to the "worthless." These films are sequences of events that could never possibly happen; in fact, the artist wishes us to take them as such. A second kind of comedy uses events that could indeed occur in reality (*Bringing Up Baby, College, The Palm Beach Story, The Rules of the Game*), but even this kind often deliberately introduces coincidences, plot twists, and individual pieces of business that rupture human probability. The two kinds of comedy can be seen in clear oppositions: Old and New Comedy, Shakespearean comedy and Jonsonian comedy, *Waiting for Godot* and *The Importance of Being Earnest*, *Rhinoceros* and *The Caretaker*. The former of each of the pairs might be thought of as a metaphoric representation of an impossible action, the latter as a literal imitation of a possible (but not necessarily plausible) action.

That we do not believe in comedy's reality, that we consciously recognize the imitation as imitation, produces an intellectual-emotional distance from the work that is the essential comic response. It is this attitude that Olson calls "katastasis"—a relaxed, unconcerned detachment.

Banishing emotion (sentiment and suspense) from comedy is an extreme oversimplification—as Shakespeare and Chaplin, among others, show. Both artists inject pathos into their comedy at crucial moments. But even when Charlie gets sad (and we feel sad with him), we still remain in the region of the comic. First, the comic climate of the work assures us that we will not feel sad for long. Second, Chaplin will deliberately slam the audience (and Charlie) with a joke out of their sadness and back into their roles as detached, laughing observers. Shakespeare similarly alternates sentiment and farce to maintain the essential comic distance.

This detachment, which artists as diverse as Ben Jonson, Shaw, Brecht, Ionesco, Chaplin, and Renoir have consistently traded upon, allows our intellect to roam over comedy's events and characters, enabling us to make connections, see parallels, become aware of ironies, perceive contradictions, consequences, causes and effects. This may very well sound like a restatement of Brecht's *Verfremdungseffekt,* and indeed it is. Brecht's theory of "Epic Theatre" is essentially a comic theory: make the audience aware of stage artifice; reveal the workings of lights and sets; turn the humans into puppets on stilts; use mechanical gimmicks such as slides, placards, and follow-spots. The baring of theatrical artifice stimulates reflection by reducing illusion. Although Brecht thought that our reflection would probe the political and social causes of the events depicted on stage, that reflection might just as well probe the artist's emphasis on the artificial. Nevertheless, a kind of reflection it is.*

One way that film comedies communicate serious thought about human values is to stimulate audience reflection on the ironies, ambiguities, and inconsistencies presented in the comedy. This kind of stimulation is the intention of most comedies that depict an impossible

*It is worth noting that many so-called Brechtian films—for example, Godard's—are much less "Brechtian" than Chaplin's comedies.

action that must be taken as a metaphoric representation of human action rather than a literal one. *Boudu sauvé des eaux* urges on us the contradiction between the bookseller's humanistic clichés and the way he actually lives. *Modern Times* ironically calls attention to the different ways people feed and are fed upon: Charlie fed by machine in the factory; Charlie feeding lunch to his co-worker who has, himself, been accidentally fed into a machine; Charlie stealing a huge meal so he can return to a comfortable prison cell; Charlie and the Gamin eating in the department store where he is night watchman; Charlie as a waiter trying to deliver a roast duckling to a hungry customer in a crowded restaurant. *Doctor Strangelove* notes such ironies as nations using "doomsday machines" to preserve the human race; our nation's dependence on a "reformed" Nazi scientist; pilots working feverishly to repair a damaged bomb door so they can destroy not only themselves but the entire human race; lines like, "You can't fight . . . in the War Room," when the Russian ambassador tussles with Pentagon personnel; the Russian's insistence on taking photographs of "secret" military maps just before the earth is about to evaporate.

This style of comedy—dark irony; metaphoric, almost allegorical examinations of human and social values; outrageously outlandish or horrifying events presented with the most good-humored matter-of-factness—is the particular gift of our own century. Although death and comedy are traditionally mutually exclusive (for the horror or sadness of a human death usually violates comic detachment), these grimly comic films treat death as a bitter or foolish joke, thereby reducing death (that supremely important fact of human existence) to the merely "worthless." They are similar in spirit to Kafka, Beckett, Brecht, Ionesco, Flannery O'Connor, Faulkner's *As I Lay Dying*, Ford's *The Good Soldier*, Heller's *Catch-22*, and other literary manipulations of comic grimness.

Yet another irony about this kind of comedy so dependent on irony is that although the intentions of such a work are clearly intellectual—to stimulate reflection, to ask the audience to perceive ironies—the works never tell the viewer precisely what to think, reflect about, or perceive. The viewer is free to roam over the work's details, picking out the important ones for himself, then doing his own addition. The artist, of course, if he has built his structure and patterns properly, has subtly guaranteed the sum.

A second way that film comedies communicate ideas is with a more traditional, familiar method. The film's action, dialogue, or both can explicitly describe or even promote certain values. A classical example of such a comedy is Jonson's *Alchemist,* whose action depicts how easily the greedy get gulled and then introduces an authorial spokesman (Lovewit) to state the case plainly. The same is true of Ibsen's *Wild Duck,* that foreshadowing of our century's deadly comedy, which dramatizes the danger of destroying functional illusions and includes an authorial spokesman (Dr. Relling) to tell us precisely the same thing.

Preston Sturges's *Sullivan's Travels* is a series of adventures aimed to show us that (*a*) wealthy, sophisticated moviemakers are incapable of telling stories about unhappy, starving people; and (*b*) even if they could, such a film would serve no useful purpose since the unhappy, starving people would rather laugh their troubles away than see accurate depictions of their own misery. In support of the action, Sullivan directly states what he has learned as a result of his travels. Frank Capra's *Mr. Deeds Goes to Town* contrasts the human, folksy, sensitive ways of the rural Mr. Deeds with the sophisticated, snobbish, money-hungry, callous ways of big-city people. The action concludes with an almost-peroration, a courtroom climax in which Deeds (seconded by the impartial judge) directly states the superiority of his values. Whereas the audience must infer the moral values of the ironic comedy, this second kind of comedy directly hands the audience every intellectual morsel it is expected to swallow, usually by making each incident in the plot revolve about the central moral issue and often by including some spokesman to provide a summation.

A third way that film comedies communicate serious ideas is also a descendant of older forms. Even the most lighthearted, escapist piece of fun inevitably implies serious values. The audience, however, might fully understand the comedy without examining any of its values; and the artist (or artisan) might not care whether anyone can find a serious implication in it, might not even know what values he used to build it. Whereas the first kind of comedy allows the audience to infer values (but insists that they do so) and the second kind tells the audience its values, this third kind only implies values, and it may make no difference to the comic effect whether the audience sees those implications or not. For example, it is perhaps possible to enjoy *As You Like It* greatly without speculating that two brothers are doing nasty things to two other brothers, that a clown and a shepherd debate amusingly about appropriate behavior in the court and in the forest, that the characters include a literary, pastoral shepherd and a real shepherd, that all the trouble occurs in court and all the solutions in a mythical forest, that a misanthropic gentleman doubts the value of any human action. Though one might find the play amusing without considering the implications of such facts, its structure and intentions cannot be understood without doing so.

But then, *As You Like It* is Shakespeare. What about brainless television comedies, Broadway comedies, and Hollywood comedies which imply serious values and moral assumptions even if their creators wouldn't recognize an "idea" if they stepped in it? It is impossible to construct an "imitation of a human action" without implying the moral values on which that action is based. The reason that so many popular works do not raise speculation is that the creator has purposely used the most commonly accepted formulas and clichés of morality, so as not to cause speculation, but to drown such speculation in pleasantries.

Finding the moral values of a work in which they are only implied and might not even ask to be inferred is a tricky business for the critic. Such exercises lead to political interpretations of the "Little Orphan Annie" comic strip; to productions of Shakespeare's comedies that present the director's view of the "spirit of the play's implications" rather than the apparent spirit of the text; to ingenious interpretations in which the critic seems to put his own values above the author's. In film criticism, some of the most comic results (and the laughs are unintentional) come from critical evaluations of "pure" comedies such as Mack Sennett's, the Marx Brothers', or Laurel and Hardy's.

Raymond Durgnat, for example, parallels a Laurel and Hardy short, *The Music Box,* in which the two clowns must haul a heavy piano up an immense, steep, narrow flight of steps, to the Sisyphus myth.[1] One might just as well liken the task to Christ's carrying the cross up Calvary, or to Capitalism's oppression of the Worker's Spirit. One can find such interpretations interesting, but it is impossible to agree or disagree with them because their assertions are not based on evidence in the film. Durgnat also calls *The Music Box* "a study in absurdity that one has not the slightest hesitation in ranging alongside the few best examples of the theatre of the absurd."[2] His "one" would indeed be a single opinion in search of a second (*The Music Box* alongside *Waiting for Godot*?).

Durgnat, in the attempt to make his subject seem significant, has been guilty of overstating the case for comedy—or for that comedy. There are many serious implications in *The Music Box*—the psychological relationship of the two clowns as they grow more and more frustrated; the attitude of the film toward the nurse, the cop, the "professor," and toward material objects of any kind. On the other hand, a very early Chaplin film for Essanay, *Work,* begins with a sequence in which Charlie hauls an immense wagon all through town and up a steep hill; he stands in the place usually reserved for a horse or mule; the owner of the wagon sits inside it, cracking his whip—Charlie must transport the boss as well as the goods in the boss's wagon. Chaplin photographs the scene in an extreme long shot, making little Charlie and the large wagon two black silhouettes against the sky, emphasizing the steep incline of the hill. Now this must surely be interpreted as a visual translation of the class system—Capital and Labor, Master and Slave, the man with the wealth and power, the man with nothing but the guts to pull that wagon. One could even begin to make parallels with Pozzo and Lucky of *Waiting for Godot.* For reasons in the films themselves, one is on safer ground with Chaplin than with Laurel and Hardy.

To recapitulate, comic films, because of their "worthlessness" and often deliberately flaunted incredibility, detach the emotion of the spectator from the illusion of the work, leaving the intellect free to perceive the issues of the work. The spectator perceives those issues either by (1) inferring them from the intentional ironies and incongruities of the film; (2) seeing and perhaps hearing those issues specifically represented; or (3) inferring them from unstated but implied values on which the characters and events of the film are based. This last method requires a special effort on the part of the critic, because such a comic film is often not conscious of its serious values and seeks only to produce laughter and pleasure. Such an admission might well contradict the premise of comedy's appeal to intellect unless I postulate (as many theorists have) that laughter is itself a physical-emotional response produced by intellectual recognition. The intellectual basis of comedy's emotional effect (laughter) is precisely what gives it its power as an intellectual tool.

Categories and Definitions

Inevitably, the comic film "says" something about the relation of man to society. The comedy either (*a*) upholds the values and assumptions of society, urging the comic character to reform his ways and conform to the societal expectations; or (*b*) maintains that the antisocial behavior of the comic character is superior to society's norms. The former function of comedy underlies most pre-twentieth-century theory (and practice). Jonson, for example, presented characters of "humours," whose overzealous preoccupation with a single need or desire was an offense against both nature and society. Jonson's plays and prologues urge the offender to purge the "humour" and return to balance. Bergson similarly finds laughter a social cure (even the metaphor parallels Jonson's) for the disease of "mechanical inelasticity"; when the comic figure fails to exhibit the elasticity that social life demands, our laughter serves to turn the human machine back into malleable flesh and soul.

Underlying such a definition of comedy is an assumption about the relationship between nature and society. Although Jonson and other Renaissance thinkers may have been engaged in a "nature-nurture controversy," Jonson seems to avoid the dilemma by implying that the demands of society and of nature are allied, that it is inherent in *human* nature to live socially (hence his use of animal names for antisocial behavior in *Volpone*). Bergson similarly equates social behavior and natural behavior, as opposed to antisocial behavior and unnatural ("mechanical") behavior.

Modern thought, however, makes very different assumptions; rather than allying nature and society, the twentieth-century thinker sees the two as antithetical. The hero of modern comedy is the natural rebel who, intentionally or unconsciously; exposes the shams of society: Shaw's Dick Dudgeon and Saint Joan, Ionesco's Berenger, Brecht's Azdak, Heller's Yossarian, Mann's Felix Krull. In such comic works, the central figure's errors in society's eyes are his virtues in the eyes of his creator. Even anti-heroism is a virtue in a world in which heroism either does not exist or has no value. In Bergsonian terms, one might say that in modern comedy, society and its representatives have become entrusted with the mechanical, rather than the comic protagonist with a comic flaw. Only he, because of that "flaw," is elastic enough to expose society's petrifaction.

In this same tradition, the most thoughtful film comedies are iconoclastic. The movies are, after all, a twentieth-century medium. The greatest comedies throw a custard pie (sometimes literally) in the face of social forms and assumptions. The greatest film comedians are antisocial, but in this antagonism they reveal a higher morality. Ironically, these iconoclastic comedies are products of a commercial system that depended on the support of mass audiences composed of anything but iconoclasts. Perhaps the enjoyable silliness of a comedy muted the underlying attack; perhaps comic iconoclasm provided the audience with a useful emotional release, an opportunity to indulge their own antisocial urges without damaging the social fabric; perhaps the iconoclast was free to speak against social and moral values because he used the entertaining comic form—a traditional privilege of comedians since Aristophanes.*

Many other film comedies—often very entertaining ones—do not confront the mores of the status quo. Some avoid any appearance of a social or moral issue by basing the action and the characters' motivations on literary formulas and moral platitudes: rich people are invariably unhappy; man must work to be happy; self-indulgence is necessarily self-abuse; fate inevitably rewards the virtuous and punishes the vicious. Such comedies cannot be said to contain "thinking" at all, since their value systems defy serious reflection and since an audience accepts such systems (if at all) solely because they are the hackneyed descendants of so many other books, plays, films, and political speeches.† Other comedies tackle moral and social issues without overturning the prevailing order by making error and evil the result of a single human's warping or perverting of that order (Frank Capra is the master of this method). But the comedies that look best today are those which challenge society's ability to make human experience meaningful. That also implies something about today.

One distinction, then, among "serious" comedies is whether they are iconoclastic or apologetic. Another is whether the film transmits its values exclusively by comic devices or by serious sections interspersed with comic ones. Frank Capra and Preston Sturges frequently split their films into comic and serious servings, the success of the film varying inversely with the quantity of serious footage. *Mr. Deeds Goes to Town* seems less labored than *Mr. Smith Goes to Washington* because *Mr. Deeds* contains few purely serious passages, whereas *Mr. Smith* abounds with loving shots of Washington's buildings and monuments and culminates in jingoistic speeches inside the Lincoln Memorial and Senate chamber. *Mr. Deeds* generates its ideas *through* comedy—comic dialogue, characters, business, human interaction—whereas *Mr. Smith* provides serious ideas *and* comedy. Chaplin's *Monsieur Verdoux* is a schizophrenic mixture of 14 comic reels and two sermonizing ones.

Chaplin's great gift was his ability to convey moral attitudes without moralizing. A one-second piece of comic business could reveal a

*Chaplin's iconoclasm eventually caught up with him. As it became more overt, the public became increasingly hostile.

†Films using such platitudes often earn the hoots and howls of a later audience that no longer accepts the same clichés. Given enough of these, the film transcends the realm of platitude into the stratosphere of camp.

whole philosophy of human experience, as, for example, in *The Pilgrim*. Because Charlie is an escaped convict, he takes refuge by impersonating a parson. Called on by villagers to deliver the Sunday sermon, Charlie walks to the pulpit. He leans on the rostrum and then, *instinctively*, lifts his right foot to set it on a bar railing (which, of course, isn't there). The gesture of lifting his foot and then jerkily trying to find a railing to support it economically suggests the similarities and differences between churches and taverns, and the nature of human instinct, which, regardless of disguise, reacts to new situations in terms of familiar ones. Because Chaplin was so brilliant at creating seriousness through comedy, the final reels of *Monsieur Verdoux* are a startling departure from his artistic objectivity—though not enough of one to nullify the brilliance of the first 14.

The greatest film comedies communicate serious values through the comedy itself; they do not serve a comic *digestif* between the serious courses. Indeed, a comedy that sermonizes at us might well be more banal, less complex, less serious than a totally wacky film that goes about its silly business without a conscious idea in its head (or its characters' mouths). The lunacy might contain a very complex underlying view of human experience, whereas any ideology that can be summed up neatly in a piece of explicit, terse movie dialogue is going to "say" less than it says.

As a result, the most effective film comedies—as well as the most thought-provoking ones—are mimetic rather than didactic, descriptive rather than prescriptive. They present a picture of a particular social or human condition without tacking on a simplistic moral solution to the comic problems, and without telling the viewer to apply the solution to his own life. The human problems depicted in *Modern Times, The Rules of the Game, Trouble in Paradise, The General, The Italian Straw Hat, Mr. Hulot's Holiday,* and *Smiles of a Summer Night* do not admit easy solutions. Often when the comic filmmaker does provide one— the utopian idyll at the end of *À Nous la liberté*, the reformation of all the crooks and the eradication of poverty at the end of *Easy Street*—it deliberately shows the ridiculousness of expecting easy solutions.

Not only does the effective comic film present its serious values through the means of comedy itself, but its comic and serious matter are inseparable. Indeed, the film's view of human experience is a function of its comic technique, and its comic technique is a function of its view of human experience. Keaton and Chaplin films "say" different things about human experience because Keaton and Chaplin have different comic styles, find different things funny, use different comic principles. And they are different as comics because they have different views of human experience. When we add cinematic style—angles and distances of shots, lighting, pace and style of cutting, principles of combining sound and image—as a function of comic style (and vice versa), we get the three mutually dependent elements that form the compound of the greatest comic films. Cinematic style is a function of comic style is a function of philosophic vision is a function of cinematic style and so forth around the perfect and unbreakable circle.

Silence and Sound

The great silent comedies revolve about the body and the personality of its owner; the great sound comedies revolve about structure and style—what happens, how it happens, and the way those happenings are depicted. Film comedy, as well as film art in general, was born from delight in physical movement. The essence of early filmmaking was to take some object (animate or inanimate) and simply watch it move. The essential comic object was the human body, and its most interesting movements were running, jumping, riding, colliding, falling, staggering, leaping, twirling, and flying. The early comic filmmakers soon learned that to make better comic films, they needed better comic bodies that could do interesting and surprising tricks. They needed athletes, not wits; men who could turn in the air and take a fall, not turn a phrase. The university for such athletes was not the legitimate stage but vaudeville, burlesque, the music hall, and the circus. Many of the great film clowns later paid fond tribute to their alma maters (Chaplin's *The Property Man, A Night in the Show, Limelight;* Arbuckle's *Backstage;* Keaton's *The Playhouse*).

In the vaudeville house the film clowns learned valuable physical lessons that they never forgot—even after the greatest ones had added a head to the body. Chaplin's most famous routine with the Karno Pantomime Troupe was his impersonation of a comic drunk. That drunk act recurs throughout Chaplin's 50-year career in films. In *The Rounders* (1914) he sways, slides, and staggers while linked to Fatty Arbuckle (and Chaplin is drunk in over a dozen other Keystones). In *A Night Out* (1915) he re-creates the Arbuckle routines with Ben Turpin. In *One A.M.* (1916) he plays the routine alone—except for a house full of objects. And so on, until he staggers into a fancy nightclub in *City Lights* (1931) with his millionaire friend and, 20 years later, enters his boarding house drunk in the opening scene of *Limelight*. The solidity of Chaplin's schooling shows in the eternal usefulness of his basic routines.

The silent clown began with magnificent physical control. Although he usually tried to look funny, it was what he could do with his body that really counted. Ben Turpin's crossed eyes were his trademark, but Turpin could take tremendous falls, turn his legs into rubber bands, or, conversely, stiffen his frame into an unbendable plank. Although Arbuckle was famous for being Fatty, no fat man could move so fast or fall so hard as Arbuckle. This physical control explains why many sound comedies that try to evoke the Sennett spirit fail. They may use Sennett's undercranked camera; they may manipulate pace and non-sense and non sequitur; they may conjure up chase after chase after chase. But they (Kramer's *It's a Mad, Mad, Mad, Mad World*, for example) must depend on funny-looking comic personalities rather than human pretzels, balls, and rubber bands.

The sound comedy is far more literary. Given the opportunity to use the essential tool of literature, words, as an intrinsic part of the film's conception, the filmmaker did not hesitate to do so. In silent films, the use of words in titles was intrusive, a deliberate interruption of the cinematic medium and a substitution of the literary one. We stop look-ing and start reading. But the sound film provided the means to watch the action and listen to the words at the same time. Whereas the silent performer was a physical being—and only through the physical an intellectual one—the sound performer was both physical and intel-lectual at once.

Another difference is that because he could talk, the sound per-former was more like all ordinary human being in society than a spe-cially gifted comic-athlete-dancer-gymnast-clown. Further, the visual interest in sound films was not the physical motion of the performer but the visual juxtaposition of the people with their social and phys-ical milieu. Images and imagery replaced movement. All such shifts were in what can be termed a "literary" direction, making the film far more like a play or novel. And as in the play or novel, the underlying unity of such comedies was provided by structure—what the charac-ters did, what happened to them as a result, contrasts between the char-acters, conflict between the characters and the social milieu, stylistic contrasts, oppositions, parallels, and balances. This style of comedy reached its full development in France in the 1930s, but it is also the comedy of Lubitsch, Capra, Ophuls, late Chaplin, Hawks's comedies, Bergman's, Kubrick's *Doctor Strangelove,* and many others.

Early American sound comedy was not so quick as the French to desert the old silent forms. The great American clowns of the 1930s and their films—W. C. Fields, Mae West, the Marx Brothers—were curious hybrids of silent and sound principles. Theirs are comic films of personality (like the silents) in which the central clown primarily uses his mouth rather than his body (like the talkies). The Marx Brothers and Mae West came to Hollywood from Broadway, and Fields, great vaudeville buffoon and juggler that he was, became more celebrated in films for his misanthropic, under-the-breath mutterings than for his deftness at juggling cigar boxes, pool cues, croquet mallets, whisky bottles, or whatever came to hand. Perhaps the reason the "American Comedy," the comedy of personality, died is that as a style of physical comedy its natural medium is silence. The first decade of sound was close enough to the silent era so that the American physical comedy of personality retained much of its vitality.

But if silent comedy was dominated by physical personalities and sound comedies by more complex structures and careful manipulations of style, there are unique and revealing exceptions to this rule. Lubitsch and Clair made structural, stylistic comedies in the 1920s. It was therefore no accident that they made the best early sound comedies in the 1930s. Tati and Chaplin made comedies of physical personality in the sound years. But Chaplin's one structural comedy of the 1920s—*A Woman of Paris*—sorely misses the vital presence of his personality. And after making two comedies of personality in the 1930s without synchronized sound, Chaplin, beginning with *The Great Dictator*, built his dialogue comedies on structure and style—even when his personality also dominated them. Indeed, Chaplin's refusal to use synchronized dialogue in his first two sound films was a realization of the antithesis of the comedy of physical personality and the structural demands of a comedy that uses words to communicate the characters' feelings and thoughts.

The Art That Conceals Art

Finally, a word must be said about one of the most difficult aesthetic questions about comedy, a question so closely related to personal taste and audience psychology that aestheticians usually avoid it altogether. When is a film (or gag, or line, or character) that is intended to be funny truly funny? What is the difference between meaning to be funny and *being* funny?

Imprecise as it may be, the only answer seems to be this: A film (or gag, or line, or character) is truly funny when the audience is not conscious that it intends to be funny. As soon as one becomes aware of artifice and fakery (not the kind that often functions as an integral part of the comic climate), comedy disintegrates into banal and obnoxious posturing. Although intellectual detachment is crucially related to the experience of successful comedy, when the detachment becomes so great that the mind is no longer amused and engaged but notes the gap between intention and accomplishment, conception and execution, the comedy fails to amuse and entertain.

Perhaps the only term for describing the successful marriage between comic intention and execution is one of the key concepts of the Renaissance—*sprezzatura*. *Sprezzatura* might be defined as the art that conceals art, the supremely artificial that strikes us as supremely natural. The great comedy endows the most contrived and artificial situations (comedy has always been dependent on artifice) with the impression of spontaneity. Although the events and characters of a comedy might seem improbable in relation to reality, they must seem probable, lifelike, and "real" in relation to one another.

To get an idea of this *sprezzatura* at work in a comic film, one need only recall some of the supreme moments of comic films—Chaplin's fantasy ballet with the globe in *The Great Dictator*, Keaton's montage sequence in *Sherlock Jr.*, the dinner table sequence in *Bringing Up Baby*, Tati's tennis game in *Mr. Hulot's Holiday*, the raucously farcical and complicated evening party in *The Rules of the Game*—all of which are totally unnatural and contrived, yet feel spontaneous and alive. Or rather, they feel that way for those who find them funny. Conversely, those who do not find Jerry Lewis or Danny Kaye or Red Skelton funny (and I am one of those) are really saying that their attempts to be funny are obvious and hence do not succeed at making comic life out of contrived business.

As with any other matter of artistic creation, there are no specific rules or formulas for converting comic contrivance into comic life, for endowing a comedy with *sprezzatura*. In general, the impression of *sprezzatura* is a matter of rhythm and emphasis—when to cut and when not to cut, what to emphasize and what to gloss over. And the comic develops this perfect rhythm and emphasis in the handling of all those comic elements discussed above: when to use the close-up to reveal a human reaction or concrete detail, when to stay farther away to allow the viewer to infer it; how long to remain with that close-up; what kinds of business are genuinely funny, what angle and distance illuminate that humor; when to cut quickly away from a facial reaction, a piece of business or a line and when to prolong the shot.

Failures to produce comic life in a film, to create *sprezzatura*, are inevitably failures of rhythm and emphasis—usually failures of overstated emphasis and underpaced rhythm, which produce effects commonly known as "heavy-handed," "overdone," and "doing too much." Understatement seems to be the key to comic-film success. In a form in which intelligence plays such an important role, it is a mistake to insult the audience's intelligence.

NOTES

1. Raymond Durgnat, *The Crazy Mirror* (New York, 1970), 94–95.
2. Ibid., 95.

DAVID MARC

14 | Television Comedy

Along with the comic strips in the daily newspaper, television is the medium that brings humor into American homes on the most consistent basis. Although television broadcasts much that is not humorous, such as sports, drama, and news, David Marc contends in "Television Is Funny" that comedy has been central to television programming since its beginnings in the 1930s, not only in such intentionally humorous forms as the situation comedy, but also in the obvious artificiality of staged wrestling and even in the amusement we may feel when watching out-of-date "serious" programs. The situation comedy, which Marc analyzes in some detail, has been an enduring form of television humor since the 1950s, and the intimacy of television has also made it ideal for presenting stand-up comedy, as he points out in "In Front of the Curtain." Marc is also the author of *Comic Visions: Television Comedy and American Culture* (1989).

Television Is Funny

Comedy is the axis on which broadcasting revolves.
            —Gilbert Seldes, *The Public Arts*

Though network executives reserve public pride for the achievements of their news divisions and their dramatic specials, the fact remains that comedy—entertainment of a primarily humorous nature—has always been an essential, even dominant, ingredient of

From David Marc, *Demographic Vistas: Television in American Culture* (Philadelphia: University of Pennsylvania Press, 1984), 7–29, 168–70. © 1984 by the University of Pennsylvania Press. Reprinted by permission of the University of Pennsylvania Press.

American commercial television programming. The little box, with its squared oblong screen, egregiously set in a piece of overpriced wood-grained furniture or cheap industrial plastic, has provoked a share of titters in its own right from a viewing public that casually calls it "boob tube." Television is America's jester. It has assumed the guise of an idiot while actually accruing the advantages of power and authority behind the smoke screen of its self-degradation. The Fool, of course, gets a kind word from no one: "Knee-jerk liberalism," cry the offended conservatives. "Corporate mass manipulation," scream the resentful liberals. Neo-Comstockians are aghast, righteously indignant at the orgiastic decay of morality invading their split-level homes. The avant-garde strikes a pose of smug terror before the empty, sterile images. Like the abused jester in Edgar Allan Poe's "Hop-Frog," however, the moguls of Television Row make monkeys out of their tormentors. Their deposit slips are drenched in crocodile tears; the show must go on.

In 1927, TV inventor Philo T. Farnsworth presented a dollar sign for sixty seconds in the first public demonstration of his television system.[1] The baggy-pants vaudevillians Farnsworth televised in 1935 have been joined by a host of modern cousins, including the sitcom character actor, the stand-up comedian, the sketch comic, and the gameshow host. No television genre is without what Robert Warshow called "the official euphoria which spreads over the culture like the broad smile of an idiot."[2] Police shows, family dramas, adventure series, and made-for-TV movies all rely heavily on humor to mitigate their bathos. Even The News is not immune to doggerel, as evidenced by the spread of "happy-talk" formats in TV journalism in recent years. While the industry experiments with new ways to package humor, television's most hilarious moments are often unintentional, or at least incidental. Reruns of ancient dramatic series display plot devices, dialogue, and camera techniques that are obviously dated. Styles materialize and vanish with astonishing speed. Series such as *Dragnet, The Mod Squad,* and *Ironside* surrender their credibility as "serious" police mysteries after only a few years in syndication. They self-destruct into ridiculous stereotypes and clichés, betraying their slick production values and achieving heights of comic ecstasy that dwarf their "serious" intentions. This is an intense comedy of obsolescence that grows richer with each passing television season. Starsky and Hutch render Jack Webb's Sgt. Joe Friday a messianic madman. The *Hill Street Blues* return the favor to *Starsky and Hutch.* The distinction between taking television on one's own terms and taking it the way it presents itself is of critical importance. It is the difference between passivity and activity. It is what saves TV from becoming the homogenizing, monolithic, authoritarian tool that the doomsday critics claim it is. The self-proclaimed champions of "high art" who dismiss TV shows as barren imitations of the real article simply do not know how to watch. They are like freshmen thrust into survey courses and forced to read Fielding and Sterne; they lack both the background and the tough-skinned skepticism that can make TV a meaningful experience. In 1953 Dwight Macdonald was apparently not embarrassed to condemn all "mass culture" (including the new chief villain, TV) without offering any evidence that he had watched television. Not a single show is mentioned in his famous essay, "A Theory of Mass Culture."[3] Twenty-five years later it is possible to find English professors who will admit to watching *Masterpiece Theatre*. But American commercial shows? How could they possibly measure up to drama produced in Britain and tied in form and sensibility to the nineteenth-century novel? There is an important reply to this widespread English Department line: TV is culture. The more one watches, the more relationships develop among the shows and between the shows and the world. To rip the shows out of their context and compare them with the works of other media and cultural traditions is to deny their history—their American history—and misplace their identities.

The influence of other American media in the genesis of TV programming is obvious. Radio and movies immediately come to mind. In the early days of network telecasts, however, viewers were treated to generous doses of "exhibition sports," such as professional wrestling and roller derby, phenomena that were new to electronic media. The outrageous antics of the performers on these shows were more in the realm of burlesque or the dance than sport. Wrestler Gorgeous George (the late George F. Wagner) was an early superstar of the genre who was capable of sending pre-space-age viewers rolling off their couches. Borrowing a page from Max Fleischer's cartoon hero Popeye, he would struggle to his corner at the point of defeat, take a few hits from an oxygen tank marked "Florida Air," and, born again, return to the center of the squared circle to defeat his perennially wide-eyed opponent. The carnival-freak-show ambience of the program was enhanced by special matches featuring midgets and women. Wrestling was TVs first original comedy, a grotesque comedy of violence. Not only did the performers have to be excellent acrobats possessing numerous circus skills in order to execute their complex ballets of flying dropkicks, atomic skull-crushers, and airplane spins, but they were also called upon to prove their mettle as character actors and stand-up comedians during the "interview" segments of the show, which can take up as much as half of a wrestling telecast. Playing various archetypal American figures, including ethnic stereotypes that date back to minstrelsy and the vaudeville stage, such characters as Killer Kowalski, Baron Fritz von Erich, and "Country Boy" Haystacks Calhoun would rant and rave, threaten their opponents' lives, and make promises to their fans, never for a moment stepping out of character. Roland Barthes has compared the technique of wrestling with that of the *commedia dell'arte*.[4]

The early tone that wresting set in television comedy is in direct opposition, however, to the comic framework that eventually won commercial favor. As television strove to legitimize itself as a medium worthy of the attention of a middle-class sensibility (circa 1950s U.S.A.), programming came packaged in more identifiably respectable wrappings. The "play area" or stage of the wrestling show was vague and undefined; the viewer could not automatically distinguish between stage and world. Was that wrestler leaving the arena on a stretcher truly unconscious? Was the blood on his face real? Were those women actually tearing chunks of hair out of each other's heads? The ring announcer said yes. Many viewers had their doubts. Could television lie? Was this any way to sell a Chevrolet? Previous to 1955, all four networks (including the now defunct DuMont Network) had offered coast-to-coast wrestling telecasts during the heart of prime time.[5] Though wrestling continues to be locally produced in many U.S. markets and has even reappeared nationally on superstations, it has disappeared from the network programming taxonomy. The only wrestling matches carried by the networks today are occasional telecasts of amateur wrestling on such shows as *The Wide World of Sports* and *Sportsworld.* Barthes likens the experience of watching this "respectable" sport to attending a suburban cinema; it is devoid of the spectacular distension of the professional variety.[6] The present-day descendants of professional wrestling on television are such shows as *Real People* and *That's Incredible!* These schlockumentary magazines (*TV Guide* calls them "sit-life shows")[7] perhaps fill the void left by the cancellation of the wrestling spectacle. Just as wrestling played on its superficial resemblance to the relatively respectable sport of boxing in order to establish a framework of legitimacy for outrageous spectacle, the schlockumentaries borrow their form from the respectable TV newsmagazine (notably *60 Minutes*).[8] These shows stage phony sporting events (e.g., man in tug-of-war with the Goodyear Blimp; daredevil attached to giant rubber band leaping off bridge), and freaks are gratuitously displayed (two-headed man; child savant, etc.); all is presented by a straight-faced ersatz newsman, the successor to wrestling's ersatz sports announcer.

Enter the Proscenium

The forms that came to dominate television comedy (and therefore television) were video approximations of theater: the situation comedy (representational) and the variety show (presentational). The illusion of theater is a structural feature of both. It is created primarily by the implicit attendance of an audience that laughs and applauds at appropriate moments and thus assures the viewer that the telecast is originating within the safely specified walls of the proscenium stage. Normal responses are thus defined. The audience may be actual or an electronic sound effect, but this is a small matter. The consequence is the same; the jokes are underlined. The ambiguities of wrestling are thus avoided.

The situation comedy has proved to be the most durable of all commercial television genres. Other types of programming that have appeared to be staples of prime-time fare at various junctures in TV history have seen their heyday and faded (the western, the comedy-variety show, and the big-money quizshow among them). The sitcom, however, has remained a consistent and ubiquitous feature of prime-time network schedules since the premiere of *Mary Kay and Johnny* on DuMont in 1947. The TV sitcom obviously derives from its radio predecessor. Radio hits such as *I Remember Mama, The Burns and Allen Show, The Goldbergs,* and *Amos 'n' Andy* made the transition to television overnight. Then, as now, familiarity was a prized commodity in the industry. In terms of preelectronic art forms, the sitcom bears a certain physical resemblance to the British comedy of manners, especially in terms of its parlor setting. A more direct ancestor, as Jack Gladden has shown, may be the serialized family comedy adventures that were popular in nineteenth-century American newspapers.[9] Perhaps because of the nature of its serial continuity, the sitcom had no substantial presence in the movies.[10] Though *Andy Hardy* and *Ma and Pa Kettle* films deal with sitcomic themes, their feature length, lack of audience response tracks, and relatively panoramic settings make them very different viewing experiences. Serial narratives in the movies were usually action-oriented. *Flash Gordon,* for example, was constructed so that each episode built to a breathless, unfulfilled climax designed to bring the patrons back to the theater for the next Saturday's resolution. The action of the sitcom is far too psychological for this. Urgent continuity rarely exists between episodes. Instead, climaxes occur within episodes (though these are not satisfying in any traditional sense). In the movie serial (or a modern television soap opera) the rescue of characters from torture, death, or even seemingly hopeless anxiety is used to call attention to serialization. The sitcom differs in that its central tensions—embarrassment and guilt—are almost always alleviated before the end of an episode. Each episode may appear to resemble a short, self-contained play; its rigid confinement to an electronic approximation of a proscenium-arch theater, complete with laughter and applause, emphasizes this link. Unlike a stage play, however, no single episode of a sitcom is likely to be of much interest; it may not even be intelligible. The attraction of an episode is the strength of its contribution to the broader cosmology of the series. The claustrophobia of the miniature proscenium, especially for an audience that has grown casual toward Cinemascope, can be relieved only by the exquisiteness of its minutiae. Trivia is the most salient form of sitcom appreciation, perhaps the richest form of appreciation of any television series. Though television is at the center of American culture—it is the stage upon which our national drama/history is enacted—its texts are generally unavailable upon demand. The audience must share reminiscences to conjure the ever-fleeting text. Giving this the format of a game, players try not so much to stump each other as to overpower each other with increasingly minute, banal bits of information that bring the emotional satisfaction of experience recovered through memory. The increased availability of all-rerun stations being brought about by cable services can only serve to intensify and broaden this form of grass-roots TV appreciation. Plot resolutions, which so often come in the form of trite didactic "morals" in the sitcom, are not very evocative. The lessons that Lucy Ricardo learned on vanity, economy, and female propriety are forgotten by both Lucy and the viewer. A description of Lucy's living room furniture (or her new living room furniture) is far more interesting. The climactic ethical pronouncements of Ward Cleaver conjure and explore the essence of *Leave It to Beaver* less successfully than a well-rendered impersonation of Eddie Haskell does. From about the time a viewer reaches puberty, sitcom plot is painfully predictable. After the tinkering of the first season or two, few new characters, settings, or situations can be expected. Why watch, if not for a visit to the sitcosmos?

The sitcom is a representational form, and its subject is American culture: It dramatizes national types, styles, customs, issues, and language. Because sitcoms are and have always been under the censorship of corporate patronage, the genre has yielded a conservative body of drama that is diachronically retarded by the precautions of mass marketing procedure. For example, *All in the Family* can appropriately be thought of as a sixties sitcom, though the show did not appear on television until 1971. CBS waited until some neat red, white, and blue ribbons could be tied around the turmoil of that extraordinarily self-conscious decade before presenting it as a comedy. When the dust had cleared and the radical ideas being proposed during that era could be represented as stylistic changes, the sixties could be absorbed into a model of acceptability, a basic necessity of mass marketing procedure. During the historical sixties, while network news programs were offering footage of student riots, civil rights demonstrations, police riots, and militant revolutionaries advocating radical changes in the American status quo, the networks were airing such sitcoms as *The Andy Griffith Show, Petticoat Junction, Here's Lucy,* and *I Dream of Jeannie.* The political issues polarizing communities and families were almost completely avoided in a genre of representational comedy that always had focused on American family and community. Hippies occasionally would appear as guest characters on sitcoms, but they were universally portrayed as harmless buffoons possessing neither worthwhile ideas nor the power to act, which might make them dangerous. After radical sentiment crested and began to recede, especially after the repeal of universal male conscription in 1970, the challenge of incorporating changes into the sitcom model finally was met. The dialogue that took place in the Bunker home was unthinkable during the American Celebration that had lingered so long on the sitcom. But if the sitcom was to retain its credibility as a chronicler and salesman of American family life, these new styles, types, customs, manners, issues, and linguistic constructions had to be added to its mimetic agenda.

The dynamics of this problem are perhaps better explained in marketing terms. Five age categories are generally used in demographic analysis: (1) 0–11; (2) 12–17; (3) 18–34; (4) 35–55; (5) 55+.[11] Prime-time programmers pay little attention to groups 1 and 5; viewing is so prevalent among the very young and old that, as the joke goes on Madison Avenue, these groups will watch the test patterns. Prime-time television programs are created primarily to assemble members of groups 3 and 4 for commercials. While members of group 4 tend to have the most disposable income, group 3 spends more money. Younger adults, presumably building their households, make more purchases of expensive "hard goods" (refrigerators, microwave ovens, automobiles, etc.). This situation was profoundly exacerbated in the late sixties and early seventies by the coming of age of the "baby-boom" generation. The top-rated sitcoms of the 1969–70 season included *Mayberry R.F.D., Family Affair, Here's Lucy,* and *The Doris Day Show.* Though all four of these programs were in Nielsen's Top 10 that season, their audience was concentrated in groups 1, 4, and 5. How could the networks deliver the new primary consumer group to the ad agencies and their clients? Norman Lear provided the networks with a new model that realistically addressed itself to this problem. In *Tube of Plenty,* Erik Barnouw shows how the timidity of television narrative can be traced directly to the medium's birth during the McCarthy Era. If the sixties had accomplished nothing else, it had ended the McCarthy scare. The consensus imagery that had dominated the sitcom since the birth of TV simply could not deliver the new audience as well as the new consensus imagery Norman Lear developed for the seventies. This break in the twenty-year-old style of the genre self-consciously defined itself as "hip." The historian Daniel Czitrom has called this phenomenon "Lifestyle."[12]

In the fifties and sixties, the sitcom had offered the Depression-born post-World War II adult group a vision of peaceful, prosperous suburban life centered on the stable nuclear family. A generation that had grown up during hard times, and that had fought what Herbert T. Gillis always referred to as "The Big One," had seen its desires fulfilled on the sitcom. The economic, political, and social travail of the thirties and forties had been left behind by the brave new teleworld. Instead, there was a family: a husband and wife raising children. This family was white and had a name that bespoke Anglo-Saxon ancestry and Protestant religious affiliation. Surprisingly enough, the darnedest things happened to them. Each week a family member—usually a child—would encounter some ethical crisis or moral dilemma in the course of this relentlessly normal state of affairs. Dennis (the Menace) Mitchell hits a line drive through Mr. Wilson's kitchen window after being warned not to take batting practice in the backyard. Beaver unwittingly discovers a copy of tomorrow's history test, which Miss Landers has dropped in the school corridor. The man of her dreams finally asks Patty Duke out for an evening; should she send her twin cousin Cathy to keep her regular date with Richard? These families were all above the pressures usually associated with financial uncertainly. The father was comfortably placed in the professions—lawyer, doctor, insurance executive—or sometimes just amorphously well fixed (e.g.,

Ozzie Nelson). Furthermore, Dad was never in short supply of moral provisos, bromides, and panaceas to alleviate the anxiety of his little citizens-in-training. Mom, who worked for love not wages, though she was rarely shown doing any household tasks more demanding than serving dinner, managed to keep the family's spacious quarters in a state that can be best described as ready for military inspection; she could do it in formal attire to boot.

In these shows—*Father Knows Best, Ozzie and Harriet, The Donna Reed Show, The Trouble with Father, Make Room for Daddy,* et al.— actual humor (jokes or shticks) is always a subordinate concern to the proper solution of ethical crises. They are comedies not so much in the popular sense as in Northrop Frye's sense of the word: No one gets killed, and they end with the restoration of order and happiness.[13] What humor there is derives largely from the cuteness displayed by the children in their abortive attempts to deal with problems in other than correct (adult) ways. Sometimes an extra element of humor becomes the task of marginal characters from outside the nuclear family. Eddie Haskell (Ken Osmond) is among the best remembered of these domestic antiheroes. A quintessential wiseguy, Eddie's deviation from the straight and narrow—as walked by Wally Cleaver—is implicitly blamed on his parents. The fact that Eddie is uniformly punished by the scriptwriters makes his rebellion all the more heroic.

A transformation on this model is the single-parent sitcom. Here the same moral universe remains intact. Instead of the traditional mom-and-dad, however, a widow, widower, aunt, or uncle is raising the children (divorce would not come to this subgenre until Norman Lear's *One Day at a Time* [1975]). This narrative format, pioneered in such shows as *My Little Margie* and *Bachelor Father,* makes it possible to augment the cuteness of the children's moral educations with situations involving romantic possibilities for the adult. Though Hays Office standards are rigorously adhered to, some relief is offered from the sexless picture of married life that otherwise prevailed in the genre.

Beneath the stylistic variances of *Father Knows Best* and *All in the Family* (and *Bachelor Father/One Day at a Time*) these shows are bound together by their unwavering commitment to didactic allegory. Lear indeed updated the conversation in the sitcom living room, but his sitcoms were actually quite conservative in terms of their form. Like the sitcoms of the fifties, Lear's shows reinforce what Dorothy Rabinowitz calls "our most fashionable pieties."[14] "Fashionable" is the key term. As Roger Rosenblatt has pointed out, the greatest difference between *Father Knows Best*'s Jim Anderson and Archie Bunker is that Jim, the father, is the source of all wisdom for the Anderson family while Archie is more likely to be the recipient of lessons from Mike, Gloria, and Edith.[15] In marketing terms, the representation of the higher spending power is consistently heroic.

Though didacticism may be a structural feature of the sitcom (and all storytelling), a strain of situation comedy has developed that is less emphatically moralistic and more concerned with being funny. *I Love Lucy* is one such sitcom; it is the prototype of the "zany" variety. Here, father still knows best, but his task is not so much to preach sermons to the children as to restrain his wife from doing "crazy" things that threaten middle-class order. Lucy is in no way the imperturbable wife and mother embodied in her contemporary, Margaret Anderson. She overspends her budget, acts on impulse, and does not hesitate to drop Little Ricky with Mrs. Trumble at the slightest hint that her dream of something more than a hausfrau existence might be satisfied by an audition for a show at the Tropicana. Lucy refuses to allow bourgeois role destiny to stifle her organic desires, no matter how often she is repressed. Her attempts to escape from what Ricky and society define for her as "her place in the home" turn her into a buffoon, and this is the center of the show. By the end of each episode she has been whipped back into middle-class-housewife shape. Her weekly lapse into "childish" behavior, however, makes her into a freak whose comic talents are far more compelling than the dismal authoritarian morality that controls her.[16]

Though Lucy was copied in such shows as *I Married Joan* and *Pete and Gladys*, the imitators could not easily come by the comic talents of Lucille Ball. To compensate for Lucy's personal magic, they frequently turned to the supernatural. In shows such as *Bewitched, I Dream of Jeannie, Mr. Ed,* and *My Favorite Martian,* an otherwise realistic (or at least scientifically feasible) vision of middle-class life is invaded not by a mere madcap but by a character (woman, animal, or alien) possessed of supernatural powers. Magic is both the cause of and the antidote to the much-feared curse of zaniness. The relatively naturalistic Lucy often becomes the victim of her own harebrained scheming and has to own up to Ricky in humiliation before the final credits. On the other hand, Samantha Stevens, a witch, can set things right with a twitch of her nose—with husband Darren often none the wiser. In each case the wife possesses energies and desires that tempt her to rebel against the constraints of middle-class-housewife status. The husbands, both the immigrant striver Ricky Ricardo and the Madison Avenue executive Darren Stevens, are determined to keep their contractual slaves/lovers locked safely away at home. Though a bandleader himself, Ricky simply forbids Lucy from pursuing a show business career. Darren is an even crueler sexist. He constantly expects Samantha to entertain his business contacts at home but forbids her to use her magical powers. Though she can prepare an elegant banquet with a spell (usually one heroic couplet) and a twitch of her nose, he forces her to slave over a hot stove all day for no other reason than to satisfy his incorrigibly puritanical "principles."

The domestic sitcom has strayed from its compelling middle-class center upon occasion. Though the conventions of teleculture define the middle class as a vast amalgamation of all those Americans who neither depend on welfare payments nor have live-in servants, there have been self-consciously proletarian sitcoms, including such early shows as *The Life of Riley* and *The Honeymooners*. As the titles suggest, there is little of Clifford Odets in them, though the Kramdens' stark two-room flat is notable. Interestingly enough, the working-class sitcom was virtually absent from the networks during most of the sixties. It was Lear who revived the idea with *All in the Family*. The black sitcom has a similar history. It appeared in TV's pioneer days (e.g., *Amos 'n' Andy, Beulah*), only to disappear from view during the sixties and then make a comeback under Lear's tutelage. In acknowledgment of the protests of civil rights organizations against the lily-whiteness of the sitcosmos, NBC premiered its *Julia* series in 1968. This was a single-parent situation starring Diahann Carroll as a widowed, professional, middle-class mom; the tokenism of the series was as obvious as its resemblance to *The Doris Day Show*, which made its debut that same season. Lear and his Tandem Productions restyled and resurrected the black sitcom in *Sanford and Son*, which premiered in 1972. Other black sitcoms, such as *The Jeffersons* and *Good Times*, followed.

Faced with the problem of seeming fresh and different without upsetting expectations of the familiar formula, sitcom-makers have attempted to bring the form to various settings. In addition to the ubiquitous contemporary middle-class living room, sitcoms have taken place in military barracks, prehistoric caves, tenement flats, mansions, extraterrestrial space, junkyards, offices, police stations, and high school and college classrooms; in New York, Los Angeles, Minneapolis, Mayberry, Bedrock, Indianapolis, Moscow, Milwaukee, a Nazi prison camp, and Any-town, U.S.A. The military sitcom has been a strong subgenre.

Sgt. Bilko, McHale's Navy, F Troop, Gomer Pyle, U.S.M.C., I Dream of Jeannie, Hogan's Heroes, C.P.O. Sharkey, M*A*S*H, and *Private Benjamin* (to name just a few) have extended the military setting through war and peace, present and past, and every branch of the U.S. armed services, save the Coast Guard. Deviation from "normal" (that is, nuclear family) life also occurs in a subgenre of the sitcom that focuses on single career girls. Early examples include *Our Miss Brooks* and *Private Secretary* (also known as *The Ann Sothern Show*). Like the blue-collar and black sitcoms, the career-girl sitcom faded from the homescreen during the halcyon days of the middle-class domesticom, only to resurface in the late sixties. *That Girl* (1966) was at the crest of the revival. Marlo Thomas starred as Ann Marie, a young woman who leaves her parents' suburban New York home to move to Manhattan and pursue a career as an actress. Ann's ties to her family, however, were emphasized. Both her father and mother were series regulars who kept a close watch on their daughter's fortunes in Sin City. Her thoroughly innocuous steady boyfriend stood between Ann and promiscuity. It was *The Mary Tyler Moore Show* and the MTM Enterprises spin-offs that finally presented a picture of women out in the world on their own. The career-woman sitcom became a staple of the seventies. The heroine, freed at last from her role as chief cook and bottle washer, as well as from the moral authority of a husband or father, entered the pantheon of telemythology.[17]

For all the stylistic variations on a theme that have characterized sitcom history, the comic success of a show ultimately has depended on the talents of its actors and their collaborative success as a troupe. As performers as diverse as Don Rickles and Jimmy Stewart have learned, the sitcom simply does not work as a one-star vehicle; the laughs—and usually the ratings—have gone to the well-formed ensemble. Andy Griffith's "stardom" fades from memory if isolated from Don Knotts's woefully neurotic Deputy Barney Fife, Howard McNear's apoplectic Floyd the Barber, and the other citizens of Mayberry. Compare the brilliant Kabuki-like choreography of the original *Honeymooners* to the awkward, misplayed revival in the sixties; Audrey Meadows and Joyce Randolph were never quite replaced. Though Lucille Ball was able to stay atop the ratings throughout her sitcom career, she would never again attain the comic heights she had achieved with Desi Arnaz, Vivian Vance, and William Frawley. Lucy's artistic demise was due not only to the inferior comic technique of her later efforts (*The Lucy Show* and *Here's Lucy*), which can be explained in show business terms as "inferior timing," but more importantly to the absence of the mythological syntheses of *I Love Lucy*: male and female (Ricky/Fred vs. Lucy/Ethel); native-born and immigrant (Lucy/Ethel/Fred vs. Ricky); old and young (the Ricardos vs. the Mertzes); and organic and genteel (Lucy vs. the middle-class world she lived in). These paradigms tightened the interstices of the field of American comedy. The later shows invested all comic tensions in the conflicts between Lucy and the hyperbolically genteel Gale Gordon; they pale in comparison.

Perhaps the reason that the sitcom has been looked down upon by critics as a hopelessly "low" or "mass cult" form is that a search for "the best which has been thought and said" is a wild-goose chase as far as the genre is concerned. R. P. Blackmur, though certainly no TV fan, commented germanely that the critic "will impose the excellence of something he understands upon something he does not understand. Then all the richness of actual performance is gone. It is worth taking precautions to prevent that loss, or at any rate to keep us aware of the risk."[18] Television is not yet a library with shelves; it is a flow of dreams, many remembered, many submerged. How can we create a bibliography of dreams? Blackmur also wrote that "the critic's job is to put us into maximum relation to the burden of our momentum."[19] As a culture, television is the engine of our momentum. It has heaped thousands upon thousands of images upon the national imagination:

> Gleason rearing back a fist and threatening to send Alice to the moon.
>
> Phil Silvers's bullet-mouthed Sgt. Bilko conning his platoon out of its paychecks.
>
> Jack Benny and Rochester guiding an IRS man across the crocodile-infested moat to the vault.
>
> Dobie Gillis standing in front of "The Thinker" and pining for Tuesday Weld.
>
> Carroll O'Connor giving Meathead and modern philanthropic liberalism the raspberry.
>
> Jerry Van Dyke settling down in the driver's seat of a Model T Ford for a heart-to-heart talk with *My Mother, the Car*.

[Walt] Whitman, in *Democratic Vistas*, called for a new home-grown American literary art whose subject would be "the average, the bodily, the concrete, the democratic, the popular."[20] The sitcom is an ironic twentieth-century fulfillment of this dream. The "average" has been computed and dramatized as archetype; the consumer world has been made "concrete"; the "bodily" is fetishized as the unabashed object of envy and voyeurism; all of this is nothing if not "popular." The procession of images that was Whitman's own art, and which he hoped would become the nation's, is lacking in the sitcom in but one respect: its technique is not democratic but demographic. The producers, directors, writers, camera operators, set designers, and other artists of the medium are not, as Whitman had hoped, "breathing into it a new breath of 'life'."[21] Instead, for the sake of industrial science, they have contractually agreed to create the hallucinations of what Allen Ginsberg called "the narcotic . . . haze of capitalism."[22] The drug indeed is on the air and in the air. Fortunately, the integrity of the individual resides in the autonomy of the imagination, and therefore it is not doomed by this system. The television set plays on and on in the mental hospital; the patient can sit in his chair, spaced-out and hopeless, or get up and push at the doors of consciousness. This is the happy ending for the sitcom.

In Front of the Curtain

"The virtue of all-in wrestling," wrote Roland Barthes in 1957, "is that it is the spectacle of excess."[23] I have tried to show that the sitcom, on the other hand, is a spectacle of subtleties, an incremental construction of substitute universes laid upon the foundation of a linear, didactic teletheater. Even the occasional insertion of the *mirabile* or supernatural is underlined by the genre's broader commitment to naturalistic imitation. Presentational comedy, which shared the prime-time limelight with the sitcom during the early years of TV, vacillates between these poles. The comedy-variety show has been the great showcase for presentational teleforms: stand-up comedy, impersonation, and the blackout sketch. This genre is similar to wrestling in that it too strives for the spectacle of excess. Its preelectronic ancestors can be found on the vaudeville and burlesque stages: the distensions of the seltzer bottle and the banana peel; the fantastic transformations of mimicry; the titillations of the physical, psychological, and cultural disorders that abound in frankly self-conscious art forms. But the comedy-variety show does not go to the ultimate excesses of wrestling. Like the sitcom, it is framed by the proscenium arch and accepts the badge of artifice.

While the representational drama of the sitcom and its cousins, the action/adventure series and the made-for-TV movie has flourished to the point that these genres consume almost all of the "most-watched" hours, the comedy-variety show has been in steady decline since the 1950s, when it was a dominant genre of prime-time television. Since the self-imposed cancellation of *The Carol Burnett Show* in 1978, the new presentational variety hours that have appeared in prime-time have been hosted by singers (Barbara Mandrell, Marie Osmond), and comedy has been relegated to a rather pathetic secondary concern on these programs. The demise of the genre has deprived prime time of some of television's most promising possibilities. Stand-up comedy, as developed in the American nightclub, is one of the most intense and compelling of modern performance arts. Eschewing the protection of narrative superstructure and continuity, the stand-up comedian nakedly faces the audience. He truly works in the first person, making no distinction between persona and self. When successful, the monologist offers an awesome display of charismatic power: the lone individual controlling the imaginative and physical responses of millions. By the same token, nowhere is failure more pathetic or painful. The rhythm of the stand-up monologue demands the punctuation of the audience's response; when it is missing, the spectacle of impotence is shattering. The stand-up comedian laying an egg is one of the few phenomena on television or in mass entertainment in general where the visible pressure to produce the desired effect emerges through even the slickest production values. That pressure is unrelenting. Like the wrestler who must continue to play his role during "interviews" outside the ring, the television stand-up comic is expected to remain in character at all times. After doing "five minutes," he must join Johnny and his guests as "himself," a clown, a wit, a funnyman. The ability to do this often provides satisfying performance art. Failure cracks apart the smooth veneer of TV "normalcy."

Television as a medium is particularly well suited to the presentation of stand-up comedy. The comedian is easily framed on the small screen. Perspective can be spontaneously shifted by the director from the full body portrait, which gives the comic the authority of a public speaker, to close-ups that are advantageous to mimicry and face-making. The intermediary teletheater is devoid of drunken hecklers and clattering dishes, making it a propitious showcase for the carefully rehearsed, well-timed routine (though admittedly, for some stylists, this loss of spontaneous give-and-take is regrettable). The structure of the show business industry, however, has inhibited stand-up comedy as a television art. Comedians, even the handful who employ writing staffs, must beware the plague of overexposure. A powerful nightclub monologue can become worthless in Las Vegas and Atlantic City after even a single television appearance. Furthermore, the fetishization of "dirty words" on television puts severe limits on stand-up text. It is perhaps principally for these reasons that the stand-up comedian has been largely squeezed out of prime time into what the industry terms "marginal hours." On daytime television, for example, stand-up performers abound as players on gameshows and as guests on *Merv* and *Mike*. Gameshows such as *The Hollywood Squares* and *Battlestars* have even been tailored as stand-up vehicles. The real stronghold for presentational comedy on television, however, has become the late-night spot.

In May of 1950, NBC premiered *Broadway Open House* in a late-night time period (i.e., 11:30, eastern time), and ever since, this segment of the NBC schedule has been reserved for presentational comedy. It has even become a relatively safe zone for artistic freedom (or at least TV's equivalent of "blue" material). Alex McNeil describes *Broadway Open House* as "a heavy-handed mixture of vaudeville routines, songs, dances and sight gags."[24] The cohosts were vaudeville veterans Jerry Lester and Morey Amsterdam, and much of the humor derived from their interplay with the Dolly Parton of early TV, "a buxom blonde named Jennie Lewis, better known as Dagmar, who played it dumb."[25] By the midfifties, the program had evolved a more sedate format: a 105-minute, Monday-through-Friday, "desk-and-sofa" talk show known as *The Tonight Show*. It was hosted by *bon mot* comedians such as Steve Allen, Ernie Kovacs, and Jack Paar. The opening monologue became an institution, television's only daily comic paratext to The News. In 1981 Johnny Carson continues to deliver the only regularly scheduled comedy monologue on national television, but Johnny's ever-expanding vacation schedule has made even that an iffy proposition; the show has dwindled to a mere one hour due to Johnny's seemingly unquenchable thirst for recreation. The *Tonight Show* sofa, once filled with guests, including two or three comics a show, is relatively empty these days.

Weekly late-night comedy shows, such as *Saturday Night Live* and *SCTV*, have taken up some of the stand-up slack, but the great work of these shows has been to grandly resuscitate TV blackout. The blackout sketch, or short skit, was pioneered as a distinctive teleform in the early days of TV. Before two-hour television movies ate up such a large chunk of network prime time, the viewer did not have to wait for the wee hours of the weekend to see sketch comedy. Milton Berle, Jimmy Durante, Jackie Gleason, Sid Caesar, Ernie Kovacs, Martha Raye, and

Ed Wynn were just a few of the comedians who hosted their own weekly comedy hours. These stars were the pampered children of Television Row. Jackie Gleason was able to get CBS to build him a Hudson River mansion during the fifties; later, when he got Sunbelt Fever, CBS chairman William Paley granted him a complete new production facility in Miami Beach. Milton Berle, "Mr. Television," was signed to a thirty-one-year contract by NBC in 1951. The role of Uncle Miltie in the early proliferation of the medium itself is, of course, legendary. His subsequent fall from Nielsen grace parallels the decline of the genre. From 1948 to 1956, the Berle show was a Tuesday night ritual. The first official ratings season was 1950–51, and A. C. Nielsen ranked Berle's *Texaco Star Theater* as the Number One attraction on television.[26] General Sarnoff's multimillion-dollar investment seemed to be paying off as the show consistently finished among the Top 5 for the next three seasons. However, in 1954–55 it slipped to Number Thirteen, and in 1955–56 it dropped out of the Top 20 altogether.[27] It is too easy to dismiss the Berle phenomenon as merely a case of the public's fickle favor. Not a single comedy-variety hour made the Top 10 in 1955–56.[28] Few variety shows hosted by comedians would finish in the Top 10 ever again. At the end of the 1955–56 season, the unthinkable happened—Berle was yanked off the air. After a two-year layoff, NBC tried him again, this time in a reduced half-hour format; the new show was not renewed for a second season. By 1960, stuck with an expensive long-term contract, Sarnoff was using Milton Berle as the host of *Jackpot Bowling*. Finally, with over fifteen years remaining on his contract, Berle and NBC came to an agreement, and the once indomitable star was let go. Last-place ABC promptly signed him for a comedy-variety comeback, but *The Milton Berle Show* could not survive six months in 1966. The early rush to sign the stars for eternity ended as the networks entered the age of entropy.

The reasons for the failure of Berle and his "hellzapoppin'" burlesque style of presentation are not obvious. What can be said with some assurance is that this failure took place amid increasing demand for a "product" as opposed to a "show" in the growing television industry. As the prime-time stakes rocketed upward, sponsors, agencies, and networks became less tolerant of the inevitable ups and downs of a star-centered presentational comedy. The sitcom and other forms of representational drama offer the long-term rigidities of shooting scripts, which make "quality control" easier to impose. Positive demographic responses to dramatic "concepts" are dependable barometers. Performance comedy is only as good as an individual performance; the human element looms too large. Furthermore, the dreaded extremes of presentational comedy can be avoided. Kinescopes of *The Texaco Star Theater* reveal Berle in transvestite sketches whose gratuitous lewdness rivals wrestling at its most intense. The passionate vulgarity of these sketches could not have been wholly predictable from their scripts. Instead, it derives directly from Berle's confrontation with the camera—his performance. Censorship of such material presents complex editing problems, which are easily preempted in representational drama by script changes. It is my own feeling that the high-tech mystique of television itself—the sterile promise of the machine—is what kept the show from crossing the border from "family fun" to pornography in the early days of television. Gilbert Seldes described Berle's comedy as "good clean dirt."[29] Seldes called the early Berle a "stag entertainer," offering this observation: "The basic material of the stag entertainer, whether he dresses in women's clothes, pretends to be homosexual, or develops some other specialty, is still the off-color story, and the basic style is always the public one of maximum projection."[30] Perhaps the blinding gloss of the "modern miracle" of television was becoming subdued during television's second decade. Time, boredom, and the further technicization of the American household were making the future banal enough to generate a critical response. Were the full implications of burlesque beaming into the home becoming a bit too clear for Berle's family audience? Brooks and Marsh have indeed attributed the undoing of Uncle Miltie to increasing "sophistication" among the viewing public: "By 1956 the steam had run out for 'Mr. Television.' TV was by then becoming dominated by dramatic-anthology shows, Westerns, and private eyes, and the sight of a grinning comic jumping around in crazy costumes [i.e., women's clothing] no longer had the appeal it did in 1948."[31] When NBC gave Berle his second chance in 1958, the show was considerably toned down:

> Two years after his departure from the Tuesday line-up, Berle returned to prime time with a half-hour variety series for NBC. He was a more restrained performer this time—no slapstick or outrageous costumes—attempting to function more as a host than the central focus of the show.[32]

The consequence was clear: Berlesque, like wrestling, had been blackballed from television's increasingly genteel prime-time circle. The late fifties, of course, was the heyday of *Playhouse 90*, *The U.S. Steel*

Hour, and *The Armstrong Circle Theater,* the "Golden Age" of respectable drama. TV then, as now and always, was on the verge of becoming sophisticated. The NBC late-night spot had passed from the wacky vaudevillian Jerry Lester to the neurotically urbane Jack Paar. Berle was certainly neurotic; he simply could not be urbane.

A survey cited by Sterling and Kitross shows the number of "Evening Network Television" hours given to comedy-variety shows declining from a high of 21.5 hours in 1951 to 5 hours in 1973.[33] The censorship problems I have mentioned have checkered the history of the genre. The case of the Smothers Brothers provides an example. Tom and Dick won their network wings with an innocuous sitcom in the 1965–66 season. When CBS gave them their own comedy-variety show, *The Smothers Brothers Comedy Hour,* the network suddenly found itself with a severe Standards and Practices crisis. As Brooks and Marsh have written, the show "poked fun at virtually all the hallowed institutions of American society—motherhood, church, politics, government, etc."[34] Controversial guests, such as folk singer Pete Seeger and Dr. Benjamin Spock (after his conviction for aiding draft evaders), were invited to appear on the show. Many segments were severely censored or deleted. An embarrassed CBS canceled the series on a technicality: A tape was delivered past the usual deadline. That tape contained a sequence in which Joan Baez dedicated a song to her husband, David Harris, who was serving a sentence in federal prison for draft evasion.[35] In 1981 the Smothers Brothers were back on the air, the stars of a short-lived representational drama series, *Fitz and Bones.*

Nat King Cole was a singer, not a comedian, but the peculiar case of his ill-fated variety series makes a stark point about the qualitative distinctions between presentation and representation on network television. Black actors and actresses were not complete strangers to television in the 1950s. Ethel Waters had played the title role in *Beulah* (ABC, 1950–53), and Tim Moore, Spencer Williams, Ernestine Wade, and the rest of the cast of *Amos 'n' Andy* (CBS, 1951–53) were of course black (the radio cast had been white). Amanda Randolph played the part of Louise (the maid) on *The Danny Thomas Show* from 1953 to 1964. But when Nat King Cole was given his own variety show in 1956, not a single sponsor could be found. NBC affiliates in the North as well as the South declined to carry the program.[36] Even the appearances on the show of such mainstream white stars of the day as Tony Bennett, Frankie Laine, and Peggy Lee could not dissuade affiliates from their boycott. To its credit, NBC continued to air *The Nat King Cole Show* as a sustaining program for more than a year, juggling its time slot twice in an attempt to find a place for it. But a black entertainer stripped of the representational mask would not be successful in prime time until *The Flip Wilson Show* (NBC, 1970–74).

The comedy-variety genre never completely died off in prime time. A handful of hits such as *The Carol Burnett Show, The Flip Wilson Show,* and George Schlatter's innovative *Rowan and Martin's Laugh-In* managed to keep it alive. But pop singers, including Sonny and Cher, Tom Jones, Englebert Humperdinck, Tony Orlando and Dawn, the Captain and Tennille, and Donny and Marie, took over the lion's share of the dwindling hours given to vaudeville-style presentation in the sixties and seventies. A later full-fledged attempt to revive the comedy-variety hour was *The Richard Pryor Show,* which premiered on the NBC fall schedule in 1977. It was destroyed by the old comedy-variety devil—censorship—after only five airings.

Generally speaking, the comedian has had to step back from in front of the curtain, cross the proscenium arch, and don the mask of a representational character to find a place in prime-time television. The networks have thus provided themselves with a modicum of protection from the unreliability of individual personalities. Presentational comedy—performance art—may simply be too dangerous a gamble for the high stakes of today's market.

Interestingly, the disappearance from TV of the clown who faces the audience without a story line has occurred more or less simultaneously with rising interest in and appreciation of performance art in avant-garde circles. In "Performance as News: Notes on an Intermedia Guerrilla Group," Cheryl Bernstein writes:

> In performance art, the artist is more exposed than ever before. The literal identification of artistic risk with the act of risking one's body or one's civil rights has become familiar in the work of such artists as Chris Burden, Rudolf Schwarzkogler, Tony Schafranzi and Jean Toche.[37]

Burden, for example, invites an audience into a performance space where spectators sit atop wooden ladders. He then floods the room with water and drops a live electrical wire into the giant puddle. The closest thing television offers to a spectacle of this kind is Don Rickles, who evokes audience terror by throwing the live wire of his insult humor into the swamp of American racial and ethnic fears. Rickles, for the most part, has been prohibited from performing his intense theater of humiliation in prime time. Twice NBC has attempted to contain him in sit-com proscenia, but these frames have constricted his effect and turned his insults into dull banter. In recent years he has been unleashed upon a live studio audience only during his infrequent appearances as a guest host on *The Tonight Show*. The erratic quality of Rickles's performances on *Tonight* offers a clue to the networks' reluctance to invest heavily in the presentational comedy form.

Bernstein points to The News as the great source of modern performance art on television. She deconstructs "The Kidnapping of Patty Hearst" by the Symbionese Liberation Army as a performance work. The SLA was a troupe that was formed to create a multimedia work—the kidnapping—principally for television. The mass distribution of food in poor neighborhoods in the San Francisco Bay area (one of the SLA's demands), as well as the shoot-outs and police chases that occurred, were all part of a modern theatrical art that can take place only on television. Perhaps the proliferation of The News on television can be tied to the decline of presentational comedy: the two have seemed to occur in direct proportion to each other. The sit-life schlock-umentary is the point at which the two genres meet. Furthermore, the bombardment of the homescreen with direct presentations from every corner of the earth has created a kind of vaudeville show of history. The tensions of the nuclear Sword of Damocles create a more compelling package than even Ed Sullivan could have hoped to assemble. The nations of the world have become a troupe of baggy-pants clowns on TV. They are trotted out dozens of times each day in a low sketch comedy of hostility, violence, and affectation. The main show, of course, is the network evening news. Climb the World Trade Center. Fly an airplane through the Arc de Triomphe. Plant a bomb in a department store in the name of justice. Invade a preindustrial nation with tanks in the name of peace. Can Ted Mack compare with this?

NOTES

1. Christopher H. Sterling and John M. Kitross, *Stay Tuned: A Concise History of American Broadcasting* (Belmont, CA: Wadsworth, 1978), 147.
2. Robert Warshow, *The Immediate Experience* (Garden City, N.Y.: Doubleday, 1962), 128.
3. Dwight Macdonald, "A Theory of Mass Culture," *Diogenes*, no. 3 (1953), 1–17; reprinted in *Mass Culture: The Popular Arts in America*, ed. Bernard Rosenberg and David Manning White (New York: Free Press, 1957), 59–73.
4. Roland Barthes, *Mythologies*, trans. Annette Lavers (New York: Hill and Wang, 1972), 17.

5. Tim Brooks and Earle Marsh, *The Complete Directory to Prime Time Network TV Shows, 1946–Present,* rev. ed. (New York: Ballantine Books, 1981); see "Prime Time Schedules."

6. Barthes, *Mythologies,* 15.

7. David Chagall, "Reading the Viewer's Mind," *TV Guide,* Nov. 7, 1981, 48.

8. Barthes comments on this subject: "The public knows very well the distinction between wrestling and boxing; it knows that boxing is a Jansenist sport, based on a demonstration of excellence. . . . A boxing-match is a story which is constructed before the eyes of the spectator; in wrestling on the contrary, it is each moment which is intelligible, not the passage of time. The logical conclusion of the contest does not interest the wrestling-fan, while on the contrary a boxing-match always implies a science of the future"; *Mythologies,* 15–16.

9. Jack Gladden, "Archie Bunker Meets Mr. Spoopendyke: Nineteenth Century Prototypes for Domestic Situation Comedy," *Journal of Popular Culture* 10, no. 1 (1976): 167–80.

10. A notable exception to this is the silent "Mr. and Mrs. Jones" series made by D. W. Griffith for Biograph in 1908–9. Robert Sklar describes these films as "situation comedies" in *Movie-made America* (New York: Vintage Books, 1976), 106.

11. Groups 4 and 5 are sometimes constituted as "35–49" and "49 + "; in recent years, "35–55" and "55 + " have been increasingly in use.

12. Daniel Czitrom, *Media and the American Mind: From Morse to McLuhan* (Chapel Hill: University of North Carolina Press, 1982), 190.

13. See Northrop Frye, *Anatomy of Criticism: Four Essays* (Princeton, N.J.: Princeton University Press, 1957).

14. Dorothy Rabinowitz, "Watching the Sitcoms," in *Television: The Critical View,* ed. Horace Newcomb (New York: Oxford University Press, 1979), 55.

15. Roger Rosenblatt, "Growing Up on Television," in Newcomb, *Television,* 351.

16. In 1961 Saudi Arabian State Television refused to show *I Love Lucy* on the grounds that Lucy dominated her husband. This misinterpretation of the text was later revised, and *I Love Lucy* was shown on Saudi Arabian TV in the seventies. See Bart Andrews, *Lucy and Ricky and Fred and Ethel: The Story of "I Love Lucy"* (New York: Fawcett Popular Library, 1977), 13.

17. For a review of the changes in the image of the American woman signaled by the popularity of *The Mary Tyler Moore Show,* see Carol Traynor Williams, "It's Not So Much 'You've Come a Long Way, Baby'—As 'You're Gonna Make It after All,' " in Newcomb, *Television,* 64–73.

18. R. P. Blackmur, "A Burden for Critics," in *Lectures in Criticism,* ed. Elliot Coleman (New York: Harper and Brothers, 1949), 189.

19. Ibid., 188.

20. Walt Whitman, *Democratic Vistas* (1871; rpt., London: Walter Scott, 1888), 83.

21. Ibid., 5

22. Allen Ginsberg, "Howl," in *Howl and Other Poems* (San Francisco: City Lights Books, 1956), 11.

23. Barthes, *Mythologies,* 15.

24. Alex McNeil, *Total Television: A Comprehensive Guide to Programming from 1948 to 1980* (New York: Penguin Books, 1980), 112.

25. Ibid.

26. "Ratings," in *TV Guide Almanac,* ed. Craig T. Norback and Peter Norback (New York: Ballantine Books, 1980), 546.
27. Ibid., 547–48.
28. I am including neither *The Ed Sullivan Show,* which was a "straight variety" show, nor *The Jack Benny Program,* which was an eccentric self-reflexive sitcom, in the comedy-variety category.
29. Gilbert Seldes, *The New Mass Media: Challenge to a Free Society* (Washington, D.C.: Public Affairs Press, 1968), 143.
30. Ibid.
31. Brooks and Marsh, *Complete Directory,* 496.
32. Ibid.
33. Sterling and Kitross, *Stay Tuned,* 528–29.
34. Brooks and Marsh, *Complete Directory,* 692–93.
35. McNeil, *Total Television,* 647.
36. Ibid., 502.
37. Cheryl Bernstein, "Performance as News: Notes on an Intermedia Guerrilla Group," in *Performance in Postmodern Culture,* ed. Michel Benamou and Charles Camamello (Madison, Wisc.: Coda Press, 1977), 79.

LAWRENCE E. MINTZ

15 Ideology in the Television Situation Comedy

While David Marc provides an historical overview of the television situation comedy in Chapter 14, Lawrence E. Mintz, in the essay that follows, is concerned with how such comedies convey certain values in American culture. Examining the structure, themes, characters, and messages of a variety of situation comedies over a period of several decades, Mintz assesses whether such programs reinforce or challenge the dominant values of American culture.

Popular culture has emerged, in the modern world, as a primary purveyor of ideology, supplanting as much as supplementing the traditional authority of family, church, and formal education. For obvious reasons, television is the most powerful communication medium of our popular culture, and over the years situation comedy has consistently been the dominant television genre.[1] Yet it is hard to take sitcom seriously. Except for the overtly thematic offerings of Norman Lear and his imitators, the genre seems to be trivial, silly. The viewer may be aware of simple "morals" contained in the stories, and of character-stereotypes, conventional portraits of urban and rural lifestyles and other potential meaning, but only a few sophisticated critics have realized that decoding this banal entertainment is a complex and rewarding task.[2] David Marc, one of the best analysts of the importance of television to American culture, does not

From Lawrence E. Mintz, "Ideology in the Television Situation Comedy," *Studies in Popular Culture* 8, no. 2 (1985): 42–51. Reprinted by permission of *Studies in Popular Culture* and the author.

overstate the case when he observes, "television is America's jester. It has assumed the guise of an idiot while actually accruing power and authority behind the smoke screen of its self-degradation. . . . The sitcom dramatizes American culture: its subject is national styles, types, customs, issues, and language."[3] In this chapter I propose to show how sitcom broadcasts messages through its *structure, premises, characterizations, plot-themes,* and *semiotic elements,* using selected examples to illustrate the process rather than attempting a thorough account of all of the issues raised by the investigation of the subject.

Probably the most important meaning we can find in the situation comedy is implicit in the structure of the genre itself. Situation comedies are weekly half-hour plays involving a recurring cast of familiar characters who face new adventures initiated and resolved in each episode.[4] The program opens with the characters in a state of normality, that is, going about their business in their usual place, manners, and roles. Frequently this point is made emphatically by the opening thematic scenes in which recurring images both visually and orally suggest such continuity. For instance, Archie and Edith, seated at the piano singing "Those Were the Days", or the subway train leading to the Brooklyn high school class in *Welcome Back Kotter* let us know that, for the moment, at least, things are progressing normally. The "situation" of the sitcom is the interruption of this normality, attempts at coping with the intrusion or problem, and the resolution of it allowing for what we *could* call "the return to normalcy" (but of course we won't).

The problem of the situation comedy is almost always a minor threat—either an embarrassment, a confusion or misunderstanding created by a failure to communicate or an opportunity for change which equally threatens the common, familiar pattern of existence for the characters. Faced with the threat, problem or opportunity, the characters act, and invariably make things worse, complicating and compounding the difficulty, creating new, secondary dangers. The plot thickens until there is a miraculous, unexpected, almost always unearned rescue; the situation is resolved as artificially as any *deus ex machina* ending in a classical Greek drama. All is explained, all is corrected, all is forgiven, all is restored to the condition of normality.

We could illustrate this process by picking just about any sitcom from the earliest Molly Goldberg episodes to the most recent activities of Bill Cosby. The structure embraces the kidcom of *The Brady Bunch* and the "social dramas" of Norman Lear. Lucy Ricardo, bored with her role as a housewife, embarks on a quest to help Ricky or to succeed in a venture of her own. She gets herself in increasingly hot water (e.g., the salad dressing she is going to bottle and sell is indeed popular, but it will cost more to make and ship than the already advertised price, and orders are piling up). But Ricky doesn't kill her, despite her recurring fear. He vents a little steam, helps her pick up the pieces, and life goes on.

Riley is sitting in his apartment minding his own business. "Ding-dong" goes his doorbell. It's his best friend and co-worker informing Riley that he (the friend) has been laid off from the job. Riley suggests that *they* (he involves himself in the problem) open a gymnasium. They secure a lease on a loft, rent equipment and await the customers who fail to appear. Now they have an investment of their life savings at stake, compounding the problem. Riley enrolls his boss as a client, after the latter has warned that a back condition makes it impossible for him to work out. Riley recommends the steam cabinet, the old-fashioned iron-lung-like contraption where only the victim's head is visible. Predictably the boss becomes stuck in the cabinet, allowing for the physical comedy element in the show as they try to get him out while the pressure (his as well as the steam's) mounts. He fires Riley as well. A shapely young woman signs her son up for some exercise lessons, but the boy refuses to cooperate. The woman decides to use the lessons herself and she enlists a friend. As Riley and his friend show the two attractive, sweat-suited ladies the ropes (and the other equipment), the two men's wives show up (right when the coaches are in innocent but apparently compromising contact with their charges). Now Riley is *persona non grata* at home as well as at work. "Ding-dong" goes the doorbell. The boss shows up to announce that his bout with the steam cabinet has cured his bad back, and in gratitude he is going to rehire the two men. "Ding-dong" goes the bell again. The landlord arrives to beg for the termination of the lease, offering to cover any expenses incurred by the erstwhile entrepreneurs. No more gymnasium, no more threat to the wives, no more life savings in jeopardy, no more unemployment. Back to normal.

In episode after episode of situation comedy, the threat of change—for better or for worse—is thwarted. Kotter gets his big break to try and make it as a stand-up comedian, but the sweathogs confront him with his own statements about the primacy of education and he voluntarily returns to the classroom about which he continually complains. But the last thing we see is his smiling acknowledgment that this is really the best possible solution. Ralph Kramden will never get off of his bus nor will he ever abandon his absurd hopes which exasperate his commonsensical wife. But while he may threaten her with non-scheduled trips to the moon in the heat of his struggling, in the end he will acknowledge that she is "the greatest," and that the best he can really hope for is what he has already at the beginning of each episode.

Most of the critics who have written about situation comedy have noticed and discussed this structural element in the genre. Indeed, David Grote argues that it is this aspect which makes the genre unique, different from traditional comedy.[5] Horace Newcomb, Roger Rollin, and John Bryant have recognized the social conservatism implied by the emphasis on the normal domestic scene as the epitome of happiness for the characters.[6] The ideology of the situation comedy is an interesting contrast to the idea of the American dream as one of achievement, opportunity, growth, mobility. Here such volatility is seen only as threat, as a dream which cannot be realized, which creates only conflict and disappointment. The characters are encouraged to accept their lot, to "let it be," to replace ambition with the solace of love, friendship, and the promise that in a limited, static way, everything will work out all right eventually. Perhaps a different version of the American dream is recalled, Jefferson's "forty acres and a mule." The foolish characters struggle, connive, and dream; their wise counterparts attend to business, accept their lot, give solace to the fools when inevitably the plans blow up, and remain of good cheer. Sitcom ideology reconciles the viewer, as well as the characters, to a social situation in which vertical mobility is a dream unlikely to be realized, in which chance is merely threat, in which domestic tranquility is the highest ideal. It graphically illustrates a shift in national attitude from the more aggressive nineteenth century-early twentieth century hopes to an acceptance of the actual lot of most middle-class citizens.

Students of the situation comedy often sub-divide the genre into groups by similar premises. Rick Mitz, for instance, writes about "domcoms," "kidcoms," "couplecoms," "Scificoms," "corncoms," "ethnicoms," and "careercoms," and John Bryant identifies eleven program types including domestic, man-woman, professional/military, ethnic, hick, town hall and others.[7] Program types themselves are subject to interpretation as having ideological significance. Racial and ethnic sitcoms, as an example, tend to portray minority cultures as quaint, amusing, but not essentially different from "mainstream" America. Even the early shows such as *The Goldbergs* and *Amos 'n' Andy*, more derogatory in their acceptance of ethnic stereotyping and linguistic mockery, presented only a superficial view of their respective (Jewish, Black) cultural subjects while the familiar fare of the sitcom remained dominant and undifferentiated.

A later program, *Julia,* seems on the surface to have been an attempt at a late-sixties public affirmation of the legitimacy of the civil rights movement—the protagonist is an integrationist fantasy of a perfectly acculturated yet unassimilated Black woman. But aside from Julia's obligatory remarks that remind us of her race and the fact that members of it are not always accepted by all Americans, the program asserts that life for Black people in America is not any different than it is for whites. Still later programs, *The Jeffersons, Good Times, Sanford and Son* and others update the surface references to racial identity and grudgingly give more credence to the idea of racial tensions' antipathies, but here too there is no question that a primary covert message in the premise is that Black people have the same needs, problems, and, for the most part, beliefs and behavior, as the rest of the population. Ethnic comedies reflect a similar pattern and a similar meaning. Such generalizations gloss over differences in individual shows, individual characterizations, particular episodes, of course (and as we will discuss below), but there is an important statement made by the basic premise of the racial/ethnic situation comedy.

Military comedies have been popular for quite awhile, but with the partial exception of *M*A*S*H* they have little or nothing to do with war or the Army *per se.* The soldiers of *Sgt. Bilko, McHale's Navy, Gomer Pyle, Hogan's Heroes*—and to some extent *M*A*S*H* as well— are really in a men's summer camp or sports club where gambling, drinking, joking, and other camaraderie is the most important feature of their existence. To be sure, Hogan and company have a mission, subverting the stereotypically stupid and/or brutal Nazi soldiers, but they are also comfortably in charge of a rather happy clubhouse which their captors foolishly regard as a prison.

If we look at workplace comedies such as *Our Miss Brooks, Cheers, Taxi, Alice* and others in a similar light, we realize that they, too, are not about the business-at-hand; rather, their subject is the making of a pseudo-family or club out of the fellow workers or neighbors. Even Mary Richards's newsroom is subordinate to her overlooking her "family," the team which develops personal loyalties and emotional ties which readily spill over the boundaries of the workplace, work-situation. Bosses are presented as inept tyrants—Mel, Mr. Conklin, Louis—who are saved by their efficient, loyal, long-suffering employees, but it is clear that the bonds between worker and boss, as well as among co-workers, are more familial than professional.

In a sense all of the program premises are merely subcategories under the general thematic proposition, "the family is the most important thing." This, then, is really a companion message to the one projected by the sitcom's structure: acceptance into the group or family is a part of the serenity of a changeless situation. But the majority of situation comedies deal with families literally as well as figuratively. One kind, illustrated by such shows as *Father Knows Best, The Brady Bunch, Leave It to Beaver, Eight Is Enough* and many other popular shows, boasts a formula which is as tightly followed as any other in popular culture. Children make mistakes or get into low-grade trouble which is compounded by their parents. The parents guide the children to a peaceful, simple rectification. The program's appeal is in the models of behavior: children who learn to be open, trusting and parents who are caring, calm, positive, and warm. Single-parent families follow a similar pattern, but they also face the additional problem of reconciling social and professional needs with the domestic ones. The message which emerges is that one must always be attentive to the demands of the family, always ready to listen and to communicate. Programs popular with young children virtually always adhere to this theme, even when the "family" is defined more loosely as it is in *Happy Days* or when additionally there are other non-traditional elements present as well, such as in *Three's Company,* a program very popular with kids despite sexual themes which are aimed at an older (chronologically if not emotionally) audience. Subordinating all to the needs of the family has been an important part of the American ideology since the Second World War, if not before, and the sitcom no doubt has an important role in acculturating us to that norm.

Characterization is yet another way for the sitcom to express social values and beliefs. Sitcom incorporates all of the traditional American comic characters, various kinds of fools, wise fools, "little men," "termagant wives," bullies, conmen, tricksters and the like, and it employs stereotypes, racial and ethnic, sex-role, professional, and others, to generate understanding as well as laughter. The wise fool tradition provides one good example.[8] Sitcoms have negative fools such as Archie Bunker, for example, whose errors of speech and judgment represent an ignorance or a stupidity to be scorned. But the wise fool—either the naif like Archie's wife Edith or commonsense philosophers whose practical, experiential wisdom belies their lack of formal status (e.g., Alice Kramden)—is also represented. The wise fool represents the democratic credo that the common man has an innate wisdom superior to the "book learning" of the upper classes and intellectuals (note the *Beverly Hillbillies* as one example of this theme's prominence). Indeed, the often-discussed ambiguity of Archie Bunker's reception reflects this issue in American humor's history. Like John Downing, Simon Suggs, Sut Lovingood and a host of others, Archie begins with a set of negative traits, but because he is a common man— i.e., a democratic "hero"—our sympathies are at least divided. He is as often victim as victimizer (for example, of Mike's parasitism), and even his ignorance reflects a misguided but positive inclination. Archie wants a simple, proper, orderly positive world, and his opinionated bluster is just his stubborn insistence that there is a clear truth and that he understands it despite his impotence in having his views prevail.

Ralph Kramden provides a similar insight. Loud, aggressive, arrogant, he is a traditional braggart-bully figure whom one might have encountered in the *commedia dell'arte*. He is also a fool whose lack of understanding of "reality" leads him on perpetually doomed quests. But he is also a "little man" who is frustrated by his inability to cope with a world with so many false promises. Like Riley (at one point Jackie Gleason had both of these roles), Ralph keeps plugging away (cf. Chaplin, Keaton, Langdon, Lloyd), undaunted if unrewarded. The viewer may feel superior to Ralph and derisive toward him, but there is doubtlessly some sympathy mixed in as well.

Sympathy must also be extended to his wife—poor, suffering Alice. While she is the victim of his backfiring schemes, she is also a critic in the tradition of the nagging wife. She is practical and down-to-earth, but she is drab. Her counterpart in the domestic sitcoms are similarly boring (though they are usually a little more cheerful at least). Their husbands are not quite the fools and losers of the traditional male characters discussed above, but they are only visitors in their homes, more often than not. Well-meaning and full of advice, the men are entirely dependent upon their wives for valid information concerning anything going on around the house (hence in the show). Working women are also often portrayed in the same way, going back as far as the *Private Secretary/Ann Sothern* days and up through Mary Richards at least. Ostensibly subordinate, it is the women who get things done while men issue orders, create problems, worry about potential disasters and take the credit.

As many critics have pointed out effectively, contemporary shows which consciously seek to alter the stereotyped, sexist view of women are at best only partially successful toward that end.[9] Mary Richards, as has been said, is as much a traditional mother as she is a dynamic professional, though she did grow with the show to some extent. Even Ann Romano in *One Day at a Time* presents only, as Roxanne Mueller puts it, "a facade of feminism" under which we can find a very traditional sex-role portrait.[10] "Jiggle-coms" such as *Three's Company, Too Close for Comfort,* and *WKRP* (at least as far as Loni Anderson's role) retreated to familiar roles taken from film and theater (cf. Lorelei Lee), and along with Gloria Stivic, Margaret Houlihan (another character who grew, however, it should be noted), Maude, Laverne, Shirley, Alice, Rhoda and all of their sisters, offer little in the way of positive role models for contemporary women. Once again there is the illusion of change undercut by the prevalence of conventional perspectives.

Themes expressed in particular episodes are more varied and difficult to categorize for ideological consistency. In the early years of the genre this was not a problem since the concerns faced in a particular show were not particularly topical. Prior to the 1970's the ideological content of most sitcoms was limited to the non-inconsequential messages of structure, premise, and characterization already discussed. Much of the credit (or blame, perhaps) for the increasing moralizing in the genre is often given to Norman Lear. Lear's Tandem Productions gave us *All in the Family* (1971), *Sanford and Son* (1972), *Maude* (1972), *Good Times* (1974), *The Jeffersons* (1975), and a half-dozen or so less remembered offerings during the decade. Lear consciously and overtly dealt with topical issues in his programs, including such subjects as racial conflict, homosexuality, abortions, sexism, political conflict, crime, the problems of the elderly and many others. A great deal has been written concerning their possible impact on the audience.[11] His critics emphasize the ambiguity of his positions and his defenders underscore the difficulty of dealing with controversial topics in the television medium and the comedy genre.

In the long run the contribution of Norman Lear is certainly going to be less in the issues he aired or the way he confronted them than in his role in establishing the genre as an appropriate vehicle for discussing social mores and concerns. For instance, several of Lear's shows dealt with homosexuality—an *All in the Family* episode in which one of Mike's friends seems to Archie to be gay, but Archie learns that the effeminate young man is a heterosexual while the "macho" ex-football player at the neighborhood bar is in fact a homosexual, or the episode of *Maude* where Arthur confronts the issue of licensing a gay bar in his community. Both shows avoid any real position. The *All in the Family* episode has as its overt theme the idea that one cannot judge the sexual preference of any individual by masculine/feminine stereotyped behavior, but it says nothing at all about the issue of the homosexual's place in society, or for that matter about the nature of the phenomenon. The *Maude* show is even thinner. It boils down to a legal technicality allowing the bar because it is outside the town's limits, but the only communication on the ostensible topic under scrutiny are some covert implications that otherwise admirable and creative people might be indeed gay and that gays can be as intolerant of the straight community as vice versa.[12] On the face of the programs, nothing constructive has been aired dealing with the issue, but the significance is really in that this taboo topic was discussed at all; the discussion opened the way for so many other programs in which homosexuals are featured, directly and prominently such as in *Soap* or in an episode of *Kate and Allie,* to cite just a couple of cases among many, or in which sexual identity is an acceptable topic for humor (*Three's Company, Bosom Buddies, Love Sidney* et al). Indirectly the point is made very clearly; homosexuality is a significant phenomenon in our culture and society. It cannot be ignored and it need not be faced with anger, fear, or scorn.

Lear's success spawned, in the usual TV process of imitation, a wave of issue-oriented situation comedy. *Mary Tyler Moore* and the various MTM spin-offs, *M*A*S*H, Barney Miller, Chico and the Man* and dozens more sought to captivate the audience by mixing traditional sitcom conventions, humor, and social analysis. But the trend was not limited to the obviously topical programs. Even programs which seemed to be consciously counter to the "engage" group—*Happy Days, Laverne and Shirley, Welcome Back Kotter, Mork and Mindy, Different Strokes—* just about every sitcom, in fact—features moralizing as prominently as any other aspect. Garry Marshall, producer of *Happy Days, Laverne and Shirley, Mork and Mindy* among others informs us of how conscious this preaching can be: "We tried to be useful. We did shows about mental health, about diabetes, about death, blindness, epilepsy," and "the most clearcut comments are Mork's soliloquy at the end, which was designed for just that reason, to say it head-on. I scared the network. They don't understand the ice-cream theory. If you give them ice cream, they'll listen."[13]

Marshall's messages are rather muddled more often than not. For example, a *Mork and Mindy* show attempted to deal with the issue of aging and the role of the elderly in America. Mindy's grandmother becomes depressed when she considers her advancing years. Mork seeks to console her, so using his extraterrestrial powers he ages himself to seventy (as he puts it, perpetuating a popular misconception about senility, he sets his age control for senility minus ten years) and proceeds to court the elderly woman. She responds as he had hoped, becoming young in spirit again, hopeful and happy. When Mork is forced to reveal the trick (neither he nor the show's writers could figure out any way out of the situation), she has learned her lesson, which she articulates as the popular cliché, "you're only as old as you feel." The message of the show is actually closer to "pretend you are young or emulate the young and you'll fit in just fine," but just how far off the writers are in understanding their own communication becomes clear when Mork reports to Orson, on Ork, with what we are supposed to accept as the message: "They don't know how to treat the elderly on Earth like we do on Ork, with positions of respect, meaning." Needless to say, nothing in the show whatsoever dealt with meaningful roles for the elderly in society, on Ork, Earth, or even Hollywood.

Such mixed and/or sloppy moralizing is far from an isolated example. Indeed it is the rule rather than the exception in the genre. In *One Day at a Time,* Ann Romano's daughter faces the issue of pre-marital sex. Her boyfriend has confronted her with an ultimatum, so she comes to her mother for advice. Mother tells her that the decision must be personal, carefully thought out, and based upon what she thinks is really best for her, establishing clearly that such "situation ethics" have replaced traditional moral and parental authority, but this important statement is completely undercut by the mother's hysterical conduct (played for laughs but unmistakenly significant nonetheless) when her daughter does not come home at the expected hour and the evasiveness with which the daughter treats her decision.

An episode of the seemingly innocuous kidcom *Different Strokes* provides another good example. A teenaged girl (a friend of the daughter in the family) believes that she is pregnant. She confides in her friend, noting her fear that her father will react violently if he finds out. (A possible ideological message may be slipped in during this dialogue when the two girls discuss the options for what can "be done about it," and seem to consider abortion as a possibility, perhaps one which will be eliminated, but the ambiguity of the actual remarks makes this interpretation questionable.) The show develops into a predictable confusion comedy. The two brothers think it is their (step)sister who is pregnant, they tell her father, mistakes compound until a direct confrontation solves the whole thing. The girl's father is informed, he reacts calmly, understandingly, constructively; it turns out to be a false alarm after all, and the problem disappears leaving the overt message that a) children should be open and honest with their parents, and b) parents should be calm and understanding in their dealings with their children. But even in permissive contemporary America, one wonders if the program would have been aired if anyone connected with it realized its covert message: "nice girls—even very young middle-class teenagers—do."

Almost every situation comedy episode in the past fifteen years could be analyzed in a similar way. Themes are "dealt with," but in anything but a clear, consistent, coherent way. The ideology of episode content is not part of a systematic, conscious communication; rather, it is a reflection of the values held by the people who make and distribute the fare and/or what they believe the American people want to see and hear.[14] The degree to which these images are manipulated in the interests of the dominant social groups is debatable, but that the shows set up stories to allow for an exploration of contemporary social beliefs is not. Consciously and unconsciously the situation comedy expresses the audience's values, attitudes, dispositions, fears, and hopes. Its structure, recurring premises, characterizations, themes, dialogue, humorous "shtick" or action, settings and other semiotic elements all communicate ideological meaning, perhaps the most significant content in the most effective form of all such communication in contemporary America.

NOTES

1. For a more thorough definition, description, history and discussion of the genre, substantiating this contention, see Lawrence E. Mintz, "Situation Comedy," in Brian Rose, ed., *TV Genres: A Handbook and Reference Guide* (Westport, CT: Greenwood Press, 1985).
2. E.g., David Grote, *The End of Comedy: The Sit-com and the Comedic Tradition* (Hamden, CT: Archon Books, 1983); David Marc, *Democratic Vistas: Television in American Culture* (Philadelphia: University of Pennsylvania Press, 1984).
3. David Marc, "Understanding Television," *The Atlantic Monthly* (August 1984), 35, 37.
4. Horace Newcomb provides an excellent basic definition of the genre in his *TV: The Most Popular Art* (Garden City, NY: Anchor Books, 1974). See also my chapter cited in note 1; John Bryant, "Emma, Lucy, and the American

Situation Comedy of Manners," *Journal of Popular Culture,* 10:2 (Fall 1979), 248–56, and Grote, *The End of Comedy.*

5. Grote, *The End of Comedy,* 67.

6. Again, see Newcomb, *TV;* Grote, *The End of Comedy;* Bryant, "Emma, Lucy"; also Michael Apter, *"Fawlty Towers:* A Reversal Theory Analysis of a Popular Television Comedy Series," *Journal of Popular Culture,* 16:3 (Winter 1982), 128–37.

7. John Bryant, "A Checklist of American Situation Comedy," *American Humor: An Interdisciplinary Newsletter,* 5:2 (Fall, 1978), 14–31; Rick Mitz, *The Great TV Sitcom Book* (NY: Perigee Books, 1983), 5.

8. A discussion of the importance of the Wise Fool character for American humor can be found in Lawrence E. Mintz, "Brother Jonathan's City Cousin," Ph.D. dissertation, Michigan State University, 1969.

9. There are many useful discussions of the images of women in television. Two which deal with the sitcom specifically are K. Edgington, "Classicism, Sexism, Racism, and the Sitcom," *Women: A Journal of Liberation,* 8:3 (1983), and Roxanne Mueller, "Sitcom Morality: From Beaver to Ann Romano," *Journal of Popular Film and Television* 9:1 (Fall, 1981). I am also indebted to two excellent undergraduate papers on sexism done for my American Studies senior seminar on the sitcom by Karen Gardiner and Iris Soppa.

10. Mueller, "Sitcom Morality," 50.

11. See, for a starting place in the body of Norman Lear criticism, Richard P. Adler, ed., *All in the Family: A Critical Appraisal* (NY: Praeger, 1979).

12. Another student paper for the seminar mentioned in note 9, on homosexuality as represented in the genre, was done by Jonelle Coley, contributing greatly to my appreciation of the issue.

13. Garry Marshall in Horace Newcomb and Robert Alley, *The Producer's Medium* (NY: Oxford University Press, 1983), 248, and Marshall, in "Our Happy Days Together," *TV Guide* (April 28, 1984), 5.

14. A consideration of the various theories of responsibility for the messages in mass communication is not possible here, but it is indeed pertinent. A good place to investigate the issue is Michael Gurevitch, Tony Bennett, James Curran, Jenet Woolcott, eds., *Culture, Society and the Media* (NY: Methuen, 1982). Also interesting and more immediately concerned with the production of American television are Ben Stein's *The View From Sunset Boulevard: America as Brought to You By the People Who Make Television* (NY: Basic Books, 1979), and Newcomb and Alley, *The Producer's Medium.*